Prai:

CU00970930

"Few people have taken a ⌐
in this country than Matthew Collins. You know it's personal
with him and you know by the far right's reaction to him that
it runs both ways. *Hate* is Matthew's personal story, brilliantly
told, incredibly funny and occasionally bawdy. It's a stark
reminder of waste, but also a skilful and agonising confrontation with life, class, poverty and identity. Reading it leaves a
lump in the throat at times, because it will confront you, as
Matthew has confronted me numerous times, personally!"
Jon Cruddas MP

"Hard-hitting and often darkly comic prose of the years
he spent with those who planned world domination."
Metro (Book of the Week)

"Fascinating memoir ... peppered with bizarre
and often achingly funny paragraphs."
Belfast Telegraph

"Unashamedly bawdy, always witty, often dark."
Sunday World

"A tale told with humour with nothing left sacrosanct."
The Morning Star

"What comes out most clearly from Matthew's walk through
the world of far right extremism is the seediness. The
tackiness. The pettiness of prejudice ... walk out the
door, find a bookshop, buy it and read it."
Labour Uncut

"Kicking in the heads of old ladies at a public meeting in
a library [is] an event he details with chilling candour."
Brisbane Times

"A story of smoky pubs, drunken punch-ups, mindless
hooliganism and paranoid conspiracy ... a timely riff
on the past 25 years of the UK far right."
The Independent

MATTHEW COLLINS

HATE

My Life in the British Far Right

Biteback Publishing

First published in Great Britain in 2011.

This edition published in Great Britain by
Biteback Publishing Ltd
Westminster Tower
3 Albert Embankment
London SE1 7SP
Copyright © Matthew Collins 2012

Photo credits: Photo of Charlie Sargent copyright and by kind permission of Nick Lowles/*Searchlight*. Photos of MC selling *The Flag* and at
conference, Bermondsey, Eltham copyright and by kind permission of
Daphne Liddle. MC with Billy Bragg, MC with guitar, and Billy Bragg
copyright and by kind permission of Peter Dunwell. Photos of Ian
Stuart Donaldson, Nick Griffin and Newcastle copyright and by kind
permission of Hope Not Hate. All other photos by kind permission of
Searchlight and from the personal collection of Matthew Collins.

ISBN 978-1-84954-327-9

10 9 8 7 6 5 4 3 2 1

A CIP catalogue record for this book is available from the
British Library.

Set in Sabon and Helvetica

Printed and bound in Great Britain by
CPI Group (UK) Ltd, Croydon CR0 4YY

CONTENTS

ACKNOWLEDGEMENTS

I began writing the first draft of this book on the second day of my honeymoon, 26 February 1996. It took considerably longer to finish than the marriage itself. They both got shelved sometime in 1998.

As is always the way, there are numerous people to thank and countless others that I cannot thank publicly, who should know that I am eternally grateful to them for their contributions, honesty and most of all their bravery.

Those who can be thanked publicly include Nick Lowles, who pretended to read the manuscript despite the constant distractions of football, sunshine and curry. Often we were joined by 'Titus' Batty who chopped wood, drank red wine and complained. Without their constant encouragement and duplicity this book may well have never seen the light of day.

To Dan Hodges, to whom there would appear never to be a closed door, and who convinced the great Iain Dale that he really needed to publish a book with a lot of profanity. And to the memory David Greason, from whom I learnt so much and of whom I was so in awe until his untimely death in 2011. Many thanks to my very patient and liberal-minded editor Sam Carter.

Thanks must also go to those people in Melbourne who mothered, fathered and occasionally fed me during those years I lived there. In particular, but not only, Robyn and Noel, Ross and his girls, Leanne, Greg & Titty, Conn, Gavan, Warren, Chris A, Heathcliffe and his family, the Day family and those many others who I do not forget.

In television land I cannot go without mentioning Roger

Childs and Jane D, who both put up with my smoking, temperamental bowels and quite occasional foul language. This was particularly tough on Jane D in her mission to get me to Oldham. And then there are Quentin McDermott and Andy Bell who put up with the same sort of stuff which eventually got me sent to Australia.

Thanks must go to those who inspire me: my brothers and their beautiful families, especially. For his music, eternal patience, friendship and access to his rider, there is, of course, only one Mr Billy Bragg (and family). To Gregg McDonald and Pete Dunwell who captured the whole journey.

For reading the manuscript and giving advice where needed (and where not), it would be remiss not to mention Vicky O, Nick Ryan, Dr G, Ruth S and Romeo. The wonderful staff and volunteers at *Searchlight* and Hope Not Hate, in particular the 'A team'. Special thanks to Andy V and Daphne Liddle for hunting down long-lost pics, and to Ben Speroni for attempting to spell check,

I should also thank Derek Sherwin, Kate Smith, Tim Joyce, Martin Collier, Elliot Furneaux and Paul Heaton who taught me right and learned me good. And a special belated thanks to Steve Hales, Danny Fisk and Tony King, we were the fourth best gang in school.

For sound financial advice, curry and lager, Cormac H and Simon T were superb encouragement. So too was my father.

But this book is for my mother. It's both a recollection and an apology.

Matthew Collins, London 2011

FOREWORD

Billy Bragg

Back in 2003, the BBC asked me whether I'd come and meet this bloke who'd flown in from Australia to talk about his time with the National Front, the BNP and Combat 18. The Beeb was making a documentary about him but I wasn't particularly keen to be honest. These were the sort of people engaged in the ongoing intimidation and harassment of people who bought my records and used my website as a fanbase and I wasn't in the mood to sit down with somebody who wanted patting on the head.

But after talking to the good people at *Searchlight,* curiosity got the better of me about his story and how he'd changed sides from fascist to anti-fascist and passed valuable information on without his comrades knowing anything about it. I ended up in a café in Shepherds Bush that specialised in Thai and traditional English cuisine, having breakfast with Matt Collins, talking about football, Englishness, page three girls and my music. He told me that he'd previously shaken my hand in the toilets of Melbourne Town Hall.

So here finally, is his roller coaster ride. A brilliantly candid memoir of being a confused and isolated teenager witnessing the far right's terrifying acts of violence and depravity during the Thatcher years and later those of John Major, as they plotted their seemingly impossible dream of one day sitting in the council chambers of England and the European Parliament.

Matthew's story is as emotive as it is horrifying and,

of course, always viciously witty, warm and poignant. But this book should sound a warning too; that we should not ignore the fascists or ever think they'll go away.

Since that fateful full English in Shepherds Bush, I've had Matthew come on tour with me, speak on stage with me and even organise and promote benefit gigs for me. We've stood shoulder to shoulder on numerous occasions in the face of those fascists, none more memorable I suppose than in Barking and Dagenham in 2010, where we came face to face with the BNP's council leader in the street and I ended up in heated discussion in front of the media with people who really would tell any lie and say and do anything to win over the hearts and minds of ordinary, disaffected working class people. We went on to help remove every single one of the BNP's twelve councillors and defeated Nick Griffin's parliamentary ambitions during that same campaign.

Matthew Collins should be the first port of call for anyone serious about understanding how people so isolated, driven by fears they cannot understand or comprehend, can be so taken in by racism and fascism. Taking that other brave step, as he did, to then go and spy on them gives us also an edge-of-the-seat thriller.

He's pulled no punches. If he ever has a guest list, you'll wanna be on it.

WHAT IS WHAT

ANTI-NAZI LEAGUE (ANL): Broad-based group founded in the 1970s, ostensibly under the control of the Socialist Workers Party (SWP), to counter the National Front. Wound itself up in 1981 before relaunching again in 1992.

ANTI-FASCIST ACTION (AFA): Coalition of socialists, trade unionists, leftists and anarchists often, but not always, militantly opposed to the far right. 'The reds'.

BLOOD AND HONOUR: Worldwide neo-Nazi music network formed in England by Ian Stuart Donaldson in the 1980s after he split from the National Front. In early 1992 it aligned itself with the terror group C18. Donaldson died in 1993 and B&H split in the late 1990s, along with C18. Some continue to use the name to pursue a musical direction; others prefer to use the name for terror purposes.

BRITISH MOVEMENT (BM): Hard-line and openly Nazi organisation that engaged in vicious street violence during the 1970s and 1980s. Formed by Colin Jordan in 1968, the organisation wound itself up in the mid-1980s though some persist in using its name.

BRITISH NATIONAL PARTY (BNP): Formed in 1982 by former hard-line members of the National Front (NF) who left or were removed from the NF in 1980. The BNP's founder, John Tyndall, was an unrepentant Nazi who had previously headed the NF. He moulded the BNP into a violent and undemocratic street army using Nazi imagery and led violent confrontations with political opponents. In 1999 Tyndall was replaced as leader by Nick Griffin, who modernised the party, going on to make the BNP the most successful post-war fascist party in UK. The BNP is currently suffering savage internal and financial difficulties.

COMBAT 18 (C18): Formed by Charlie Sargent in 1992, C18 was initially a security wing for the BNP. Its name was formed using the initials of Adolf Hitler, represented by their place in the alphabet (first and eighth). Active in London, it eventually took on a life of its own and turned against the BNP as its violent reputation gained notoriety both nationally and internationally. The group was responsible for a series of violent attacks on internal political rivals, trade unionists, anti-fascists and celebrities both at home and abroad. In 1997 the organisation violently split, leading to the murder of a south-London man who was part of a faction led by Wilf Browning, also of south London. C18's founder, Charlie Sargent, was sentenced to life imprisonment in 1998 for murder.

ENGLISH DEFENCE LEAGUE (EDL): Far-right street movement founded by football hooligans in Luton during 2009 to protest against radical Islam. Violently racist and confrontational, by 2011 it had surpassed the BNP as Britain's largest and most active far-right group, spawning 'divisions' across Britain and Europe as part of the growing 'anti-Jihadist' network of far-right Christians, cultural conservatives and disenfranchised neo-Nazis.

HOPE NOT HATE (HNH): Hugely successful group founded in 2004 to campaign against racism, fascism and extremism. Its most significant achievement so far has been its defeat of Nick Griffin and the complete removal of twelve BNP councillors from Barking and Dagenham in 2010.

NATIONAL FRONT (NF): Formed in 1967 by merging a number of small racist and fascist organisations from around the country. By the late 1970s it had become an enormous, violent neo-Nazi, fascist and anti-immigration street movement but did not have – and has never had – any electoral success. A volatile organisation to say the least, the NF has suffered over a dozen near-fatal splits since its inception. *Hate* deals primarily with two factions formed in 1986 both using the name of the party: the Flag faction and the Political Soldiers (see below).

THE FLAG FACTION: Formed in 1986 around *The Flag* newspaper under the title of the National Front Support Group. The group was set up to counter the influence of young radicals in the NF under the leadership of Nick Griffin and Patrick Harrington. The Flag faction had three former party chairmen in its group, one of whom (Andrew Brons) went on to be elected as an MEP for the BNP in 2009 alongside Nick Griffin. The principal players – Ian Anderson, Martin Wingfield, Andrew Brons, Steve Brady and John McAuley – gained control of the name and mantle of the NF finally in 1990.

THE POLITICAL SOLDIERS: Also occasionally called the Official National Front (ONF). Between 1983 and 1986 Nick Griffin and Patrick Harrington, among others, tried to divert the National Front towards a bizarre political direction that included supporting Colonel Gaddafi. In 1986 the party split, with Griffin and Harrington declaring themselves the 'radical faction'. It wound itself down in acrimony around 1990.

RED ACTION (RA): Expelled from the ANL for 'squaddism', Red Action launched in 1981 with the belief that the fascists were not yet beaten. RA was at the centre of violent confrontations with the far right throughout the 1980s and 1990s while part of AFA. They credit themselves with driving both the BNP and C18 off of the streets of east London and predicting that New Labour would lead to an electoral rise for the far right.

ULSTER DEFENCE ASSOCIATION (UDA): Northern-Irish paramilitary group engaged in the murder of Roman Catholics and Republicans in Northern Ireland.

ULSTER VOLUNTEER FORCE (UVF): As above.

WHO IS WHO

IAN ANDERSON (1953–2011): Former NF Chairman 1985–6, 1988–95. Joined the National Front in the mid-1970s, later becoming part of the youthful leadership which took over the party in 1980. In 1986 Anderson led The Flag faction during a vicious internal feud that saw him line up against the young 'radical' Nick Griffin and his 'Political Soldiers' faction. In 1995 Anderson tried to wind the NF down and form a new party, the National Democrats. When he was unable to do so completely, the Nat Dems faltered. Anderson ended up in various anti-EU groups before succumbing to a brain tumour in 2011.

IAN STUART DONALDSON (1957–1993): Former NF member who sang in the skinhead band Skrewdriver. Founder of the worldwide skinhead movement 'Blood and Honour', Donaldson died in a car crash in 1993.

RICHARD EDMONDS (1943–): A former London school teacher, Edmonds was a founding member of the British National Party (BNP) in 1982, having formerly been a member of the National Front until the party split in 1980. A long-term supporter of BNP founder John Tyndall, Edmonds funded the opening of the BNP's controversial office and bookshop in south London in 1989. A notorious anti-Semite, Edmonds was responsible for the distribution of the controversial newspaper *Holocaust News* during the late 1980s and early 1990s. Edmonds was later suspended and then expelled from the BNP by Nick Griffin after he took over the leadership, though he was welcomed back in 2009. In 2011 Edmonds announced his was going to challenge Griffin for the leadership of the BNP, but instead left to rejoin the minuscule National Front.

NICK GRIFFIN (1959–): Leader of the British National Party. Cambridge-educated Griffin rose to prominence in the National Front in the 1980s when he led a faction inside the party calling themselves the 'Political Soldiers'. Amongst other things, the group supported Colonel Gaddafi, Catholicism and Welsh nationalism. This bizarre line of politics split the party. Griffin wound his faction of the NF down in 1990 and moved to France, returning to far-right politics in the mid-1990s and renouncing his previous political deviations. In 1999 he defeated BNP founder John Tyndall in a vicious and controversial leadership election.

(PAUL DAVID) CHARLIE SARGENT (1960–): Convicted drug dealer and long-time far-right activist within both the NF and the BNP, Sargent was the founder of the terror organisation Combat 18. In 1998 Sargent was sentenced to life imprisonment for the murder of a political rival during an internal feud. It was later alleged that Sargent had been working for government security services.

JOHN TYNDALL (1934–2005): British Nazi who led (among other groups) both the NF and the BNP. Tyndall formed the BNP in 1982 having lost control of the NF in 1980, and headed the new organisation until Nick Griffin won the leadership in a bitter election in 1999. Tyndall's defeat led to suspension and then expulsion from the party he had formed in his own image, which in turn resulted in a series of court battles. A hard-line neo-Nazi until his death, Tyndall was imprisoned a number of times during his life, including a sentence for organising a paramilitary

organisation named Spearhead in the 1960s. He published
a magazine by that same name until he died in 2005. At
the time of his death Tyndall was due to go on trial alongside Griffin for incitement to racial hatred. He was once
engaged to perfume heiress Françoise Dior.

INTRODUCTION

I ran up those stairs, breathless, my comrades behind and beside me. The saviours of our race and nation, skipping over the prostrate body lying bloodied before us. Onwards and upwards we charged towards our final destination. Watch out you reds, because here we are, heavy with tattoos and lager courage. The door was kicked open and in we fell, breathless with excitement, smelling blood in anticipation like the hound after the hare. Fists clenched, eyes wide open, weapons drawn and headlines about to be written.

It felt like going over the tops of far-flung trenches for race and nation as we charged into Welling Library. No guts, no glory; no pain, no gain. The little old ladies inside the library attempted to flee in terror but they had nowhere to go, nowhere to hide. They were forced to cower together against the walls in united, agonised anticipation of their bloody beating. Their own chairs were raised in slow motion against them. This was going to be a bloodbath, a prophetic one for them too, as they were in the library to discuss their fears about having us in the neighbourhood. Their howls of terror were drowned under the brute noises of us grunting, Neanderthal Nazis, screaming and jeering as into the ladies we ploughed.

And down they went, trying to curl into defensive little balls, covering their tortured faces as we screamed 'BNP! BNP!', stamping in time, stamping on them, kicking their heads, stamping on their bodies, dragging them off the walls and into the middle of the room so that every one of our number could feed on them. The hammers were out and everything possible was smashed and destroyed. One person dived screaming through the window and into the street but nobody stopped for even a moment. This was our glorious victory, our chance to be heard, our chance to speak up for the poor old white working class, the warrior race of sturdy Anglo-Saxons. We were fighting back; this was our democratic right to be heard and these cowards, these little old ladies, had to learn that we were not going to take their lies about us being brainless, racist thugs any more.

We left as we came in, exiting excitedly through the main door out into the early evening sun and back onto the eerie evening calm of Welling High Street.

‡

Four years later
I wasn't the most experienced of travellers. I'd only left the UK once before and, like now, that was at the magazine's expense. This time it was slightly more serious. Not for me another fortnight getting pissed and morbid in Spain while court cases were fought and won to protect my anonymity; this time I was going to Australia to – in the words of the police officer who advised me to leave – 'fuck off' completely.

I'd been planning to go for a while but perhaps, in all honesty, I would never really have gone ahead with it without being confronted with the threat of bloody revenge right outside our council house in south London. These sorts of things always concentrate the dithering mind wonderfully.

I was leaving home because I'd been a very naughty boy. For six years I had been the fresh-faced fascist, kicking in heads and getting my head kicked in in return as I rose up the ranks of Britain's blistered and permanently pissed far right. But for just under three of these years, I'd been passing information to the anti-fascists. It was hardly James Bond material – a little more like Austin Powers to be honest. There were no fast cars or women to make it exciting. It was a daily grind of telling lies to 'comrades' and eye-opening exposures to violence and intimidation leading me to hide in hotels while passing information to journalists through a series of complex drop-offs and making often tearful and terrified phone calls while wracked with self-doubt and teenage growing pains. I was the fly in their ointment but I was also torn about what I was doing. I knew so little of life, so very little of the reasons for the hatreds that had driven a younger me and I understood even less why I had kept on going and kept on doing it when all the time I had longed for and dreamed of an opportunity to get away from it all and live a life less confronting and emotionally draining. I wanted to be like everyone else my age. No one knew who we were and no one cared what we did. We'd been making plans for world domination from the very fringes of society – among the ashtrays and urinals of council estate pubs, shouting loudly into a deafening silence about our feelings of impotence. They would one day call me a traitor, rubbish my name and make blood-curdling threats, but for now, it was time to leave.

Gerry pressed an envelope into my hand with a few hundred quid in it. He was the legend who had become a friend. As the editor and publisher of the anti-fascist journal *Searchlight* he had for years and years used people like me to disrupt the far right. 'Not for getting pissed,' he said sternly. This was to be the rest of my life. I had escaped the clutches of the Nazi terror group C18 (Combat 18, the numbers representing the numerical position of Adolf Hitler's initials in the alphabet) and their loyalist friends, as well as the threats and cajoling of Special Branch officers delivering daily death threats, passed to them by their grasses in the movement.

I was now a truly free man. Well, if you can call a 21-year-old a man. As I boarded the Cathay Pacific flight at Heathrow it was plainly obvious, to me at least, that I was not an adventurer heading off to discover the world. I was a little boy lost in Departures.

I had my fears about returning one day but I also had my dreams. I wanted to be somebody. Someday, someone somewhere should want to know all about me. I hoped I could one day come back a better person, an intelligent person, anything other than the boy I'd left behind at Heathrow Airport, confused, terrified, so very young and hurting inside. The terror of what I was doing and the shame of what I had done was overwhelming. I no longer wanted to be Morrissey's *Sweet and Tender Hooligan*. I needed to know who I was and who I could be in future.

I had been the boy with a picture of Margaret Thatcher on his bedroom wall throughout the miners' strike and I had admired Norman Tebbit's call to the unemployed to 'Get on your bike' and look for work. I had also been the boy travelling to Birmingham to watch the football, with a cricket bat and bicycle chain on the back seat of a friend's car.

‡

With hindsight, I'd advise anyone with a spare six years to waste to go and get into a bad marriage. Don't get involved in marginal politics with men with drinking habits and nicknames like 'Killer' or 'Hitler'. If you fancy a wild and varied sex life, don't get married or get involved in marginal politics with men known as 'The Virgin'. Avoid, at all costs, being photographed in some high-class broadsheet, alongside quotes like 'Revolution, revisionism', or 'Hitler wasn't necessarily wrong … just misunderstood.' Don't try to act normal at parties where no one knows your politics; you have no idea what normal people are thinking or talking about; you are removed. Your thoughts are coloured by the grubby magazines that you've hidden under your bed, which only you and other men in anoraks read.

You could be single, divorced, tall, short, fat or thin but you could still find yourself, like me, ranting and raving at drunks in parks as if you were on *Question Time*. If, like I did, you think you've been at the back of every queue in your life and never pushed, if you blame it on the idea that we've been swamped by worthless, lazy immigrants, then you should take a look at the true facts and figures of the situation. Or you could put your own hands in your pocket and try being an immigrant, like I have.

I bitterly remember my time with the morons of the National Front and the BNP. For a while I'm sure I was having a good time, to be honest. Superbly transformed from ordinary under-achieving schoolboy, into spiteful little fascist with a penchant for split lips and bloody noses, for a while I was stunningly important among the rank and file members of the arse end of politics. How did I get there in the first place? Having got there, how did I wind up here? Why is it still an almost impossible question to answer?

CHAPTER 1

Patrick and Kathleen married in Forest Hill, south London in 1963. He was an Irish immigrant about to do his National Service; she was desperate to escape her tyrannical father. My paternal grandfather did not attend the wedding on account of my mother being a Protestant and instructed my future father's eight siblings not to attend for the same reason. By all accounts my grandfather was a miserable, religious old git who ran Irish dancing classes and beat dogs near to death in his back garden under the auspice of being a dog trainer.

He hated my mother and hated the English, something that he made apparent to us even when we were kids, the few times we ever saw him. With the 1960s being a great time of peace and love, perhaps Patrick and Kathleen thought that love would conquer all. Perhaps.

Nine years later I was born. We moved to a large redbrick council house on an estate in Lee, south London. I was the youngest of four boys and we settled in the four-bedroom house with a garage but no car. There was no reason at the time for anyone not to believe our lives were going to be perfect.

Sadly, I have no recollection of my father ever living with us. Apparently he did for a while but, after leaving the army, he got himself a job on the railways and continued the heavy drinking he'd learnt whilst on National Service. Occasionally he would come home late at night while we all slept. He was not cut out for marriage, fatherhood or civvy street.

By the time I started primary school, he was officially

gone. I couldn't even smell him in the house any more. Not even his Brut 33. His departure coincided with the first major loss of my young life. He took with him the babysitter from next door, barely ten years older than me herself. She and her family were the only black people I had known.

And there began a life with its differences. I was the only kid in my class without a father at home, an anomaly in a tiny Christian primary school in the 1970s.

Still, it didn't stop me singing Christian songs about a guy in a boat with a sister who was useful with the sails. I quite liked it, sitting in the school assemblies singing songs about Jesus and his virgin mother. *When I Needed a Neighbour* was a particular favourite, it reminded me of my father and the babysitter.

Like most kids, my life revolved around football. I'd play it all day at school and then again when I got home. With all the other kids on the estate we'd have massive games anywhere we could. Sometimes we played in the street, at other times against the walls in the car park of the already abandoned community centre. We kidded ourselves we had talent, but we didn't want it to take us anywhere. We weren't ambitious dreamers, we were merely children of the 1970s growing up under Thatcher. The lucky ones had the shirt of their glamorous football idols. Unfortunately, I was given a Crystal Palace shirt. Rather like my home life, Crystal Palace rarely offered a decent male role model.

My brothers and I managed a sporadic relationship with our father, who tended to turn up out of the blue at strange times, always smelling of booze. It wasn't an unattractive smell, it was more intriguing than anything else. I used to sit and stare at him in wonderment. How very strange it was to have a man in the house who I was related to but knew so little about. When he was drunk he was kind of cuddly, giving us hugs so I could feel his stubble against my face. He wasn't a happy drunk though; Patrick was a little morose. When I remember him back then I think he did care in a strange, detached way. But I always wondered why he couldn't love us and our mum as much as he loved alcohol and why he wouldn't just stay with us like the other, presumably miserable, fathers I knew of who ignored their children. Why did I not even have the shame of living in fear of him?

When my father's limited conversation would run as dry as his throat he'd slowly stand up to leave and we'd beg him to stay. I'd run to my bedroom and grab books, toys or anything I could think of to impress him. Did we bore him? Did *I* bore him?

'Look at me, I can read! I'm the best in my class, read a book with me, please,' I'd beg. But he never did. I'd dump a hundred toy soldiers onto the floor and say 'Let's play!' but he never did.

The visits stopped for a while after he crashed into a police station on the way home from a pub. Separation from my mother and all paternal responsibility came with a car it seems. He had the decency to stagger around and explain that he probably wouldn't be driving for a while, so we'd have to get a bus if we wanted to see him. He didn't do buses and was sick of the sight of trains. I didn't go. How could I get a bus or a train anywhere at my age? It didn't seem too important to him whether I visited him or not, so I decided deliberately, there and then, to lose out. He'd regret it, not me, I lied to myself in my first real experience of spiteful anger.

When I was ten, I found myself in the living room staring at our record player. It was ancient even then and hardly ever used. We weren't a particularly musical family, despite the fact that there was an old, unplayed piano in our kitchen on which we rested unread books and cups of tea. There were four Elvis albums that never got played, a very, very old recording by some foreign crooner and something else, something I'd never seen before. I pulled at its spine and out came a green album with a photo of a man holding a rifle in front of an Irish flag. It had wording in some foreign language too. How very bizarre. I played it and the words were familiar. I'd heard these songs before, songs like *The Wearing of The Green* and *The Rifles of the IRA* but where had I heard them?

Later that afternoon, the record was removed. I must have played it a dozen times staring transfixed at the speakers, then back at the album cover until my mother came stomping in the room, grabbed the record off the player and walked out without saying a word. She had the look on her face which told me that I was not even to question what she was doing or thinking. Dinner was held in stony silence that night, which was unusual. Normally there would be some kind of argument or somebody having the piss mercilessly taken out of them. Number two brother was scowling at me. He grabbed me after dinner and said 'You silly little cunt. That was Dad's record, now it's in the bin.' Curious, I decided I'd get the bus and visit him as soon as possible. My first interest in politics.

So we were Irish. Bugger me, we'd been throwing stones at the kids going to the Catholic school from the moment we could pick up a stone. The Irish families on the estate were called pikeys and we always took time to make their lives a misery. When the angry Irish residents used to run from their flats or houses shouting angrily, 'I know your father,' we used to laugh aloud at them. How the fuck would they know my father?

My old man didn't seem too surprised I didn't know about this Irishness in my make-up. I'd never noticed anything *unusual* about us before.

'There's history in our family name,' he said, leaning on the bar.

Fuck me, I was Irish. How the fuck did this happen? Is this why we were poor?

'If you had been brought up a Catholic there'd be no nig-nogs in your school either.'

Nig-nogs?

'The coons, blacks, jungle bunnies, you know who.'

He told me about being Irish and what it meant, not just to him but to millions of people who left a country where their families died in famines or were slaughtered by the British and subjected to unthinkable poverty and persecution. And they were still killing people in Northern Ireland – a country that was not Britain's to interfere in. He'd managed to get 800 years of persecution off his chest without spilling a drop of beer. Why he still stood to attention for the British national anthem, read the *Daily Mail* and polished his British Army medals was a mystery to me.

In 1982, when Channel 4 arrived, we watched it at home in black and white, while the rest of the world had colour television. I began to think that being Irish and working class was, quite possibly, shit. Why were we poor, for instance? Why did we not go away for holidays? Why did our father not bother with our birthdays or Christmas? My mother had removed his name from birthday and Christmas cards and presents. He didn't pay for them, so why should his name be on them?

Was all this the fault of the 'nig-nogs' and 'coons'? Once they had been pointed out to me they suddenly and miraculously seemed to be everywhere, even at school and on the estate. I'd never even noticed them before. One or *two* we could apparently live with, but they played loud music (not that I ever heard any) and they were taking jobs and homes away from the decent hard-working British people. We were poor because of the 'coons'. I never discussed it with my mother as she rarely wanted to hear anything about what my father thought or said. But where did that leave me? I couldn't talk about it to anyone. What a drastic turn of events. Gone was my comfort zone. I had to start secondary school soon and I wasn't looking forward to it one bit. We'd got no money and we had an Irish father. I kept those fears with me all the way through secondary school. Sure, it's not the great search for the meaning of life but it did all become desperately and inexplicably relevant for me, particularly when nobody wanted to hear or answer my questions.

I wanted to spread the good news, my new love of the white race. With this in mind, I sometimes skipped off secondary school and knocked on doors. There I would stand, canvassing you or people like you in gobby teenager garb, as if I or my party knew anything of, or gave a toss about, your lives, your credit card debts, or your perennially peeling wallpaper. I could fight myself out of trouble as easily as I could talk myself into it. So if I ever talked myself into trouble on your doorstep, one of my comrades would give you a good kicking while I stamped on your fingers and smashed any furniture in your hallway. If I couldn't get help, I never harboured bad feelings for long, because there was nothing like walking home in the afternoon covered in your own blood. Infamy seemed pleasantly stimulating.

So be wary of those beer-bellied, bald men, standing on your doorstep, canvassing your vote. Those rosettes should read: 'Friendly but dangerous bastards'. They, and their policies, are a product of what is wrong with society, not a solution to it, even if they appear to be the last plausible answer to everything that is shit about life. In such desperate times, voting for liars in the face of disappointment and political disillusionment inflames some very disturbing thoughts and resentments. Those very same thoughts just happened to have tickled me a lot sooner than anybody else.

CHAPTER 2

My secondary school was Thomas Tallis in Greenwich, one of those huge grey schools you see in cities across the country. It was vast, surrounded by muddy playing fields with tortured schoolchildren stuck in the mud in the pissing rain. It was towered over by the Ferrier estate, apparently where people even poorer than us lived, though I don't think it has ever been proven that people from Lewisham are in any way richer than those in Greenwich. They used to urinate off their balconies and throw furniture at people walking under the tower blocks, or so my brothers told me. It was a terrifying place just by reputation. Apparently, the woman who designed it committed suicide. I'm surprised she wasn't murdered.

I realised not long after my arrival at Tallis, that I was really just a small boy from a very small primary school and a comparatively tiny council estate. None of my old friends were there and I was cast alone and adrift, a unique opportunity, I remember thinking to myself, to buckle down and try to get away from this life. Brother number two was talking about going to university, away from home, away from London. Brother number one had moved out of home with a girl he'd got pregnant and the other brother had turned into a military obsessive and seemed to spend his entire life wearing army uniforms and old army boots. I think he even went through a period of saluting his dinner.

In my tutor group alone there were four different languages spoken. We had Vietnamese and Chinese kids who we all assumed spoke the same language and could understand each other. There was a Turk in his late teens who spoke no English at all but had a penchant for slapping his knob out on the table in front of terrified schoolgirls. We had a Scouse girl who was really poor, even more so than the girl with no front teeth who never showered or bathed or, for that matter, seemed to actually be at school. There was a tall girl who already had a boyfriend with a car. The rumour was that she'd let the boys put their hands down her knickers for a quid. I didn't take the bus for a whole week just so I could have a go one Friday lunchtime. She was off sick when my turn came around.

By 1985 I could actually feel myself losing control, despite the good intentions I'd had when arriving there not two years before. My mother's reign at home was tight, but never tyrannical. She kept our house warm and safe from the outside world. Imperial Leather soap was our only luxury and she worked her fingers to the bone just to get that. It was the 1980s and politics were everywhere but not in our house. It seemed the poorer you were, the more right-wing and racist you were encouraged to be by some newspapers. You could do battle with teachers for an entire one-hour lesson if you knew the right buttons to press. *The Sun* was running a campaign against the 'loony left' and you knew the sort of people they were talking about. History, humanities and even mathematics lessons ground to a halt for a heated and out of control discussion if you could make the right obnoxious, smart arse remark. But I had to be careful; phone calls or letters home from school meant a deafening silence and a look of disappointment from my mother that was too much to bear.

Was I just intellectually curious, challenging authority, testing boundaries, or what? What was it I was doing? I never even contemplated it. 'You're the worst kind of bully; you create misery for everyone,' I was told, as I sat cold in another office somewhere deep within the grey walls of

Thomas Tallis. By the time I was thirteen, they were calling me a racist too. Was I a bully? Was I a racist bully? Fair or not, being constantly told off suited me because it suited me to feel victimised.

I knew what racism was and it was not as unattractive a proposition as the trendy posters on the school's walls claimed it was. I'd already led a campaign against one teacher to remove an anti-racist poster because it had 'no white faces on it' and she had capitulated for a quieter life.

I went to the school library and stole Martin Walker's book on the National Front. It was a curious book, well the NF was certainly curious. Later, I flicked through the phone book to see if any of the big names I'd read about were listed. I rang a few Tyndalls but couldn't get the one mentioned in Walker's book, the one that wore the Nazi uniforms: John Hutchins Tyndall. He probably didn't even exist any more.

But I still didn't think I was a racist. I just thought that no one gave a toss about me because of my colour or class, least of all some trendy overpaid bastard teachers with lefty stickers on their stupid satchels. I wondered whether if I was black they'd be giving me some award for being so cocky; or if I was Chinese or Asian they'd give me exemptions from certain classes on religious or ethnic grounds. I began asking that question aloud more and more often. No one challenged me and I felt no one was listening. I was certainly becoming the worst sort of bully.

My brother came home from university and played Billy Bragg and Smiths records continuously throughout the holidays. I had my own bedroom by now; indeed we even had a spare room. Mum started dating a man who had a car. She had started working; we had a colour television and even a video recorder. Things improved but it was still an uphill struggle just to keep your head above water, minding every penny that your mother could earn, while thinking that all of the injustices in your life were surely because you were white.

What was eating at me, why was I so angry? I'd got over the Irish thing, in fact I felt it made me a little cool, but still something was not right inside. Every now and then I'd get a twinge or a sneaking suspicion about something. Perhaps it was growing pains but I'd grown to resent everything, even friends and family, and the fact that nobody seemed to be listening. I resented my brother for going to university and coming back in his holidays like he knew everything. Working class people didn't go to university and if they did they came back talking a load of bollocks down their noses at people. Did my brother's growing vocabulary compensate for his small penis? And why did he have to play poxy records about queers on bicycles with nothing to wear? We didn't talk for twenty years after his last visit home.

At fourteen I got a weekend and holiday job on Lewisham's fruit and veg market. They worked me like a bastard no matter what the weather. But they were real men to me. Not teachers or student wankers. They had huge, handsome beer guts and pockets full of cash. They would talk to me and listen to me and they never disagreed with any of the angry observations I made about black shoppers, black youths, black women...

I worked for a couple of brothers who absolutely hated black people, strange considering Lewisham's ethnic make-up. There was an ongoing campaign against South African fruit at the time, on account of the Apartheid regime. In front of the lefty paper sellers they made me stand shouting 'Cape fruit! Cape fruit! Buy a banana picked by Mandela.' Well, I made that bit up on my own but the lads on the market loved it. I was the angry clown, a £10-a-day barrow boy.

We sold cooking cherries marketed as edible and fiddled the scales to our benefit. The full-timer put cash straight into his pocket and not into the boss's. I ate as much fruit as I could because it was good for my complexion. I'd recently started masturbating furiously and frequently, which had seemed to coincide with an outbreak of acne. The endless wanking became a bit of a distraction and sometimes I had to sneak off in the middle of the day for one. The blokes there didn't seem to mind. 'He's going for a cotton wool', they'd shout after me as I went for another toilet break.

But there was something in my head apart from all of the pornography. I was constantly asking myself what I believed in. How did I feel about myself, my home, my life? What would I do when the drudgery of school, a constant and seemingly pointless distraction from wanking, ended? I'd never gone hungry, had never been left cold at home alone, or beaten black and blue like so many other kids at school seemed to be. In the 1980s, everything was on HP and the never-never. We had a large black market economy, lightning strikes and schools with their windows locked open and the heating turned up. Mrs Thatcher seemed to be god-like if equality of opportunity managed to reach your front door but it was not knocking on ours.

Who was going to listen to my complaints? What actually *were* my complaints? I couldn't articulate what I was feeling because I didn't understand it. Something had to happen, anything. The absolute and endless periods of boredom, either locked in school or locked in my bedroom, seemed to drag by while I sat plotting all the things I was going to do when I had the chance. Never once did I list what these things were, never once did I convince myself of anything. Whatever it was I was planning would only ever turn out to be another interlude before I could start beating my meat once more. At some stage I should have called the *Guinness Book of Records* to watch me go at it, Roy Castle playing his trumpet and me on my pork flute.

In August 1987, Rudolf Hess died. I had not long turned fifteen. I watched mourning German skinheads and suited Nazis on television trying to have parades and being beaten back by German police officers. Hess had been Hitler's deputy and possibly a little bit mad, but during the war he had flown to Britain in an attempt to broker peace with the British. They stuck him in the Tower of London and then after the war in Spandau Prison, where he lived a life of solitary confinement guarded by the former Allies. Was it right to keep a man who came in peace in prison? What did he do or say to deserve that punishment? How many wanks had Herr Hess knocked out between meals?

The gangs of German Nazis in their black jackets with their faces covered looked impressive to me, even brave. People my age, with courage and conviction, trying to commemorate one of their own, betrayed by liars in foreign governments. I was leaderless and I was bored. Where was my Rudolf Hess?

I pored over the books I'd stolen from the school library on British fascists and went through the phone book once more for numbers for the National Front. But still there was nothing, not even a clue to where those angry thousands of British patriots had vanished to not ten years before. In Lewisham, on our very doorstep, in 1977 the National Front had caused a ground-breaking riot. The police had used riot shields for the first time against the mighty National Front, resplendent behind large flags, like an army of avenging angels, trying to liberate white families from the torment of a multiracial Britain. But they were gone it seemed, no longer the salvation of the white race. If only I could have been ten years older, I would have joined the Front on that march. I would have stormed the barricades, I would have been our Rudolf Hess if necessary.

And then, at last, something happened. *British Nationalist* was posted through my door one Saturday afternoon. It was a grubby-looking newspaper with a red and blue masthead. It pronounced itself the monthly paper of the British National Party. It had a large 'BNP' encircled in the top right-hand corner and lots of stories and dire warnings about blacks and Asians. Oh joy! What common sense would now prevail! I breathlessly smuggled it upstairs, hid it under the bed with my most prized copies of *Razzle* (Readers' Wives editions) and waited until I could give it my full attention.

That night, I pored over the pages in awe. I read and reread the same articles. It had a picture of one of their members, a man named Richard Edmonds, sporting a black eye he'd got from fighting for his beliefs and an obituary of Rudolf Hess, as if he was their old friend. This was bigger than me alone. This was about history and people with a will (but very little ability) to change it. In the paper was the great John Tyndall, he of the Nazi uniforms and jackboots who had been to prison for his beliefs. It was astonishing. My body trembled as I held it in my hands and read every inch of its pages. This spoke to me, this said so much without actually making any real sense to me. It made me feel small and, at the same time, the more I looked at it, the more obvious it was that this was my calling. I would just have to meet the people behind this newspaper and offer them my services.

After school on Monday, I fired Mr Tyndall off a letter from my mother's typewriter and waited for his response. And waited, and waited. There was nothing.

By now, a few of the guys from school had found a pub that would serve us. We could even drink there in our school uniforms. On Friday and Saturday nights, a dozen off us would be in there propping up the bar and talking teenage bollocks like we knew everything. It worked out I could have three pints a night on my limited barrow-boy budget.

If we didn't want to go to the pub, we'd go up to Blackheath and sit on the common by the ponds with

plastic bags full of cans of beer and bottles of cider. Some
of the pretty girls from school came along too and there
was always kissing and bragging going on. They christened me 'working class hero' on account of the fact I was
fifteen and had a job, but mainly because I was crude and
a slob. It was a beautiful, warm summer and I was almost
in danger of being distracted from everything but relentless masturbation, when the phone call came. It was a
Wednesday evening and I was locked in my bedroom with
my favourite magazines. I rarely got phone calls. 'Some
bloke, I dunno,' I was told when I asked my brother who
it was. He always answered the telephone with military
precision but had been unable to glean exactly who was
on the other end of the call to me, to his obvious chagrin.

'Matthew?' asked the voice, 'Matthew, would you like
to come to a meeting this Thursday in Bromley, a meeting
of the British National Party?' Too right I did. I put the
phone down calmly and went back to my bedroom. This
was where it was all going to start, I just didn't know what
it was yet. I was going to meet John Tyndall for sure. I went
back to Walker's book and read about Tyndall again. John
Hutchins Tyndall. I wondered whether we'd be going for a
curry afterwards like other blokes did.

CHAPTER 3

The meeting was rather like a poor man's *Magnificent Seven*, except I was not overly impressed by my company. Four men in raincoats, one of whom was pissed and muttering to himself and a couple of slightly younger blokes behind me whose faces were already weathered by the Nazi constants of alcohol abuse and violence. Where had all the people from the mass movement I'd read about – marching resplendent behind our national flag not ten years before – gone? This was impossible to comprehend. Had that mass movement really shrunk in only a few years to little more than a few old tossers in the back room of a pub?

There had been an argument before the meeting and some people had walked out over something trivial, apparently not an uncommon occurrence. This was dreadful. We retired to the front of the pub and I was offered some books about the Jews and the Holocaust, the Jews and cancer, the Jews and the poisoning of the water supply and so on. I began to get the picture.

'Whatever happened to the National Front?' I asked.

'They're still around, just,' said one of the raincoats.

Sitting drinking orange juice and holding court was a tall bald man in his forties, eyeing me curiously. He had a pursed, angry mouth and yellow swelling under his eyes, obviously as a result of him having been smacked in the face recently. It was Richard Edmonds, the man from the picture in the paper and he'd obviously been fighting again! I sat at his table and he stared straight through me. He had an air of supreme confidence about him and very gracious manners. He was a little curt perhaps, rather like an old-fashioned schoolmaster. He was wearing a plain, generic dress shirt with plain, generic slacks and shoes. He was balding and his face was slim, with pronounced cheekbones. It was as if he had done everything at great effort to look as normal as possible at the least expense, something I'd been trying to do in my own way. I quickly decided he was not really father material for me.

Eventually he addressed me: 'Take these stickers. A young man like you should be able to put a few hundred of these up.'

He was obviously important but why did he feel he needed to make me feel smaller than I already did? He pushed a bundle of white stickers across the table towards me. The others grunted in agreement. It was like a meeting of Dibley Parish Council, without the Vicar.

'Do you want to ask me something?' he said, sitting upright as if waiting impatiently for the dunce at the back of the class to respond. I tried to think of something to ask but I couldn't. What was wrong with me? This guy could have had all of the answers to everything I ever wanted to know but I was frozen. He sensed my reticence and his eyes warmed slightly but his facial expression didn't change a bit.

'Do they teach you about the Holocaust at school?' he asked.

'No, not really,' I mumbled.

He reached inside a plastic bag and pulled out a newspaper called *Holocaust News*.

'Well, when they do, remember the Jews have told lies for centuries and that's probably what has brought you here tonight without you even knowing it.'

He was leaning forward to deliver the message, his face nearly touching mine. His cheeks were red, perhaps a little bit of a shaving rash or perhaps the excitement of telling the truth about the Jews had given him a flush. Everyone at the table nodded and agreed that I needed to know about 'the Jews'.

What a curious fucking nutter this bloke was. I had a quick look inside the newspaper. Was it really saying that the Holocaust never happened? I looked up to ask a question but he spoke before me and said abruptly: 'Good day to you sir.' I got the impression I was being told to piss off.

I'd snuck out on a Thursday night and caught a bus to Bromley to be redirected to a near-empty meeting of loonies, angry loonies at that. I hadn't learnt anything, maybe I was dressed incorrectly, maybe my hair was too long? I began my regular ritual of wondering if I was too thick. How could I not think of anything to ask or contribute? The stickers were crude and racist which I liked. It was quite clear to me that only the nutters were left from those halcyon days I had read and fantasised about. I didn't get to meet John Tyndall or go for a curry but I did get his magazine *Spearhead* to read before my ritual flicking through girlie mags and going to sleep.

Spearhead kept me awake for most of the night. I thought it was awfully boring but I also had the constant nagging suspicion that I was probably a bit too thick to understand it. There seemed to be a lot of references to things I was supposed to know about but didn't. Of course, it was talking about the Jews but I didn't understand the obsession. Were the BNP Nazis and if they were, why were they saying the Holocaust didn't happen? They hadn't struck me as Nazis, just as mildly strange people who seemed to have the ability to communicate with each other using some kind of telepathy I had yet to learn.

I read more and more magazines and newspapers from the BNP but I was still unsure of myself. I had met Richard Edmonds, Tyndall's de facto number two and had not asked him anything. They'd probably forgotten about me but I wasn't sure if I was ready to forget about them.

I'd been convinced for years that the Labour Party were errand boys for Russians to invade our country and make us submit to sodomy. Surely the BNP were the only people who could save the country from being bummed by some comrade from Moscow.

Most of my mad theories were backed up by the *Daily Mail* (our family bible) and, the rare times I was allowed to peek into it, a copy of *The Sun*. I began to reread *Spearhead* and having adjusted my tiny mind, the articles began to make sense. They were still boring but their secrets started to be revealed. There were other obscure characters to read about in the stolen school library books. And there were paramilitary groups, hiding in Wales or the like, blowing up cars in fields and running along the hills, like a danger-ous version of the boy scouts. While conventional learning passed me by, I convinced myself that, as a result of poring over boring academic books on post-war fascism that had never previously been checked out of the school library, I had suddenly and overnight became smarter.

Maybe all the wanking had finally gone to my head. I began scrawling NF or BNP on the tables, lockers and walls of the school and exploding violently and controver-sially with teachers and other pupils. School, and its shite attitudes towards whatever or whoever I was, was the source of my frustration. They shunted my classes a little as I found myself falling headfirst into the comprehensive school abyss, joining the educational subnormal in staring at walls for hours on end whilst being babysat through whatever lesson I had been removed from. Black and Asian people went from being my neighbours and classmates to parasitical leeches I could barely bring myself to acknowl-edge. They were not worth my time. I was beginning to understand what the stickers and the newspapers had meant. I was beginning to understand that deep sense of frustration that these people were stealing my history and my birthright. Why couldn't they just fuck off to where they truly belonged? And their 'protectors', the teachers and civil servants with their bleeding hearts and cheap, shit, French cars were little more than university-educated scum from the middle classes sent to suppress my freedom.

The lads from school had started following the Charlton hooligan crew and we had had a few scuffles. God knows why I went, as a life-long Palace fan but, as I had no one to go and see them with, I joined the guys from school at games. The feel of the pack, the stupid songs and the making of threats was magical. We even exchanged blows with QPR fans on the Underground one day. And so over to Upton Park we went, knowing they would stand us next to the West Ham hooligans who would invariably attempt to rush into our enclosure.

With burgers in hands we walked towards the away enclosure, past the scarf sellers and programme boys until I saw them. The National Front! Just stood there. Five badly dressed men with newspapers held up and a little board with badges on.

'For Christ's sake, fucking leave it!' one of my mates said, pulling at my jumper.

No way. I missed the first half hour of the game chatting to them. I told them I'd been to a BNP meeting and they laughed.

'How was that?' they asked, winking. I told them it was a little weird. 'You must have met Richard Edmonds then?' asked a man named Ian. Indeed I had. This guy was bright, even if he did have a lot of ink on his hands, trousers and shoes.

'If you want to join us, just write to the PO Box in the paper and somebody will be in touch. There's nothing to worry about, *we're perfectly normal people.*'

Christ, I wish I'd taken that as an omen. I took a copy of their paper *The Flag*, a glossy professional-looking newspaper with normal sorts of stories in it about normal sorts of things. There were pictures of party activists without black eyes, selling newspapers or handing out leaflets and, as I discovered later, a picture of that same bloke, Ian, who was only the bloody Chairman of the NF!

They gave me a badge that said 'Smash The IRA', so I stuck it on and went into the game and caught up with the lads.

'You're fucking sad,' said one. 'You don't wanna get messed up with that lot.'

But I desperately did. I had a copy of *The Flag*, their magazine *Vanguard* and an anti-IRA badge. I don't even remember the score, but I do remember running from the West Ham hooligan crew the ICF afterwards.

A week later, some men from the NF came to our pub and propped up the bar. They seemed ordinary blokes like me, with ordinary concerns. It had been a good omen that I'd made contact when I did. After some more arguments in the local BNP, some of its members were thinking of joining the NF. One of those there was a BNP member who knew Richard Edmonds and as we spoke he told me what a wonderful person Edmonds was but that they had a bit of a beef with John Tyndall, the party supremo.

It was friendly. They asked questions about school, my family, did I like sport and so on. By the end of the night, almost every Nationalist in south London was in there. People from the large Croydon branch made up the majority, with four or five BNP members also there. In all there were twenty of us. To me it was the most magnificent drinking club in the world but even then it struck me that it was not a very happy one. I began to feel that I had that magic telepathy I had been missing in Bromley, at the BNP meeting.

I sat with the organiser of Croydon NF and the man from Bromley BNP who were old friends and they answered my questions. They explained that the NF had disintegrated after the 1979 general election when they felt they should have made a breakthrough. John Tyndall had left to form a party, which later became the BNP, and the NF carried on without him. Some felt it was his fault that the party had not made the expected breakthrough. Margaret Thatcher was partly to blame they said, she stole the racist vote, but there had already been problems inside the party.

The National Front had split again in 1986. The other lot still survived and were led by a bunch of middle class clowns, including someone named Nick Griffin. 'Fucking loonies, lunatics, poofs etc.' It had been an ideological split. The BNP unashamedly followed the 'Führer' principle. They followed their leader John Tyndall out of the National Front because the NF's elected body would not let Tyndall be Chairman forever. Tyndall was supposed to lead the BNP until his, or its, death. As a matter of cosmetic surgery it was inserted in the BNP's constitution that there could be leadership elections. JT couldn't have envisaged Nick Griffin joining the BNP back then.

I reluctantly accepted an invitation to go to another Bromley BNP meeting where I would be introduced to Richard Edmonds properly. The NF guys shrugged their shoulders as, although they respected Edmonds, they were not interested in hearing him speak. I got the impression that people considered him to be a bit mad, as opposed to terrifying like I did. I made the NF lads a promise that I would definitely be joining them. They gave me a large bundle of newspapers and stickers and every one of them shook my hand when they left. I had definitely made new friends. Every other person in my life could go and fuck themselves. They were probably very glad of it too.

Richard Edmonds was, in effect, the BNP's number two and national organiser. He also turned out to be adorable. A violent, unrepentant Nazi, a Holocaust denier, a man with convictions for criminal damage and violence was, without doubt, the most generous person I had ever met. He would give you the last baked bean off of his plate. If you could engage him, he'd listen to you for hours, nodding and encouraging you, empathising with every pathetic moment of your life. He was sincerely warm and encouraging, humorous when required, a man who took pity without mocking and would pour scorn on every single one of your enemies, lifting you up by his very company.

Two days after agreeing to join the NF, I was watching the BNP's second-in-command speaking to a crowd of ten or so in another back room of a pub. It was very different from the last time I met him. He foamed at the mouth as he ran through the newspapers, relaying stories of black crimes and unashamedly quoting *Mein Kampf* and John Tyndall's own offering, *The Eleventh Hour*, where the solutions to my sufferings and insecurities were properly explained. He was spectacular, draped in clothes patched and unironed, railing against the Jews in the media offering the news and hiding the solutions, rallying us into action as we headed off to the bar and he to his minibus and into the night.

I was easily hooked. Aghast as I was at Edmonds' predictions about the modern world, he'd plotted perfectly our response, the building of a resistance movement that would one day lead to a race war whereby the lazy old white man would get off of his backside and strike back against the Jews, lefties and liberals who were grinding down our great race and our great people. He described as a 'pollutant' those blacks and Asians who were a sore in the blue, Aryan eyes of the British people. Edmonds had originally been a teacher and then had a high-paying job in industry. Now he spent his entire life cooped up with copies of *Mein Kampf* and *The Eleventh Hour,* totally and unselfishly dedicated to bringing about his master's moment of glory which would lead to my moment of glory too. When our time came, this green and pleasant England would be ours again, my country would be mine to share with kith and kin. Edmonds had a selflessness I would very rarely experience or witness in any other person in any other political organisation again.

But he'd also made me take to my bedroom in panicked rage. I stared at my bed and my little black and white television. They meant nothing to me now. We lived in a home without superstitions or hatreds and my home life continued in its ignorance. I sat on my bed, shaking with excitement. Finally I felt I had a life with purpose.

The next Thursday night, I joined the Croydon NF branch for a leafleting session in white enclaves on the south London and Surrey borders. Twelve of us with 100 leaflets, each working in groups of four. Here I was, finally doing something useful. We were like a secret army. If one piece of literature through my door could get some-one like me interested, then it surely would not be long before there were thousands of us, ethnically cleansing our country.

I met Paul Ballard who had the nickname 'Trotsky', which at the time meant nothing to me. Like most people I'd come across he was dressed blandly and had a thin face. His hair set him apart however. It was as white as the snow, slightly receding and looked as if it had never seen a comb. He had carrier bags full of reading materials with him at all times but this couldn't disguise the fact that, in reality, he was a challenged forty-something who had somehow missed out on a decent life of his own. I didn't feel sorry for him. I wanted to admire him. I thought that it was selfless to be bland, nasal and uninteresting to the general public while on the inside secretly dedicating your life to the betterment of white people.

I needed to share this complete change in my fortunes with somebody. A few meetings in a few pubs, a few hours walking around housing estates with leaflets, and I was a permanently changed individual. I felt I should share this news with another person in need of a good change in their life.

My old man barely raised his head. Normally, flying visits meant we kids wanted money for some hare-brained scheme that he could dissuade us from. He didn't even laugh at me.

Instead, he gave me the only speech from him that ever had any constructive passion in it.

'No Irish, no dogs.' Grandfather Paddy, with my Dad and loads of other Paddies in tow, looking for somewhere to live a long way from home was constantly thwarted with this refrain. No Irish, no dogs? Thank god for the blacks really. Eventually they found somewhere to live. 'No dogs, no blacks' became the new mantra. This proud union man, proud Irishman, with a British passport, overall second in the Royal Artillery marksmen championships, with a medal to prove it, proud consumer of Irish rebel music and Carling Black Label. The same man who had, not long before, run from an Indian restaurant where we had been eating, citing overtly racist reasons.

What a conman. All those years he had spent complaining about immigration and law and order. All those years he had, in all honesty, been no different from the purveyors of fine bongo music. He was taking the piss out of me, chiding me like I was just some teenage idiot. I'd thought that fascism was for him. This was *his* way of thinking articulated after all. But now all he could do was sit in the pub and make fun of me spitefully. As I left the pub in disbelief he told me, 'The Irish have been described as the niggers of Europe, do you hate them too?' Well, I was beginning to now.

I decided to make my mark in the Front by volunteering to help the East London branch stuff Tina Wingfield's election address into what seemed like a million envelopes. In 1988, the East London branch of the National Front had two members and only one was active. It was the responsibility of the local branch to support any local candidates, so Tina Wingfield, resident of Worthing, Sussex, was standing in Epping, Essex, in a by-election, ably supported in her campaign by Ian Anderson, Chairman of the National Front and the only active member of the East London NF.

I volunteered to help because I had bugger all else to do, with no job or schooling to continue. I spoke with Anderson on the phone and put on the Burton's suit my mother had purchased for me in the hope that now I'd left school, I would find a job and stop tossing off in my bedroom all day. For months I'd toyed with various business ideas, with redoing GCSEs or maybe even taking an A-Level or two but I was kidding no one. I had four GCSEs at C or above and a few Es and Fs. Someone, somewhere had put a hand on my shoulder to voice their surprise that I didn't do better and no doubt some cheeky fucker had also sneered in the staff room that I was, after all, a thick, working-class, white twat.

On the same day, my mother forced me onto a train to Victoria for an interview for a job with the Metropolitan Police Civil Staff that she had found advertised in the *Daily Mail* a week before. Then I was off to East Ham to visit Ian Anderson. The interview was a success. They offered me the job on the spot. I knew it would make Mum happy but I didn't really care much for it. The salary offered was something like five and a half grand a year, with all public holidays etc., etc. However, I was sure that work would just get in the way of my upcoming revolutionary activities.

I took the District line across London, squeezed into my little suit, with all of the other suits and the Bengalis and Pakistanis. Sounds funny, but racists never seem to notice other white people. As per my instructions, I alighted at East Ham some forty minutes later and began the long walk to Anderson's house.

There were two doorbells on Anderson's unremarkable terraced house. The tiny front garden was unkempt, with bags of rubbish piling up and spilling over the low front wall; the windows, net curtains, front door and window frames were all filthy. The front gate was hanging on its hinges so it had to be lifted in order to pass through. If there was no answer on the first bell, I was to ring the second and wait a long time. Thankfully, he came on the first bell and shook my hand warmly, having remembered me from a paper sale we had been to together in Orpington a few weeks before. Anderson's home was no Reich Chancellery on the inside either, nor even as comfortable as Hitler's bunker might have been. The carpet was 1970s brown and green, and the wallpaper peeled off from the wall. It was so cold I kept my coat on the whole time I was there. It was grim and I was a little disappointed. After all, Anderson was not a native Eastender but, as he almost immediately told me and mentioned to anyone who cared to listen, Oxford bred, *and educated*.

The living room floor was scattered with copies of broadsheet newspapers with huge chunks cut from them. It looked like he'd never thrown a newspaper away in his life but instead of filing them had left them all there in some mad and pointless exercise to protect his shag pile. I sat on his couch, that had no springs or cushions so my arse was on the floor anyway, while Anderson prattled on about his busy day; his long chat with the newspapers that morning; a bloke from Newcastle who was bringing his entire family and pets into the Front from the BNP; and loads more stuff that didn't interest me in the slightest because I wanted to do all the talking.

There were a million things I wanted to ask Anderson but he treated the whole two hours I spent in his company like a party political broadcast. First, he knew the BNP members who were also active in the NF and warned me not to trust them. According to Anderson, who had served under Tyndall too, people in the BNP were always falling out with Tyndall but could never stay angry with his number two, Edmonds. In light of the lack of NF Christmas activities planned, I decided to attend the BNP do, and Anderson agreed I should go too.

'Report to me anything unusual, or unusual by BNP standards anyway,' he demanded. Within two hours of cementing our friendship, I was going to spy on the BNP for the Chairman of the NF.

Anderson was nowhere near as mad, or as likeable, as Edmonds. He had the air of a poor Tory about him, reasonable but unexciting and not very inspiring. He could be my mentor for all the normal stuff, I decided, but Edmonds would be my mentor for all the stuff that was exciting and dangerous. I couldn't discuss ideology or the Jews with Anderson but with Edmonds I could explode like a firecracker and he'd be off up and away. Anderson was an unremarkable plodder with a thin face and a high-pitched voice. Still, horses for courses and all that.

I had joined the NF just as the bloody and bitter sorting out process had cooled down. The two NFs agreed to carry on separately and let the results decide. It didn't mean they were immune to kicking the shit out of each other whenever possible, a fascist tactic that continues to this day, by the way.

But the 1986 split was the most damaging to the Front, the name that had become synonymous across Europe with racial hatred. Within two years the Official National Front based around the admiration for Italian terrorists and Roman Catholicism would be gone. Griffin and Harrington had driven it into ideological oblivion after leading it up a revolutionary garden path. The NF never got back the hundreds of active members who quit in disgust. I would later go on to do my damndest to finish it off completely.

The skinhead culture was having a rebirth in the late 1980s, more mindless and violent than ever before. Apart from in the Leeds division, there were no skinheads openly active in the National Front and, although they turned up on the few marches and events, they were never members or encouraged to be so. In recent years, however, they had deserted en masse, in part for financial reasons. This pleased the BNP members who were still close to the NF because, though Tyndall hated skinheads and made no secret of it, they were slowly beginning to rear their heads around the BNP. Previously the NF had relied on skinheads for cash and muscle and this was the prime reason for Tyndall accepting them back into BNP ranks. Tyndall was, after all, a Nazi through and through and a man who had never held down a proper job since deciding to become one.

I wondered if I could be a John Tyndall type and live off the movement myself? By Christmas that year I was active almost every day, putting up stickers and posting leaflets through doors during the afternoons before collapsing in front of the television for a few hours of American sit-coms and chat shows, then heading off to the strange fringe meetings I was being invited to.

And it was at one of these that I met my first terrorist. I spent a good hour in conversation with him, before Ian Anderson asked me to step outside the pub we were in while the terrorist was in the loo. A dozen or so of us left the pub and, as it eventually turned out, left Tony Lecomber in it. Lecomber, who also went by the names Wells and East, had a conviction for blowing himself up outside the headquarters of the Marxist, Workers Revolutionary Party, which was having an internal feud in the early 1980s. His idea had been to inflame this feud and get the lefties fighting one another, presumably leaving the fascists alone.

The corrupted legend had it that after carefully assembling his explosive device in the back of his car, Lecomber stepped out to get himself a Wimpy burger. Upon his return, he was given a rudimentary lesson in the basic dos and don'ts of the tilt switch. Bang! He'd written himself into the history books of stupid Nazis, though he would later go on to be a major player in the resurgent BNP.

Lecomber had been sniffing around the NF for a few months, and had been particularly keen on being lent Anderson's ear. Anderson finally put a stop to this, fearing Lecomber might be trying to ingratiate himself with the membership on behalf of elements even more sinister than John Tyndall. Although unproven, it was a common line of thinking among the paranoid far right, that people incarcerated for terror-style actions became police informants upon their return to the movement from which they originally came. It is more likely however, that getting short shrift from the BNP, Lecomber fancied his pseudo-intellectual waffling would curry more favour in the NF. Sadly for him, nobody could understand a bloody word he was on about and this just increased suspicion of him.

Lecomber returned to the BNP. I had quite liked him. I think Ballard did too but he didn't put his hand in his pocket all night and had droned on endlessly about bollocks so he was no great loss.

CHAPTER 4

All the stomping around the house I do is merely an amusement to my family. Do I wear kinky boots? Have I gassed anybody lately? Does my new-found racism mean I wouldn't give Diana Ross one? Are Hitler and Monroe enjoying their little love tryst on the moon? Perhaps I have a personal line to the Führer, and can join him at a moment's notice for a ménage à trois. They all bang their hands on the table in the absolute joy that their inappropriate humour gives them.

I have no time for this however, as I've been hiding in my bedroom since Christmas, sheltering myself from the awful conspiratorial truths passed on to me by Richard Edmonds. Richard had taken me aside at the BNP's Christmas gathering and summed up for me the overbearing evil that we faced in our quest to regain our great nation. Was he really just mad? A former schoolteacher and an educated, respected nationalist, who stood some five inches taller than me, had taken the time to simplify the struggle: we were good, Jews were evil. To believe anything else would be a waste of my time and youth. I had to get a grip on the Jewish question to really understand anything else.

The New Year, 1989, begins quite well for me in the NF. Fresh from our humiliation at Epping, every day sees me more active and more involved in fascist politics. I read *Mein Kampf*, kindly supplied by the BNP, at the family dinner table, and sell a dozen copies of *The Flag*, door-to-door on a housing estate in Downham, south London. Around a quarter of the estate's residents are black, so my comrades and I equip ourselves with useful tools should violence or a puncture befall us. I'm knocking on doors with a copy of the monthly paper in one hand and a wheel brace in a plastic bag in the other. I start attending Bromley BNP meetings as regularly as the NF ones; the crowds are the same, though the speakers are different.

Our own leader in the NF does not command as much respect as the BNP's John Tyndall. Anderson has made the mistake of being known by his members; of not being aloof enough; and of living in London, where he can't avoid all contact with other members and, more importantly, not soil himself by having black or Asian neighbours. Nick Griffin's splinter NF claim that that Ian Anderson is a drunk and his deputy – now a leading member of Griffin's BNP – a wife-swapper. Respect!

But my personal involvement is going well; the more I put myself about, the more people phone me to go on an activity with them, or attend a meeting. 'The Mad Bomber' Lecomber, back in the BNP for good, starts calling me during episodes of *Emmerdale Farm* with interesting bits of gossip about my own party and its leaders, all very scurrilous but at the same time amusing.

'What d'you think of that?' he asks.

I don't know what to think, so I don't argue but instead tut-tut as Jack Sugden moves more to the left with every episode. I also decide that if any more Asians and homosexuals turn up in *EastEnders*, I'll have to start listening to *The Archers* and do away with television altogether.

Meanwhile, we are preparing for a regular NF ritual. We sit in our rented pub back room and plot our savage attack on Irish marchers through London that January. It's not a particularly political meeting as a lot of time is given over to the question of 'giving Diana Ross one'. Eventually we get around to the real business in hand. I am going to be involved in a confrontation with supporters of the IRA. There will be violence and almost guaranteed arrests. Am I prepared for it? Too fucking right I am. For all I really care, we could be attacking conservative Christians, I just want action on a grand scale.

I had had my indoctrination to violence, throwing punches on doorsteps or even having to run away if the numbers weren't in our favour. So far I had not let the side down and why would I? I'm hardly a huge brute of a bloke but I am a 'game little fucker'.

The Irish Republicans were to march in north London. We had to stick together and be careful of a group called Red Action who would be sending spotters out to try and ambush us before we got to the march.

'They won't take any prisoners. If they get hold of you, they'll fucking bury you', the ex-squaddie organising us warned.

'What do they look like?' I asked, expecting the reply to be the usual 'like social workers'. Instead, I was told sternly and seriously, 'like everyone here', as he waved his arm around the room.

The derisory thirty of us who turned up to protest in north London were as wet and miserable as I was, probably wishing, like me, that they'd stayed at home for the *Brookside* omnibus. The Irish marchers shuffled past, protected by the police from thirty wet and cold blokes with poor dress sense standing under a banner that read 'National Front: Stand by Ulster'. Still, I do learn a new song, *Fuck the Pope and the IRA*, and buy a highly illegal magazine from a man with a sports bag full of Ulster badges, scarves and magazines. Red Action obviously didn't have spotters out that day, because if they had, we'd have been murdered the moment we came out of the Underground. A thousand or so marchers pass with their flags, banners and drums, demanding British 'Troops Out' of Northern Ireland. Bringing up the back of the march was the infamous Red Action, a large bunch of blokes with faces as angry as ours, who slowed dramatically by the barriers separating us, offering for us to have a go at them. We declined.

Just when the day was looking like a complete disaster, a stocky man, modelling the attire of a 1970s jungle fighter put his arm around me on the way to the pub and told me not to look so disappointed. I was meeting a legend. I'd seen him in pictures before and seen him at the 1988 NF march to the cenotaph on Remembrance Sunday, where he had held a wreath, dressed in a suit with white shoes, white tie, and sunglasses covering most of his face. I had just met Eddie Whicker, the man who had once given out NF leaflets at the Notting Hill Carnival.

How could I not look disappointed though? The NF's turnout had been appalling and then, like some ridiculous public relations exercise, the Chairman had made us all crowd in together for a photograph to make us look like hundreds in the next issue of *The Flag*.

The man in the jungle jacket just laughed. Red Action marched on, calling out his name.

'Eddie, give us a wave, Eddie! Eddie, give us a wave.'

And he did, still laughing. Even Red Action types had respect for Eddie.

'I work on the bins,' he announced, apropos of nothing much.

I told him that I was due to start work soon too.

'That'll be nice,' said Eddie, politely refusing a number of offers of drinks.

He then sat me down to tell me a lot of wonderful nonsense about working on the bins.

Eddie was a raconteur extraordinaire. In his forties, he was short and stocky, with a square head and a load of tattoos on his hands. He wore sunglasses although it was completely unnecessary and had an incredible amount of both menace and warm joviality about him. As we talked

I noticed his hands were like shovels and he constantly
looked you in the eye when he was talking. I also noticed
how people politely stopped by to say hello to him but if he
didn't want to talk to them, they left straight after. Under
his nose there was a very thin, red moustache, which he
stroked when he listened. This man could do somebody
some serious damage, which I suppose is why Red Action
chose to acknowledge him. That day, he just wanted to
cheer up little old me.

He told me that women, knowing that the binmen were
coming, would often change their tampons or sanitary
towels and leave then on top of the rubbish for what he
described as 'the binmen's delight'. Then, that the socialists
are all having sex with each other, which is funny as there
are hardly any women available, let alone any that would
be likeable to nationalists. Finally he said that he'd like
to come to a Croydon branch meeting more often but he
works in the evenings, as a cleaner. And *you would not
believe* the things women in big offices leave around for the
male cleaner to find.

'I could start a huge bloody collection of used tampons,'
he says. 'Apparently, they're good for toothaches!'

Everyone choked on their beer as Eddie went over to
talk to Chairman Anderson.

'I'll see you around,' he said, then he was gone.

Marginal political groups can make an enormous city
like London seem tiny. The city is divided up as to who
runs what almost by the street. Out of politeness, the BNP
and NF are expected to respect and never encroach on
each other's areas of activity. Then there's the tiny little
red groups who control certain pubs, clubs or venues.
The whole of Islington is apparently controlled by AFA
– Anti-Fascist Action, the umbrella group of which Red
Action is a part – while east and south east London are
a fairly good battleground for everyone. Now I was

learning where it was and wasn't safe to be active. Between
the NF and the BNP there were probably no more than
150 activists in London, almost all divided into their own
little cliques with their petty hatreds and distrusts. Some
were organisations within organisations, some were merely
old friendships that never die, even with all the splitting of
the main parties that had gone on. I declared my intention to start a Lewisham branch of the National Front
and everyone nodded their heads, delighted. Word of this
reached Edmonds and, in turn, Tony Lecomber, who rang
and asked if I would like to start a BNP Lewisham branch.

My Croydon branch organiser took me aside and
warned me of the dangers of becoming too closely involved
with the BNP, saying that for such a bright and intelligent
fellow as myself it would be a waste to be fooling around
with that bunch of cranks. Still, cranks are quite fun, and,
with the potential 'invasion' of our country by Hong Kong
Chinese, it was useful to know as many cranks as possible.
I also had a list of names of old Lewisham NF members
to follow up and nobody knew them better than the BNP
cranks I'd become friendly with. One of the names owned
a stall on Lewisham market, which was a bit of a surprise.
He gave me ten pounds and took ten copies of *The Flag*
from me whilst selling cheap t-shirts to black shoppers.

My new NF membership card arrived in the post the
same day I started work for the Metropolitan Police in
February 1989. Things seemed to be improving, its late
arrival was apparently due to high demand and this new
one makes last year's membership card seem seriously
dated. As for work, I'd been sent to Deptford police station.
There I was, sixteen years old, with a seat within eyeshot
of the WPCs' changing room door. For a few days I kept
my eyes open for a WPC rushing out on the job with bare
breasts flashing like sirens but it never happened. I had
ready access to all the multiracial crime statistics; every

day, another black crime was reported and circulated. It's funny how white crime never raised the eyebrows quite as much.

The Local Intelligence Office had the photographs of every known crook and pimp in south London on its walls and the property officer had an old black and white television in his office that I stopped to watch for one hour every morning. The civil service was a dream. I was owed three days' holiday from the moment I joined and every moment I worked after 4:30 was recorded until I reached eight hours and a day off. The pay was very average but the conditions and privileges were phenomenal. The job was all facts and figures and had barely enough challenges to keep a five-year-old interested. I was a clerk; facts and figures were what it was all about but with my activities with the Front keeping me up most nights, I could barely keep my eyes open at work.

My mad and angry demeanour gave me an air of mystery to the stale old ladies I worked with and before my first month was over I was ranting and raving to them about statistics, democracy and freedom of speech. It made an unusual change to their regular diet of the latest episode of *Neighbours* and they were all quite impressed by my dedication to the cause, even if I had none to the job. I was quickly talking myself into trouble but the ladies encouraged me to keep talking, keep plugging away with my racism. It amused them.

And I hardly needed their encouragement. I loved to rant. When drunk, I would engage people in heated discussions about race and immigration. The rallying cry of British Nationalism was 'For race and nation', and whether I was banging my fists in the office, home or pub I pushed strongly the fact that the British people were never consulted on immigration and had never had an opportunity to vote against it. The National Front and BNP survive solely as a reminder that democracy and freedom of speech cannot be curtailed by simply ignoring something that had quite plainly changed the make-up of Britain and the British people. To be born in a country does not make one a countryman: kittens born in a kipper tray are not kippers!

The coming New World Order would ensure that everyone looked, dressed and thought the same as it did on race and immigration. Capitalism and communism would only be served by race-mixing. As Paul Ballard and Richard Edmonds had predicted, I eventually saw who would gain from this: the Jews, the corrupt liars who controlled the media and our thoughts, the great liars who'd invented the Holocaust, where six million imaginary Jews had vanished up a chimney that did not exist.

The National Front was only formed in 1967, how could it break into a political system that had served only two parties for hundreds of years? Ian Anderson was preaching from his tatty sofa that, within the next couple of years, we would overtake the SDP as Britain's fourth biggest party. It was like an impossible dream that, against all hope, a group like the NF could ever gain power by simply pushing leaflets through doors at election times. When John Tyndall departed from the party after the Front's disastrous and infamous 1979 election results, the National Front developed a strategy they called 'Beyond Capitalism and Communism'. It was a mishmash of pseudo-intellectual ideas about distributism and the joys of rural life. Lost for a direction and a reason for surviving, the NF desperately tried to reinvent themselves. Of course, they could not reinvent the working class, they had a constant dialogue with them about confrontation and race but not on the issue of class itself.

When the Front split again in 1986, the Official NF, led by Nick Griffin, had headed for the hills and the agrarian way of life, sounding like Pol Pot, while the rest of the

NF remained concerned with racism and anti-Semitism. Anderson was constantly trying to make the NF image-worthy and had a great deal of discomfort with the party's two publications, *The Flag* and *Vanguard*, dealing solely with race. Despite his demeanour and distributist rhetoric, Anderson was building a printing empire in the East End that he was afraid of losing. Indeed, during my entire time in the National Front I hardly heard Anderson ever make a racist comment out of anger or genuine race hatred and spite. On every minuscule piece of publicity the party scraped together, he would always attempt to divert attention away from race and immigration. Not because he was not a racist but because he was a businessman. In 1989, with Hong Kong on the national agenda, it seemed that it was only the money he was making from stickers railing against Hong Kong Chinese immigration into Britain that made him bring it up at all. He much preferred stickers with the legend 'Britain's fastest growing political party'.

Having concluded with the others that a race war would be the only possibility for nationalist survival, I realised that I would have to do everything I could to make it happen. However, my job in the civil service was not conducive to revolutionary activity. Despite this I would rant and rave and exchange blows with the Socialist Workers Party at Croydon shopping centre on Saturday mornings until our time came. They were vicious, sporadic attacks. We'd approach them from behind and kick at their legs and when they hit the floor, we'd put the boot into them and walk off. We'd travel to do this too. Often we'd make a stop if we saw them and pile on top of them. It was practice on easy targets. When he was available, my new friend Eddie Whicker would turn up with his hands in his pockets. He didn't need practice but came along to give instructions anyway. He often stood away from our paper sales with his hands in his pockets, admiring the displays in Topshop or the like before flying in with an angry, shovel-like fists to deal with any opposition we attracted. It wasn't as if the rest of us couldn't look after ourselves but Whicker dished out thick, final blows that were never answered. Security, which in reality was perfectly executed violence, was his business but he seemed to think he did it with some kind of professional acumen.

'I suppose you could say I was like a trophy for the left,' he said, 'but they've never been game enough and I've been at this for years.' Whicker was also a trophy for the far right, everyone wanted him on their team.

In 1989, the National Front(s) and the British National Party had a combined membership of around 1,500–2,000. The National Front had about 800 solid, as did the BNP, with the remainder holding dual membership of the two, or even three, organisations on the right. This was not, as I had hoped, a mass organisation marching on towards victory. Apart from a very few new recruits like me, most members were old and tired, though committed to the cause. In the old publications I looked over there were hundreds of active members who had vanished without a trace, people who had stood as election candidates for Parliament or local councils, who had simply quit.

At forty years old, Anderson was gradually realising the NF had no chance. He made this clear to me. We managed to look professional on the outside, for fascists, with a glossy newspaper and magazine that were way better than what the BNP had to offer, but there was hardly anyone in the membership who could write well, hardly anyone in the membership who actually read the publications and very, very few who understood what was written inside the publications.

Anderson was continually looking for people loyal to him, people who would not ask questions about the party. I fitted the bill well because I was a newbie and could be

shaped into a relatively obedient little dog but my spending time with the likes of Richard Edmonds and the BNP's
London membership also worried him. It was at this time
he introduced me to someone he wanted me to work with
very closely in Lewisham and Bromley, Terry Blackham.
Blackham had a long record of violent criminality, so long
that whenever his criminal record was read out in court,
it took ten minutes. But Anderson liked Blackham's sense
of loyalty. The Croydon organiser and I met Blackham
for a pint in Penge, a nondescript part of London that
borders Kent.

Blackham had a large, flat face. His hair was bright red
and shorter than Wembley's hallowed grass. He had no
charm about him but an incredible amount of menace. He
was three years older and a couple of inches taller than
me but had been around the scene for years, mainly as a
skinhead who went to the odd march or rally for a punch-
up. For some strange reason he had made a decision to
get his life on track after a series of run-ins with the police
and black gangs, so he had decided to rejoin the NF after
drifting away a few years before. He had broad shoulders
and, like Whicker, had thick building-site hands that he put
to use regularly in and around Beckenham in Kent, where
he lived, and Penge where he liked to drink.

Soon, everywhere Anderson went, Blackham and
Whicker would follow as his bodyguards, with Anderson
issuing instructions. Blackham was the sort of bloke who
would help an old lady across the road, turn the corner
and punch somebody else to the ground. He looked it too,
with his ginger hair cropped short and his nose bent out of
shape, distorting his pale, freckly face.

'I failed Bromley numeracy,' he told me, 'and they give
that away!' He had desperately wanted to be in the army
but either his criminality or his lack of numeracy had put
paid to that. Whenever he pulled up outside my house my

mother would have respiratory failure but Blackham was, I felt sure, another comrade for the race war. We immediately took each other under our respective wings, sensing that we'd be better friends than enemies. Blackham became my chauffeur, driving me to and from the drunken brawls he liked to start and finish.

CHAPTER 5

Until the day I came home fully bloodied with split lips and a black eye, I thought violence was a brotherly love type thing. Sure, I stood outside school with my fists clenched but it wasn't until I was properly attacked by a political opponent that I felt any other kind of pain. Talk about the real world. More blood than the Red Cross, me. With Blackham threatening to throw a red under the wheels of a District Line train, give me brother Nobby in his grandpa's old army boots any day.

I knew violence. But political violence? It ain't for the faint-hearted. Football fans hunt in packs and most get away with just looking good while shouting abuse. But a fight amongst the fringes of the political classes was quite often a fight to the near-death. We might have enjoyed smacking up the reds but they never ran. It was as if they were always defending their little corner of Moscow or having their own battle of Stalingrad. We were no better or worse. We didn't have the cunning or the precision planning and execution of the red hit-squads, who seemed to appear from the shadows like magicians with large smiles and iron bars. Blackham feared no one and that was dangerous. He never backed down, never walked away, even when he was with his tiny gang of boys who were too young to fight.

We were looking for trouble and in 1989 the BNP felt it had enough physical presence to actually take on the left on the streets. Whilst the NF was getting turned over by the opposition for the first time in years, an uneducated media was attributing the rise of the unhinged BNP to the NF.

With Blackham leading on the streets, Anderson's softly-softly approach went begging, as paper sales turned into bloody and provocative pitched battles. The BNP were even worse. They didn't care how they were quoted or what they did. All publicity was good publicity and, of course, they'd opened their shop in Welling, south London. They were now running their increasingly openly Nazi party in full view of the world.

There are many ways to travel a country. Some do it in style but the new, useful team from south London do it in the back of Terry Blackham's car. Blackham had begun to recruit around the south London area a few former friends from his early skinhead days. Where we had hit the right areas with leaflets, a small trickle of people had begun to take notice and respond. Nothing major but in the first few months of 1989, there was a marked increase in activity by both the NF and BNP on the streets of south London. Our new branch now had something like a dozen members. We vetted them carefully, every one of them was a single white male in his late teens or early twenties and every one of them was game for a race war. Terry let me sit them down and 'educate' them about some potty policy they had a genuine grievance about over drinks and, doing our little double act, by the end of a few pints, we had convinced them that we would have to start throwing the punches and lighting the fuses ourselves.

But my favourite loony was always Richard Edmonds of the BNP. He was a sentimentalist. He'd been a Nazi since his teens and joined the National Front in the 1970s. He was losing his hair and had always enjoyed incredible misfortune. He was an unimposing six-foot Nazi who had spent his entire life reading the wrong sort of books, mixing with the wrong sort of friends. A schoolteacher, stoned off the premises by teachers, parents and pupils and then later given a large cheque by Cable and Wireless to leave their company too. If you didn't know the titles of the books, you would assume that Edmonds was well-read, sitting in his tiny BNP office surrounded by unsold copies, some up to twenty years old, of his Führer's periodical *Spearhead* and listening to Radio 4, waiting for Wagner to soothe his brow. He enjoyed his sparse existence, never tempted by drink, cigarettes or women.

Had the now defunct National Party not stood a candidate against him in the 1970s, he would have been elected to Lewisham Council with – if you included the National Party splinter vote – forty-six per cent of the vote for the NF. He would have been the NF's first, and thus far only, elected official.

Richard Edmonds was the first person to get hit on any activity, partly because he was always the first into the fight. I remember not-so-lazy Sunday afternoons with Edmonds as his small crew posted 1,000 leaflets through the doors of 'decent white folk'. In the morning the BNP and NF would sell their newspapers, *The Flag* the more readable of the two but sold with less gusto at Brick Lane market in east London. Nazis and cranks from across Britain would converge there on Sunday mornings to sell newspapers and abuse the Asian men and women who lived there. The NF and BNP would compare battle scars from the previous day's activities, before heading off to the pub at midday, together. But not Edmonds. He attracted a small, semi-literate group – the rest of the Brick Lane Nazis were illiterate – totally dedicated to political canvassing on Sunday afternoons. They were the poorest-dressed, least likeable and most anal of all Nazis. Hitler was a vegetarian and so would they be. The thuggish, meat-eating, beer-drinking and cigarette-smoking element were excused the usual canvassing on a Sunday because of their exertions the previous day. Those incapable – there are none unwilling – made do with knocking on doors just as the *EastEnders* omnibus was due.

There was no snobbery involved in this arrangement; there was a genuine admiration of the meat-eaters heading off to the pub; everyone had their duty to perform for the cause. I fell somewhere between meat-eater and semi-literate. In need of a lift home and, in those days, incapable of topping up a hangover so early in the week, my path was decided for me. The BNP's battered old minibus would pull up at some estate, Edmonds would produce a thousand leaflets and stickers and we would be off, a dozen zealots with no Sunday dinners waiting. When the leafleting was finished, Edmonds would drive us all home singing the *Horst Wessel Lied*, a famous German Nazi song. We never knew where we were going or what was planned for us. It was almost like a family drive into the country, although we were headed for council estates and tower blocks.

People would often rush out of their homes to support or abuse us. Frequently, we would be accosted by someone with a particular gripe, asking us to deal with some 'bloody Pakis' who had moved in recently. The NF used to receive a dozen requests a week in the mail from the public, asking for someone to pop round and deal with a 'problem'. If we were out canvassing for the NF and that happened, we would shoo them away, saying 'we're not the council', but in the BNP you could say anything you liked. If someone called you a Nazi, well what of it? Often people would open their windows and shout, 'That's right mate, you fucking do it, I'm with you all the way', and we felt good for it. The East End in particular was turning Nazi according to Edmonds. Accordingly, every Sunday, around three o'clock, to back up the good work done by our leafleting, the meat-eaters would leave the pubs and assault any remaining Asians on the way home. There were no BNP candidates to canvass for, we were just building the movement. 'Elections,' Edmonds told me, were 'a waste of time.'

The NF didn't feel that elections were a waste of time. They were a waste of money, yes, but you had to be in the game to win it. So one night I found myself in the small leafy suburb of Hemel Hempstead, National Front member John McAuley's heartland, at a council by-election bid, pretending I was part of the political establishment. We sat at the back of a public meeting, addressed by Anderson and McAuley himself, being heckled by the public.

Anderson, honestly believing that members of the public had given up the night to listen to his schoolboy vision of green belt England with him as its reasonable, middle-class Prime Minister, struggled to be heard but got through his speech. McAuley, slow, stuttering and unheard, gasped for breath trying to criticise a local leaflet put out by National Union of Teachers members at the local school criticising him for being a fascist. The crowd cheered so I knocked a woman over. All hell broke loose because I'd sat right in the middle of the local anti-fascist group. I ended up hitting anyone who moved with my umbrella, while Blackham and a former international sprinter fell on hard times did battle with the rump of the group.

Within a minute the entire meeting was in uproar, hurling chairs and insults at each other. Somehow the police were taken a little by surprise and took an eternity to arrive on the scene in force. As the police arrived, I immediately got the Front members present to start clapping and cheering. It worked beautifully, as the police simply dragged out those not clapping and cheering: the public. As the last protester was dragged out, screaming about their democratic rights, I gave a loud 'Three cheers for the police!' and a rousing chorus of *Rule Britannia*. It was enough to bring tears to the eyes, particularly as McAuley got to finish his speech, still stuttering and gasping for breath as he promised the deportation of every black person in the country.

It felt like a huge victory as we headed back to London, licking our lips and exaggerating our fighting prowess. But in reality, peering outside of the tiny world that fringe politics occupies, it was very small. There would be no national headlines in the morning, though the Hemel Hempstead press gave us the front page, with a picture of me with my fists clenched. We were a million miles from Lewisham and the 'Sensational Seventies'. It was deemed worthy of mention in the party publications as the NF 'defending' themselves but without the violence and tension, the meeting would have passed by like the many hundreds of others I attended, bored to tears by the National Front.

Blackham, surprisingly, managed to open a PO Box in his hometown of Beckenham, on the Kent and South London borders. He asked me to be Chairman of London NF. The Croydon & South London branch was renamed Croydon & Surrey NF, as Blackham and I were to run the new South London division, trying to outdo the BNP. On one of the three holiday days owed to me by the civil service, I took tea with Edmonds at the BNP shop-cum-head-office in Welling, another spot on the Kent-south London border.

The BNP were proud of their shop. They'd got around planning laws with the help of a dozy Tory council and opened for race-hate-business slap bang in the middle of the road into multiracial Plumstead. Behind large blue doors and boarded-up windows, Edmonds sat running the BNP. It was driving the NF crazy with jealousy, but the BNP, and in particular Richard Edmonds who ran the shop, were a law unto themselves.

Edmonds swung the door open and proclaimed: 'Enter, we are open to business. And if you're not too busy, work will set you free.' I didn't realise until years later that this was a play on the words above the gates at Auschwitz. The shop was dimly lit because there were no windows; the entire place was boarded up against possible attack by opposition groups. It was from this shop that the BNP masterminded race riots, racial violence, Holocaust denial and played a huge part in contributing to the deaths of four young men from south London. The inconspicuous little blue building in Upper Wickham Lane became a centre for race haters, Jew haters and convicted terrorists. It had the uniform Nazi look about it; newspapers scattered everywhere and magazines piled up to the ceiling. Edmonds had his tiny living quarters upstairs and his shower in the office-kitchen.

We took tea with powdered milk and exchanged the usual gossip. The phone never rang and no one popped in. Alone in the back office with Edmonds, I smoked Woodbines and asked questions.

Racism and Nazism was easy. It hardly troubled the grey matter. Socialism seemed such a difficult, almost entirely out-of-reach way to think and behave. God knows what Red Action were about but they generated the same cynicism that I felt about middle-class students preparing for life in the banking industry, sitting in cafés reading Marx and Lenin, talking about the proletariat. It's uninspiring and none too practical when real politics takes place around people's kitchen sinks. Groups like the SWP didn't inspire many to throw their weight behind the great leap forward. Banging on about the solidarity of internationalism whilst racism has its physical roots in the tower blocks of hopelessness was pointless. Instead of a difficult, and eventually thankless, campaign for better housing for all, why not campaign against people from different races being housed? At almost every white household we knocked on the door of, we were told the same thing: 'I'm not a racist but...'

The people of the East End have a marvellous tradition of fighting fascism, but fascism still always manifests itself in the East End because poverty persists at its heart. We used to believe that Arthur Fowler would have been the organiser of Walford NF or BNP, and Den Watts would be the understanding landlord with a cheap back room for hire. Dorothy Cotton was to be the disenfranchised white pensioner, and Doctor Legg a Jewish gangster. I discussed this with Edmonds but he didn't have a television and hadn't watched one in years. Even when the BBC was paying him £50 for an interview about the BNP headquarters – which the BNP protested was merely a shop – Edmonds never watched.

The people could go ahead and vote in as many Labour councillors and MPs as they wanted, but the BNP went and took a physically intimidating stranglehold on parts of the East End in the late 1980s and early 1990s. It would later – briefly – translate into electoral success. That was the moment when I realised that Labour had lost its working-class voice.

Anti-Fascist Action and Red Action articulated this dilemma first. The BNP was intimidating and ingratiating itself into static communities with real gripes. Some kids from traditionally Labour-voting families would come and stand with Nazi canvassers and candidates. This was out of blind support for racist ideology, not working class traditions that may otherwise have seen them vote Labour. No matter how often the far right get finished off in the East End of London, they always start again, always strong, always active. The NF didn't have the numbers to succeed in the East End but the BNP did. Instead of benefiting from all the good things a community could have offered itself, the BNP was allowed to tear it apart with Richard Edmonds and the slippery Eddy Butler at the forefront.

They called their campaign 'Rights for Whites', very catchy. In an area where so many basic rights were being overlooked, small vocal sections of the community were stirred into action by the BNP. There was quite obviously a fight brewing for physical control of the streets and the BNP openly laid plans for it.

Every day, free of charge, Edmonds would send thousands of pieces of literature to supporters in east London. The BNP paid for it; it was advantageous for them to have people who had no jobs, out all day posting racist posters and leaflets through doors. While the left-wing group, Militant, were sending their supporters to night school, the BNP was preparing theirs for a race war and prison. People's feelings of disenfranchisement were obvious to us, well before New Labour abandoned the working class. Just by having an office/shop, the BNP became approachable and, although Edmonds's generosity was more than likely bankrupting him and the party, people did travel sometimes enormous distances, to sit down and talk to someone who cared, someone who was not pretentious or condescending to them.

To deal with the huge growth of BNP activity on his alleged 'patch', Anderson organised the London Activities Group. The idea was to arrange an instant response to events like IRA bombings. If the IRA were to strike on a Monday, by Tuesday morning all the main train stations were to be covered in anti-IRA literature. I was to be the link man as I had a telephone at work, available to me anytime I needed it. No one seemed to mind that any such calls to action were to be made from within the depths of a police station. Anderson gave me a list of the few active members the NF had in London. From that we narrowed it down to ten people who were also active nationally.

The first test was the Deal barracks bombing. I was having a fish and chip lunch in the office when news came over the radio of a huge bomb having gone off at Deal Royal Marine barracks. Vinegar dripped onto my Burton's trousers as the news came through. It was the first time news had ever affected me. I was so angry I was speechless.

The ladies in the office chewed their lips as I sprang into action. What was I going to do? I knew I really had to do something, after all I was in the National Front. I rang Anderson immediately.

'Ian, the IRA have bombed Deal army barracks!'

'WELL, WHO GIVES A FUCK? FUCK OFF, I'M BUSY, I DON'T GIVE A FUCK.'

Anderson was hysterical. His printer was not working properly. He got another couple of phone calls, each receiving a similar response, until Terry Blackham called him. Blackham called me that night and said the group had been cancelled. Anderson had had a bad day. Thankfully the Queen had not rung and asked him to form a government that afternoon.

Anderson's uncontrollable temper had made him impossible for many people to get along with for a number of years. I had already begun suggesting to Blackham that he come along and meet Edmonds but all the Jew business seemed to concern him. I assured him it was because he did not understand the Jewish problem. Eventually he agreed to meet Edmonds one fateful summer evening in 1989.

We met up with forty other BNP activists at the office in Welling, where they were preparing to demonstrate against a meeting being held in the public library against the BNP. The meeting became known as the Battle of Welling and the BNP members who attended it have been lauded as heroes ever since. Afterwards I agreed with Blackham that we would never mention what happened in Welling Library that night. It physically shook him, which, with hindsight, I find hard to believe. At the time, however, I thought we were both going to be sick immediately after we left the library and hid in a garden as ambulances carried away women and police cars blocked off the roads around the building.

As Blackham and I made our way to the BNP office, we passed the library on Welling High Street, and I commented that this would probably be a public meeting. All meetings held on council property and deemed to be of public interest were called public meetings, because they were open to everybody to attend. It was probably just a cheap way to rent a hall and, throughout the 1970s, the NF used council property to hold provocative meetings, knowing that the opposition would have to be allowed in. Under the Representation of the People Act, councils had to allow fascists with a candidate in an election use of public facilities to hold a public meeting. It is not something widely used any more, since the vigilance of anti-fascists usually results in such meetings being turned over by the greater weight of the opposition. As far as we were concerned, ten or so of us would go to the meeting and heckle before being thrown out. Simple.

The BNP office was packed. Forty men had been shipped up to Welling in the back of a removal van and a series of cars. They stood in the shop in an orderly fashion while Lecomber arranged for transport to the library for others. In the dark kitchen where he also showered, Edmonds smoothed his bald head and washed up some mugs. There was a lingering sense of anticipation in the air. Testosterone as thick as smoke and hushed, whispering voices made the atmosphere almost unbearable. We nodded greetings to each other as we were all acquainted from other activities, or from the Sunday paper sales and punch-ups down Brick Lane.

Eventually it was decided we would all go in the removal van and Blackham and I joined the others waiting expectantly in the back. Nothing was said in the three minutes it took to get there and it was not until we decamped at the back of the library that I suddenly realised there were no posters, placards or leaflets. Nazis and libraries do not mix. If they're not burning the contents, they're throwing the occupants out of windows: it wasn't going to be protest, it was going to be a hit! My balls tightened with anticipation. There was a great deal of excitement as there was a tube strike on that day which meant that few AFA stewards would have travelled across town to protect the meeting. Blackham licked his lips (not at my balls) and I looked around at the other people in the van. Men, older than me, with crude hatred on their faces and breaths, were waiting patiently to act out as much ordered violence as they could in the time allotted to us.

'Straight in and out,' said one to no one in particular and there were quiet grunts of agreement. Lecomber called me out of the van.

We knocked on the library door and waited. Hiding around the side of the library, the rest waited silently. A cleaner came to the door and looked puzzled.

'There's a meeting on. You can't come in,' he said.

'Yes we can, it's a public meeting. Anybody can come in,' I said back.

With that he opened the door and everybody walked up the stairs behind Lecomber and me. We passed Greenwich Labour councillor Geoff Dixon looking absolutely startled. I shouted 'Public meeting' at him and he tried to block our way. Before he could speak, Lecomber punched him and, as he lay across our path, stamped on his body. The cleaner got the same treatment and has never worked again. The room was packed with women, most of them Asian, concerned about having to bring up children in such close proximity to renowned 'Paki bashers'.

They were sitting in rows in a tiny meeting room, even by Croydon NF standards. I pulled the door open and looked at them, a little bit startled. Suddenly, a voice from behind, unmistakably that of Richard Edmonds, boomed 'British National Party', as if it was a police raid, or the clearing of the Warsaw ghettos. The meeting stood up as in piled the BNP team. Blackham and I and Lecomber were the only ones actually to strike men that night. No sooner had Edmonds shouted than a man stood directly in front of me so I hit him square on the jaw. It hardly knocked him over, but before he could respond, Blackham gave him a haymaker and the rest piled in.

Tables were turned over and chairs thrown with very little physical opposition to warrant it. The members of the meeting cowered against the back wall as the BNP marched towards them, picking up chairs and tossing them at the group. A fat little bald man called Daddy waved a motorcycle helmet and hammer at them menacingly, then the BNP laid into them. They could have simply broken up the meeting by intimidation but they wanted to hurt them physically, which they did.

I thought I was having a psychedelic moment because the room was spinning but everything was actually being turned upside down, one man after the other laying into a small group of women, hitting them with chairs and hurling tables at them. There just weren't enough people at the meeting to attack, so the windows were put through with chairs. It was a bloody massacre. People were lying on the floor helpless, being stamped on, kicked and hit with objects picked off the walls and floor. A pregnant woman was locked in the toilet and the BNP were trying to kick their way in to get at her and her unborn baby.

Blackham and I left after minutes, although it felt like hours to us. The sounds of hate-fuelled aggression and shocked, bewildered terror followed us out like a sickening cocktail. We passed a man on the street, in distress and covered in blood, waiting for the police to turn up. Two policemen were with him, but neither was willing to venture into the library. As we left the scene we heard a huge crash of glass, it turned out later that someone had thrown themselves through a window to escape.

It had taken only a few minutes to leave seventeen

people needing hospital treatment; mainly women, mostly Asian, most definitely beaten. It was hardly a revenge for Stalingrad but it went into the party paper as 'Reds Routed' anyway. At a BNP branch meeting, I was given a special mention as a colleague from the NF who had helped. I was so embarrassed I nearly dived through the windows to escape too.

I decided to throw myself firmly into the NF again. It was far preferable to stand over 'Troops Out!' pickets than to face jail for assaulting women and children. At the meeting, I grabbed a copy of the anti-fascist magazine *Searchlight* to read as Edmonds was asking for donations for some of the 'heroes' who had been arrested at the library. I was a fucking coward to have done such a thing. I began to realise that this was what race wars were about, the innocent attacked and their dignity destroyed. If my mother had known, she would have disowned me on the spot.

After the library attack, I started to get to know Terry Blackham better and work with him closely. He struck me as someone with no real political motivations but, with a string of convictions for violence, at least he was quite honestly an unrelenting hater. In and around Penge and Beckenham he and his older brother had a notorious reputation for violence, even though he was only in his early twenties. Worryingly for me, most of his violence seemed to have been directed towards the Irish community.

Working as he did – labouring on building sites in and around London in the 1980s – Blackham was always being presented with opportunities to exercise his talent with his fists. He was as hard as nails and, worse still, he seemed to have absolutely no concept of fear. And you need fear, even if you are a hard man like Blackham. He seemed driven by an unquenchable thirst for violence, normally put down to an alcohol problem that seemed to be given as a mitigating circumstance at every court appearance. But Terry was not a reckless piss-head; he was an aggressive psychopath from the moment he woke up and began hitting and kicking the enormous punch bag that hung from the ceiling outside his bedroom, to the moment his head hit the pillow at night.

Terry knew little and cared even less about the history of the National Front. I had made every effort to understand what I had become involved in; Terry felt it should all evolve around himself, there and then. He didn't care for John Tyndall's BNP, he didn't care much for anything to do with any sort of history. I once read to him from Ray Hill's book, *The Other Face of Terror*, how NF members would shout 'All quiet for the Queen's speech,' before Tyndall's former sidekick in the National Front, Martin Webster, spoke at marches and rallies. He didn't find it funny.

Terry had been on the fringes of the NF when it began a period of revising its politics. He'd initially been attracted to the skinhead culture of violence, loyalty and patriotism that had become staples of a young nationalist's diet, and indeed the NF's income and output during the early to mid-1980s. I even envied Terry that he'd seen some of the radicalising of the NF by the likes of Nick Griffin but had had the chance to reject it. He'd also had the opportunity to run around in skinhead gangs while I had probably been kicking my heels at school wondering where folks like him were and what they were doing.

Terry had been part of the *Bulldog* – the paper of the Front's youth wing, the Young National Front – generation, entranced by Joe Pearce, a genuine working-class Messiah to the Front's faithful membership and leader of the YNF. Pearce had been sentenced to jail in 1982 for his editorship of *Bulldog*. While in prison, he wrote a fanciful explanation of the NF's new strategies, published later in the rather slim *Fight For Freedom*, with a wittering introduction by his friend, Nick Griffin. Pearce was one of those rejecting factional fights and preferring to keep up his own race war without silly 'politicians' talking a language he didn't understand.

Terry had always been totally unaware of what was going on. The music and magazines the NF had previously produced for people like him had seemingly just stopped one day. The more the official Political Soldier NF, led by Nick Griffin, moved leftwards into loony territory, the more it disintegrated and lost members. The traditional membership grew tired of the teachings of Colonel Gaddafi and of Nick Griffin, Derek Holland and Patrick Harrington spouting an apoplectic, wholly foreign worldview. The Political Soldier NF's final glory was an expenses-paid trip to Tripoli to meet Gaddafi's Foreign Ministry fixers. They also tried to ingratiate themselves with Welsh extremists who were implicated in the firebombing of holiday homes on the Welsh borders. Their final insult was being labelled perverts by East Belfast UDA (Ulster Defence Association) and warned to leave Northern Ireland immediately.

Paul Ballard, who had for a while been a Political Soldier, felt the young revolutionaries were the 'wrong people at the right time' for fascist politics. The influx of revolutionary ideas by new, young blood had reinvigorated a dying organisation so it must have seemed a case of 'the madder the better'.

The NF tried to get involved in more issues besides race. As with most things, the problems of the day were with race and immigration according to the Front, but post-1979 the NF realised it would have to go and find new members, not wait for another influx of Ugandan refugees to get people riled up. It had to challenge modern issues with modern solutions, still based on race but, most important, not from the pages of *Mein Kampf*. From this new strategy came magazines like *Bulldog*, *New Dawn* and the music network, Rock Against Communism. A group of Italians hiding out in London, wanted by the Italian authorities in connection with the Bologna bombings, convinced the likes of Griffin and Harrington that the NF had to appear more radical and develop policies on the environment and the economy that could distance the party from the former leadership – especially the old Nazi John Tyndall who had swallowed so much right-wing Tory policy in the 1970s – to be attractive to disenchanted Tories under Heath. They developed a deliberate policy of supporting causes that traditionally the left had been allowed to campaign on. Early on they even tried to intervene in support of Arthur Scargill's striking miners, whilst the BNP attempted to help the Coal Board.

When this strategy failed, in 1986, the Front had to smash itself to bits and try again. The result was people like me, Blackham, Whicker, the Croydon organisers, Birmingham NF, Liverpool NF – solid working-class branches and members, none of us old-time Nazis but all of us dedicated to nationalism, dedicated to our race and nation. Once inside the party, we did not care for party policies or long and odious posturing; we undertook to follow the party line on matters as long as the party provided for us an enemy and a solution. We did as we were told and followed the programme. The last thing we wanted to do was sit down in some strange farmhouse and be questioned by some Political Soldier about our revolutionary and religious convictions. Everyone was welcome in our idea of the party, particularly those with a relaxed attitude to violence. You had to keep us quiet, keep us entertained and we would perform. The minute someone started toying with the mechanics of this well-oiled machine, it fell to fucking pieces.

CHAPTER 6

As well as violent depression, a growing theme among the far right is alcohol abuse. Part of the reason for this is the obvious loneliness that perpetually single men feel. Every morning becomes the morning after the night before. Excessive alcohol consumption is a theme of everyday life for the far right. This was evident when spending time at the Croydon organiser's house.

I was crashed on a bag of unopened cement. Dignity through work or something, Marx said. The organiser was not a Marxist so, despite being a builder, he was not getting through that many bags of cement. He'd bought the house with his brother. It was large but run-down, on the outskirts of Croydon, the sort that would nowadays be converted into tiny rabbit hutches and called studio apartments; in hindsight, it was a sound financial investment. He lived there alone while renovating very gradually, surrounded by old fish and chip wrappers and empty cans of beer. He was also becoming obsessed with the fact that his neighbours might have thought he was gay. For the life of me, I couldn't see why they would think that.

I made my bed for the night out of half a dozen unopened bags of cement and collapsed into a drunken mess on top. In the morning I was to make my first ever visit to Rochdale. 22 April 1989, as Chinese students were building the protests that would lead to their eventual massacre at Tiananmen Square.

On arriving in Croydon earlier that evening, I had met neo-Nazi punk-rock god Ian Stuart Donaldson, all shaven hair and big boots, strolling through the train station on his way to the local skinhead boozer for a drink. I felt like Prince William meeting the Spice Girls at Windsor Station. Ian Stuart, as I knew him, was the John Lennon of the Nazi music scene. Well, he's dead now, so they have that in common anyway. During the 1980s, he and his band Skrewdriver helped fund the NF's political ambitions by playing 'white noise' gigs, where skinheads turned up to get pissed and stomp around hired halls to the dire noise created by skinhead 'musicians'. Where it all went wrong for Stuart I don't really know. The original line-up for the band had been signed to a progressive record label and became mildly famous towards the end of the punk era. When Rock Against Racism took off in the late 1970s and early 1980s, Stuart rebelled and ended up reforming the band under the NF's own music umbrella, 'Rock Against Communism'. He was a died-in-the-wool neo-Nazi; as the NF diminished in the early 1980s, the skinhead scene had begun to grow and so had Stuart's influence. As the Front lumbered around from pillar to post trying new ideas and radical new policies, Stuart and his band churned out crude punk-rock anthems for a German record label which the NF distributed for a tidy profit. Eventually he'd quit to do it for himself.

'How are you Ian?' I asked.

'Fucking great,' he said. 'Who are you?'

Who was I? Dedicated Follower of Fascism. The Boy With A Thorn In His Side, Charmless Man, you name it. We exchanged small pleasantries about the Rolling Stones and how easy it is to form a Nazi rock group based on a few cords ripped off an early Rolling Stones album.

'Come down and have a drink with us,' he suggested and off he wandered towards an evening's drinking pleasure in the company of his nearest and dearest. The same awaited me.

Donaldson had formed the 'Blood and Honour' music network and enjoyed worldwide notoriety between prison sentences, as a leader and spokesman for the international skinhead scene. Skrewdriver were pioneers of the Nazi-rock movement and, for the first time ever, skinhead musicians were paid real money for their musical output. He was hounded mercilessly, not just by anti-fascists who realised how dangerous this sort of counter-culture could become if left unchecked, but also by those in the political movement he and his potential funding had deserted. Politically, he punched far above his weight, having the muscle and the capital everyone wanted.

Eddie Whicker and his fat mate from London Underground are taking turns driving the Croydon NF minibus, berating each other and everyone else about their haircuts, their bad breath, their smoking. Gays take good care of their hair, Eddie tells me. And being men, they probably go at it like rabbits too. Fascinating isn't it?

'Fornicating,' he says, at the top of his voice, and everybody giggles. We wasted much of our bad breath on intelligent conversation.

We were free to smoke and fart at will, as Anderson and the only other member of Newham NF had to pick up Hemel Hempstead and Luton NF members in another minibus. I was astonished to discover we actually had to pay for the hire of the bus and petrol ourselves, but delighted that it was £5 cheaper to go with the drunks from Croydon and south London than to go with Anderson and the other contingent. As well as homosexual hair care, Whicker returned to his favourite subject: stories about tampons.

'I've given up collecting them,' he mused. 'I couldn't find any other collectors to join me at a swap-meet.'

Whicker was always light relief to the hungover. He insisted we pull over at a Happy Eater for cooked breakfasts and coffee. Stalin ran the Soviet Union over drunken, bawdy meals where a wrong comment or even a wrong glance could seal your disastrous fate. There was something not unlike Stalinism about most NF functions.

Despite the grandiose claims by party publications, the emerging BNP and their confrontational activities meant that we were slowly drowning while pretending we were only waving. The question on most of our minds was who would be the next to go over to the BNP? The Croydon organiser denounced Paul 'Trotsky' Ballard as being too close to the BNP. He had made the fatal mistake of not agreeing with some stupid dictum criticising the 'Naziness' of Edmonds and the rest of the south London BNP. He went into the car park to sulk as I quietly bit my lip. It was an attack that had obviously come from up top.

'You too,' the organiser said, pointing at me angrily, 'you're too close to them.'

Eddie coughed, leant across the table, put his thick, tattooed arm on my shoulder and glared at the organiser.

'Maff has friends, so does everyone else. Button your lip.' The organiser protested some more, though obviously without the aggression he'd shown to either me or Ballard.

The twelve of us marched back to the minibus. Whicker turned to the organiser and told him bluntly for us all to hear, 'If anyone starts slagging off any other nationalists I'll give them a clip around the ear.' And he meant it too. 'No doubt you'll be reporting this to Anderson, but if it's a choice between a wimp or a Nazi, you'd better make sure you have plenty of backing.' I sat next to Ballard for the rest of the journey.

Despite the cold weather, we had to drive with the windows down because we smelt so bad and smoked so much. Whicker didn't drink or smoke. The bins kept him fit and occupied, while his spare time was spent standing guard on Anderson. In his white shoes and resplendent, well-ironed black shirts, he was a complete contrast to Anderson, who dressed in an old pinstripe with egg stains on his tie and socks poking through his shoes. Eddie's clothes were always clean and well-pressed, Anderson's were always crinkled and dirty. On almost every activity I went on that Whicker and the Chairman attended, Whicker would bring a spare shirt and pair of trousers in case Anderson should ever truly despair of his own attire.

I didn't know the geography of a journey from Croydon to Rochdale but even an inexperienced driver like myself knew that driving on the hard shoulder was not going to get us there very quickly. The longer I sat in the van and smelt the by-products of last night's beer and kebabs, the more I thought about the Socialist Workers Party, all perfumed and nubile, heading off for a huge shagging session at somebody's stately home while their parents were in the Algarve. An experienced journalist who strayed into the NF declared: 'If you're not a Socialist at sixteen you have no heart. If you're not a National Socialist at twenty-one, you've got no bottle.' So I, just turned eighteen, had plenty of time then, eh?

Our proposed march had been banned. With a certain predictability, it transpired that we never really intended to march anyway. Ian Anderson had not even planned for one. All we would do was turn up so we could be turned away. Then we would retreat in the direction of our unassuming hotel on the outskirts of the town and make complaints about the lack of democracy and freedom of speech for us race-haters.

Rochdale played Peterborough that day. As we pulled into our designated meeting point with the rest of the motorway travellers, we decided that we would be the 'Peterborough Supporters Association' should the police pull us over. A quick head-count revealed that there were forty of us, plus at least another hundred in the town awaiting our arrival. It was like being in the cavalry, descending upon the poor defence-less white folk of Rochdale to restore their national pride. The big boys from London and the Midlands were going to show the local boys how to stir up the public, pitch whites against Asians and reclaim Rochdale as their own once more.

A quick phone call to one of our local lads told us that the news was not good. Asians with baseball bats were running riot and the police could not control them. A mob of reds from Manchester were in town whipping them into a frenzy, and our local members had decamped the area for their own safety. With nobody in the Leeds branch either competent or responsible enough to hire a minibus, they too were on their way home, having been picked up at the train station by the police.

Anderson addressed us with cool words. The game was up, we would have to do it on our own. *We* would have to save Rochdale ourselves. This was first class news. The hangover was clearing and I was in need of a brisk walk.

'I have to warn you,' said Anderson, 'that there are hundreds of Pakis armed with baseball bats causing mayhem in the town. We shall have to show great restraint.'

Restraint? Did that mean we were going to have to do a runner?

'Pakis play cricket, not baseball,' I offered, by way of light relief.

Anderson exploded like an old bitch, ranting and raving, 'fuck this' and 'fuck that'. He was still ranting and raving as I got on the minibus.

'Just get in your bus and keep your mouth shut!'

And that's what I did, red in the face and a little flabbergasted. It was from that moment on that Anderson was named 'Angry' Anderson, after a dreadful Australian pop star. Whicker offered Anderson a coat, but he refused.

'What a bitch,' said Whicker as he followed Anderson's minibus towards Rochdale, towards humiliation, towards an early bath.

The Greater Manchester Police sent a bloke with a lot of tassles and buttons on his shoulders to stop us getting into Rochdale. He stood in the middle of the road and flagged us over to the side. Anderson got out of his bus with hands on hips and argued. Then argued some more. Then got really annoyed and sat in his minibus and sulked. Another plod came and pressed his face against our window to watch our impending humiliation. We were told to leave our minibuses and stand by the side of the road while the plod looked inside. Fortunately Eddie had not brought his collection of used tampons along for the journey, because plod was desperate to arrest somebody and the theft of surgical materials is a serious offence in Lancashire. It was decided we should drive into Rochdale and pick up any stragglers whom the police were keeping behind their lines for their own safety. We moved in a convoy of two minibuses, one car and half a dozen plod vehicles, into the outskirts of town, where we decamped behind a church.

All hell was breaking loose in front of us. Angry young brown faces were running up to the mall line of police and trying to throw things at us.

'Come on let's have it!' they were shouting, wielding baseball bats.

I've often wondered where people get baseball bats from. They should probably ban them, because they appear only ever to get used to hit people with. This seems quite strange if you've ever seen them play it on television, because the professional players always drop *their* bats when it is time for fighting.

A confused young Asian strolled up to us from behind and was belted to the ground by somebody from Hemel Hempstead. 'Angry' Anderson had given up arguing and was now pleading that the police let the NF hold their pre-booked meeting in a hotel that wasn't even in Rochdale anyway. Is there no First Amendment in Britain? We were screaming 'Free Speech' and 'Hang Winston Silcott', because, after all, you may as well try and persuade the plods that you are quite decent really. No go. So off we went in disgrace, smashing the church windows as we went. Absolute losers. The National Front: as much influence as a sack of shite.

The hangovers returned as we slowly drove out of Rochdale, accompanied by a police escort until we were finally out of Lancashire. No stopping (because we were not allowed) at any more Happy Eaters. No more tampon jokes, no more quick wit. I buried my head in my lap and got the distinct impression I would have to dispose of my underwear by the time we got to Watford Gap. It could have been nerves, it could have been the chilli sauce. I'm not sure.

I left my underwear sunny side up over the bonnet of some unsuspecting French motorist and listened contentedly to Paul Ballard address everybody in the canteen. The Croydon organiser paced around the car park looking crestfallen.

Eddy suggested that with our humiliation being so early in the day, we had enough time left to travel to Southall and attempt a wrecking spree on the planned festivities in memorial of the anti-fascist campaigner, Blair Peach.

Now, at the Embankment tube station there used to be this graffiti that read 'SPG killed Blair Peach' and under it somebody had scrawled 'Good'. I didn't know who Blair Peach was, but my juvenile foolishness had taught me that the police only ever kill people who deserved it, even accidentally. It turned out that Peach was a New Zealander and a schoolteacher in Southall opposing an NF election meeting and his death had been the butt of many a bad joke in the NF ever since. What we would do is drive into Southall, find the plaque in his honour and remove it, possibly raffle it off at some function later on. We were all very keen to do so, given that we had wasted all our money on a non-event. There was only one dissenting voice: the man from London Underground was not keen.

'Have you seen Southall? Pakis everywhere. We'll be picked out straight away.'

'No, no, no,' I protested. 'All the Pakis are in Rochdale today.'

But they weren't.

When we got to Southall, Ballard got out of the bus and looked around, hesitantly. We were parked in a car park around the back of Southall market. Ours were the only white faces in town, all sitting together silently, expectantly. Ballard took a walk. Southall was preparing for the next day's activities. They were planning to march, sing, chant and give speeches before unveiling the plaque. By God we wanted that plaque too. No one was around but we whispered in case anybody realised who we were. In the background, we could hear the noise and bustle of the market.

Ballard returned with the news that the plaque was at the town hall, behind a fence. This time we drove into the town and everybody stopped and stared at us, thinking we were the police. 'Is this what Calcutta would be like?' I wondered. We would never know, so we assumed so. Ballard claimed that he'd seen them slitting the necks of goats in the market, causing us to tut-tut at the scandalous outrage that they were allowed to do this in an English town. We were doubly defeated; we couldn't find Blair Peach's plaque, and another piece of English suburbia had turned into Calcutta. Refused a march, refused a meeting, refused even a motorway stop at any Happy Eater in Lancashire.

In a poetic Russian novel, we would have rushed home and pulled our families to our breasts, sobbing uncontrollably at our sorrows, possibly drunk too much and taken our own lives. I got dropped off at my local and told my sorrowful tale of woe to the landlord, who understood everything. It was a pretty lonely drink, given that most people my age would have been out having sex at parties and listening to Acid House or something.

Rochdale was a terrible defeat for the Front. The following month the party paper tried to make a lot of noise with its headline 'MOB RULE', trying to express the anger that the members felt, encouraging them to sell more copies of the paper than in previous months, to spread the word about just how shocking Britain had become for white, law-abiding patriots. It would never work. It was humiliation that we felt, from top to bottom. Many of us just crashed into our beds, hungover and depressed by the events at Rochdale. The NF was no longer big enough, strong or capable enough to pull off such stunts. We had been humiliatingly run off the patch by Asians and reds. No propaganda would ever persuade the members it was anything else. It did nothing to encourage members to become more active and it became twice as difficult to persuade the only member with a girlfriend to ever come out with us again. Those of us who knew we would be back in such circumstances again felt embarrassed trying to persuade the few armchair members to get active.

We felt we had let down all the people we had tried to recruit. Without even the numbers for a punch-up, the entire day had been a disaster. Anderson was held up for ridicule for his shortcomings in negotiating with the police. BNP members from Lancashire who made it into Rochdale, had spread the news of our defeat to London before we'd even arrived home. Not allowing us into the town had worked. They knew we wouldn't be coming back, they knew we weren't interested in them any more.

The next day at Brick Lane we scratched our arses and sighed. The BNP was in the process of distributing the 100,000th copy of its anti-Semitic hatesheet *Holocaust News* which ridiculed the NF. Tony Lecomber issued a scathing attack on the NF in a typed circular, predicting its imminent demise and we left the Lane feeling black and sorry for ourselves. By contrast, after more successes in the East End, holding meeting after meeting, the BNP put the final nail in the coffin of the SDP by beating them into fourth place in an Essex Council election, scoring in their ward alone, just under half what the NF had polled only months before in the whole parliamentary seat. Anderson had to have a change of strategy. The members had to feel useful again. The Vauxhall by-election would be perfect.

CHAPTER 7

And so it happened that the two National Fronts would fight each other during a by-election in June 1989. No sooner had one of their officers done an interview on BBC radio claiming they were not interested in fighting elections, than the fresh-faced Patrick Harrington was nominated to stand for the Political Soldier wing of the National Front in Vauxhall.

The incumbent MP, Stuart Holland, was giving up his plum job to go to Florence. Apparently he had to do this by applying to the Crown Steward and Bailiff of the Chiltern Hundreds, the only way you can resign a seat in the Commons.

'We'll fight this one,' said Anderson, sensing a desperate need to reinvigorate our depleted activists. It would also give us a chance to rub up against Griffin, Harrington and co.

It didn't take long for the first cock-up to happen. Though our NF candidate would appear before Harrington on the ballot papers, Harrington got in there first and had himself nominated as the official NF candidate. It didn't take long for everyone to start grumbling about that. As the grumbles continued, Anderson tried to persuade everyone to turn their aggression on the Political Soldiers. And there was plenty of it.

Vauxhall was not too far from Harrington's Chelsea home, and his vanity was always stronger than his revolutionary credentials. Our candidate, Ted Budden, a former Blackshirt and *Flag* columnist, was pushing 108 years of age. He was a former trade unionist and lifelong anti-Semite with a pleasant enough grandfatherly quality about him. What was needed was for local activists to get behind our candidate. Only one man was interested: Barry 'Murph' Murphy. You guessed it: Irish Catholic. Murph was almost a radical anti-fascist. He hated the National Front and could not understand how he had ever become involved. He stayed on in 1986 out of some misguided loyalty, then quit in 1987. He was an interesting bloke, a weird romantic with a penchant for black leather and hair gel, drinking ale and abusing the NF's leadership on the telephone. He whistled Irish rebel songs and admired himself constantly in shop windows. He believed he was truly handsome.

Every night for a fortnight we would meet outside Lambeth North tube station. Murph would arrive late with his thumbs gripping his belt, laughing at us and chiding us for our enthusiasm. He would shout 'Ted Budden's an old Nazi,' at the top of his voice, then burp 'Bollocks' out loud, a wonderful gift that I have admired since I was a child. He was, surprisingly, very ordinary (except for the vanity). He was only a couple of years older than me but much more cultured in every way.

The problem with the campaign was that we spent more time pulling down Harrington's posters and stickers than we did putting up our own. The Political Soldiers always seemed to have been somewhere just after or just before us. On our ways home after the leafleting, postering and stickering, we would see all the new Harrington stickers that had gone up over ours. Our stickers had the Union Jack with 'Budden' written across the middle. By the next day, 'Budden' would have been rubbed out, or the sticker covered by one of Harrington's. Most nights there were a dozen of us, sticking together to avoid confrontations with black locals, our pockets heavy with loose change wrapped in dirty socks to be used as impromptu weapons.

The two Nash brothers made the trip over from north London most nights, partly out of courtesy to Murph but, I suspect, more because they had each purchased spiffing new anoraks that they wanted to show to the world. They were the weirdest-looking, but most harmless, people I had ever met. One of the brothers, Bob, was banned from writing articles for NF publications because they always returned to one topic, his favourite band, Whitesnake. Ask him to tackle devolution and he would come up with an article on Whitesnake. Constantly shunned for their prize-winning performances as trainspotters, the pair lived in relative isolation in a perfectly formed and perfectly run North London NF. The pair took turns holding office on the National Directorate but much preferred barn dancing, heavy metal and their mother's cooking, to Anderson's company.

The Nashes were responsible for overseas liaison and, along with two other civil servants (North London NF was run by, and as, a branch of the civil service), the NF ex-servicemen's group, of which there were two members. Rather than attend national demonstrations, they would spend their evenings picketing meetings of charitable organisations or minuscule socialist organisations with non-confrontational policies towards fascists. For them to help in this campaign meant we would have to endure Bob with his walkman playing Whitesnake and Paul moaning and complaining about Ian Anderson, having acne at the age of thirty-three and the cost of Hush Puppies. But even so, they did come.

During the campaign, I started drinking in a real ale pub which even had sawdust on the floor for good measure. Finally breaking away from evenings alone with *Razzle*'s Readers' Wives special, I discovered people were having sex while the world was collapsing around them. Every meaningless fondle with a northern student under the bridge in Borough High Street was better than any two hours with Ian Anderson or Richard Edmonds, better than stiffing up my Woolworths' socks and discarding them behind the radiator. To lie on the mattress of a lagered-up student from Grimsby was ten times better than hiding the *Sunday Sport* under the bath mat on a Sunday afternoon. Teenage years were never happy or productive for me.

It was humourless and emotionless, trudging to and from work, to and from meetings, worrying about everything, from the telephone being tapped or the IRA following me home from a demonstration, to where to hide the tissues that were mounting behind the radiator. Should I be circumcised, should I be taller, am I too dim, or am I too bright? No girl ever called me back, so I just lay in my bed at night fondling myself hopelessly, talking like a porn star, listening to Billy Bragg's *The Saturday Boy,* wondering if I would actually be happier on the other side.

When we got back to campaigning in Vauxhall, the election campaign heated up towards the end. Eddie Whicker and a few others cornered Harrington doing his own postering, and chased him on foot for half an hour through the streets of Vauxhall. A teen goon squad the Croydon branch had organised ran into some rather angry black youths and ended up in an all-in brawl near Waterloo Station. Before we could admit defeat, somebody pulled a CS gas canister from their pocket and gassed everyone within thirty feet, including our own comrades. Murph and I swiftly ran off, while a young black guy choked on his mother's doorstep, screaming for help. The entire neighbourhood came out to witness the commotion. The Croydon organiser was trying to help one of his own, while angry black faces bore down on him. I apologised and passed him, heading for the back streets, ending up in Waterloo Station toilets, sitting silently while the police searched the surrounding area. I covered my mouth because my breath was so heavy and contemplated life with a criminal conviction, all for a hundred or so votes.

During the election count, Anderson and Harrington came to blows. It was farcical as neither of them had much in the way of fighting reputations, but they went for it hell for leather. It turned out that Harrington had been learning martial arts, which came in useful as the hired security he had paid for stood motionless. Even the Revolutionary Communist Party got involved in the fracas. Thankfully the fight was broadcast on television; we'd been a bit short of TV exposure lately. We lost to Harrington by a few votes, not that it really mattered. Somewhere in their bedrooms his few members would have been delighted. Our Croydon organiser was arrested and given a minor firearms-related conviction.

Back at work in the boring old real world, it was becoming increasingly clear to me that my one hope for an interesting life was that one day the lunatics – a.k.a. the NF and the BNP – would truly take over the asylum and I would be offered an honorary doctorate somewhere like Bristol University. The police offered me a compulsory transfer to the less 'stressful' environment of Sidcup. I asked the union rep in the office to represent me as I didn't want to move. She told me that 'sadly' she could not help. She passed me a letter from the CPSA (our union) declaring that members of parties like the NF could not be union members.

'I'm sorry,' she said. 'We'll really miss your rantings in the office.'

The ladies in the office feigned varying degrees of sadness to see me go. I had kept them amused for months on end but I wasn't very nice company and I had not taken the opportunity to get to know them. Their excruciating discussions about menopause, menstruation and their endless fears of hysterectomies had never for one moment brightened my day. A teenage revolutionary doesn't need to think about the working parts of middle-aged women. We had a glass of wine on my last day and we all left the office early, but only to go our separate ways. I took the letter with me. Anderson issued a press release condemning the CPSA and the newspapers totally ignored it. He immediately lost interest in my plight.

Anderson cheered up a little at the thought of another forthcoming debacle during the European elections, where it would be the turn of the NF candidate, Martin Wingfield, to be humiliated. Wingfield had decided upon a march through the back streets of an inconsequential white middle-class neighbourhood somewhere in the Midlands that we'd never heard of.

By now, I had developed a bit of cynicism about electioneering. We didn't actually electioneer anyway, we merely scraped the surface of the electorate, crowding around local papers to scour the column inches for the name of our party. So poor had the NF become in terms of news, we were often left out of the lists of candidates when published in local newspapers. When this was the case, the BNP would stage a violent protest or a punch-up and write to the local papers about it, but not the NF, or not Anderson anyway. I still felt excited about marching and travelling in Terry's car and the opportunities for underage drinking in pubs surrounded by other lunatics, but I could also sense that our dogs of war were not getting enough battle scars and were beginning to drop off from Anderson's activities to go out on activities with the BNP instead. I'd go to bed and play out the future activity in my head. I would lead the march and make a strong speech that would lead to a bloody revolution. Along the way, I also toyed with hanging Anderson from a lamppost.

Before the march started we had an unexpected running battle with a dozen game lads in Celtic shirts. They attacked one of our cars at a roundabout, without realising there were five other cars in the traffic, full of NF members. We jumped out of our cars and clashed for a full minute, kicking off wing mirrors and jumping on and off car bonnets before they left.

The much-convicted thug team who ran Birmingham National Front shook our hands and thanked us for our presence, without which there would have been no march, due to lack of numbers, lack of interest, lack of backbone. With a total lack of dignity, I marched with 100 other dedicated, drunk – or both – patriots, singing *No Surrender to the IRA* to the lads in the Celtic shirts, on a march in support of our candidate Martin Wingfield for the European Parliamentary elections. We eventually achieved 1,500 votes, approximately 160 votes per constituency. The Green Party took most of the protest votes nationally though. Holes in the ozone layer, sheep with two cocks and some rather pointless business about hedges seemed to be considered more worthy of protesting about than immigration. Were they asleep? Could these bloody voters in white suburbia not see this awful tragedy happening before their eyes?

Blackham and I chased a man with a beard down a street with a wheel brace but we lost him when I stopped for a cigarette. The man from the local fish and chip shop came out with his hands on his hips and stared at me.

'Are you in the National Front Party, then?' he asked.

'National Front. Just the National Front,' I replied.

'Well,' he said, 'no fucker round here votes for you. Go on, fuck off or I'll fucking thump you.'

Whatever a Mexican standoff is, I think I had one. Whether it was youthful indignation or if I was just being a real tosser, I do not know but I stood there. A lanky Brummie skinhead walked up and punched the man in the face while still maintaining a full can of Tennent's Lager. Women always bloody scream. The police arrived and the skinhead departed for the hills, trying to look inconspicuous in what my brother would later identify as a genuine pair of Northern Ireland high-leg army boots. The march continued to shuffle along suburban streets while people drove past with their mouths wide open. Sometimes someone would beep their horn at us, or wind their window down and shout 'wankers'.

'You boys are Palace fans aren't you?' asked one of the Birmingham lads. 'We're coming down to your place in a couple of weeks, can you organise a welcoming party?'

I didn't know if we could or not. It wasn't like the old days with my schoolboy Charlton mates.

'We'll give you a fucking kicking if you want,' offered the sprinter-fallen-on-hard-times.

'Lovely,' said the Brummie. 'We're gonna rip up your running track.'

Blackham decided we'd go to Leicester to see Palace play after the embarrassing shuffling march. We headed off in Blackham's car towards Filbert Street, Leicester City's old ground. The teams drew, so Palace didn't make the automatic promotion place. Throughout the game a steady stream of people popped over to say hello and exchange small talk. Before the game ended there was some chanting of anti-Birmingham City songs, something that I don't recall Palace fans ever having done before.

An obnoxious army of teenagers in nice shoes and jeans were standing outside the away exit at Filbert Street, singing and chanting about Palace fans going home in ambulances. The police were nowhere to be seen, so we beat up the only person we could find in a Celtic shirt, before grabbing fish and chips.

On the way home I leant out of the car window and smoked a cigarette while Blackham told me to get as many people as I could to the Palace v Birmingham game. During the week in Beckenham and Penge, we tell every young bloke we meet to be at the game. I invited my friend, just back from a holiday in Greece ending in heartbreak after his holiday romance – a girl from Leeds called Tina – dumped him on the last day.

The Saturday of Birmingham City's visit to Selhurst Park, home of the mighty Crystal Palace Football Club, arrived with a smack to the skull from a Birmingham City supporter dressed like one of the Rocky Horror Show cast. Initially there had been a carnival atmosphere as a few hundred Birmingham fans arrived in fancy dress and sang their silly songs. I don't recall whether it was their relegation party or not, but it started off with friendly banter until, at the back of the Holmesdale terrace, lads from the local pubs arrived, with tales of running battles and how there were thousands more City supporters outside the ground. That's when the polystyrene cups of piss started being flung at them, as we watched their size swell and swell.

Most of the noise at Palace games back then came from a small area of the standing section along the side of the pitch at the front of the Arthur Wait stand. From there fans could point to the away supporters, stuck over by the corner flag in the end section of the Holmesdale terrace, behind the goal. It was in the Holmesdale, a vast terrace where those not into singing songs and being crushed on the rare occasions Palace scored stood. By the time the Birmingham City fan climbing the floodlight gave his signal for the Birmingham supporters to invade the pitch, there were forty of us at the back of Holmesdale waiting in anticipation of a fight.

The City fans poured onto the pitch and crowded at the bottom of the Arthur Wait, goading the Palace fans to come at them. Once the order was given, forty of us charged onto the pitch behind them and began picking them off. As they began to move, those at the front of their crowd were pushed right against the front of the stand and, finally, the Palace fans, who had moved to the front of the Arthur Wait began battling with the City mob too. Palace were hopelessly outnumbered and more and more fans had to pour onto the pitch from other areas of the ground, while City fans were taking over the Arthur Wait.

Any Birmingham fans in fancy dress that had not made it into the Arthur Wait were attacked by Palace fans, who were gathering on the middle of the pitch. I can still recall vividly, three enormous black lads right in the centre circle standing back to back and flattening the City fans, who seemed to be taking it in turns to have a go at them.

The mounted police came onto the pitch to a loud roar of approval from all sides of the ground. The officers riding the horses were smacking thugs on the backs of their heads. As the police headed for the Arthur Wait stand, the City supporters were trying to get back into the away end. Palace fans charged at them until nobody knew who was fighting whom.

As if walking out of some kind of mist, the Birmingham NF lads came running towards me with silly grins on their faces.

'Fucking magic, fucking magic stuff Matty, well done,' they said as they charged towards the halfway line, where they were promptly put on their arses by the black lads protecting the centre spot.

It was a hell of a picture unfolding right in front of me. There were displaced Palace and City supporters on the pitch now. I stood in front of the Arthur Wait and looked up at those still fighting, while families with young children huddled terrified. Most of the Holmesdale Road mob was by now in the Arthur Wait attacking the remainder of the City supporters. The *Croydon Advertiser* caught Terry Blackham ripping the shirt off one City fan while using his other hand to make a fist and batter him in the face. I

climbed over the barrier to get into the Arthur Wait stand
and everything went black; I was punched in the back of
the head by a man in a nurse's costume. When I woke, I
was being dragged away by fellow Palace supporters.

The game restarted after twenty minutes but no one
was watching it. All over the ground there were more fights
breaking out. The noise in the Arthur Wait was deafening
now and, in the mob mentality, anyone with a Brummie
or a Cockney accent was being attacked. Birmingham fans
were spreading all over the Holmesdale Road end as even
more City fans were arriving.

After the game the trouble continued. Mobs of locals
who had watched the violence on the television were
making their way to the ground. One small gang, from one
of the pubs in Norwood, attacked City fans with pool cues
and balls and the disorganised Birmingham hooligans, who
found themselves dumped miles from where they thought
the game was, had a nightmare moving across south east
London after the game.

For two days television replayed the scenes from
Selhurst Park. My mother videoed and paused it at regular
intervals, refusing to believe I could have been involved
in such madness so recently after the tragic events at
Hillsborough. But there I was, on television, running down
the Holmesdale terrace and then in front of the Arthur Wait
stand. Maybe this is when she gave up all her temporary
hope in me.

It was also the moment when I abandoned my interest
in football. Mum's typewriter continued to contribute to
the cause as, continuing my proper revolutionary activities,
I banged out another issue of *Lewisham Patriot*, only now
I called it *Lewisham and Bromley Patriot*. The civil service
contributed by paying for the photocopying and someone
with a handful of stolen stamps from Coventry took care
of the postage. Any normal horny teenager would have

been planning the holiday of a lifetime, trekking in Nepal or choking on his own vomit in Ibiza, but instead I went into business with Eddie Whicker as purveyors of German pornography – cash and benefits on the side. Word spread that we had a unique collection of German videos; some cranks in the BNP even asked if we had the Nuremberg Rally. But it wasn't enough: the pace of teenage Nazi life was slow, and I even thought about becoming a publican and opening a pub in Croydon called *You're Gonna Get Your Fucking Head Kicked In*. It was an idea I floated for about fifteen minutes one night before bed.

CHAPTER 8

Richard Edmonds decided to broaden my horizons. Western Goals UK, a fringe group on the right of the Conservative Party, was pleased to play host to some South African MPs. I was quite interested in this – you may recall that I liked South African fruit. Richard Edmonds and I sat together quietly, while Clive Derby-Lewis, one of the South African MPs, talked about his Scottish ancestry, black crime, Nelson bloody Mandela and some other stuff about the percentage of land owned versus percentage of taxes paid. Strong propaganda if you can stay awake. Four suited and booted men stood in the corner and winked at me, so I winked back. It was a nice place for a meeting: pleasant view of the Embankment, cool summer breeze on my neck, the man from the Tory Party sitting on my other side with his legs crossed. If my mother could see me now…

Before the end of the meeting, Richard Edmonds stood up and unfurled a 'BNP Supports White South Africa' poster, as if he were initiating his own question and answer session. Everyone looked at us, so I yawned and looked at my shoes, while the man from the Tory Party hissed, 'I told you not to do this Richard.' The suited and booted four looked amused, so I winked again and left with Edmonds and the man from the Tory Party. It turned out that it was a good ruse to avoid having to put in for the collection.

It was not long afterwards that Derby-Lewis would face the death penalty for his part in the murder of ANC leading light Chris Hani. Had we known that he would be involved in such pleasantries, we would have been far more likely to have contributed to the whip round. Later Arthur Kemp, who was also arrested but not charged in connection with Hani's murder, and controversially appeared as a prosecution witness, would eventually end up in Nick Griffin's BNP.

I met Derby-Lewis, his party leader Andreas Treurnicht and an assortment of oddball racists again, this time in the Sudeley Room in the House of Lords. Sitting two rows in front of the historian David Irving, with an assortment of Tory-right oddballs, closet Nazis and ladies in nice frocks, I listened to Derby-Lewis adopting a more diplomatic approach to his party's predicament while, with pantomime-like efficiency, everyone booed at the mention of the name Mandela. Treurnicht spoke no English, so Derby-Lewis spoke for him, accusing one F. W. de Klerk of being the true enemy of white South Africa. In hindsight, it was more probable at the time that Derby-Lewis would wish de Klerk dead than Chris Hani. With Edmonds absent, the Tories and I crossed our legs and listened intently, never quite realising that the one true enemy of white South Africa would be the one thing the Tories talked about the most: democracy.

Sitting with Richard in the tiny cramped office of the BNP was one of the highlights of my time in the far right. He explained everything purely and simply. I wanted to want the same things that Richard wanted. I wanted to reject all of things that I suppose, secretly, I actually longed for, most of all popularity and acceptance among people within the community, whatever that was. I don't know if Richard had rejected these things, or at some stage had, like me, felt that he had been rejected by them.

It was a strange time to be holding those views. We were sneaking into parliament to attend meetings with *real* politicians when it was an institution that we hated. We sat in the halls and rooms of British democracy when it was quite clear that we actually held no respect for it either ideologically or institutionally. Once the BNP came to power, there would be no more elections; there would be no time for debates, bills or legislations or lobbying and protesting. Everything the BNP did not like would simply be banned. Could I live in a society like that? I convinced myself that I could, that by using these hatreds I could strike out against all of the things I didn't understand. And that is still a powerful pull. I began to believe that under the BNP or the NF, I would be able, from some telephone box somewhere, to ring Downing Street and demand someone, somewhere got carted off and shot. I privately lined up a whole list of soap actors, pop stars, teachers and frigid and disinterested ex-girlfriends. All I would ever have to do is denounce them. If such a tiny party was so prepared to unleash such monstrous violence from such a distance, imagine what we could do when we were in power. Actually, imagine what we *would* do.

Sitting with Richard Edmonds one afternoon he explained how it would all work. There would not be any matter too small for the BNP to intervene in when in government. By all accounts, John Tyndall would never sleep. From his desk he would simply read out the names of the race traitors and Zionists who would be carted off to some shallow grave somewhere. I asked about reported UFO sightings in Somerset and he stared at me for a moment, muttered in German and offered me half a can of vegetarian mincemeat. He gave me his last slice of bread and relaxed in his chair.

'The BNP are not responsible for any alien abductions,' he announced slowly, before picking up the phone and shouting, 'Did you hear that?' into the empty receiver.

A German visitor arrived with one of Edmonds's female admirers. She was a nutty old bint and he was one of her cousins. Apparently they only discovered they were both Nazis by chance, given that their family had done all they could to keep the skeletons in the cupboard.

The four of us sat around the cramped table out the back of BNP headquarters, poring over the newspapers, circling news of black and Jewish crime, purely for misery's sake. Edmonds explained to the German that I was from the National Front and the German raised his eyebrows politely and waited for me to comment. I said nothing, so he gave me a German NF sticker and started talking about Alpine forest walking, David Irving and his second-hand car. It was almost as if we were all human beings, just sitting around in Richard's kitchen, while ten thousand copies of *Holocaust News* were delicately stuffed into envelopes, the intended recipients all Jews, politicians, councillors etc. The German almost soiled his tweeds at the fact that in a democracy, we are allowed to do this, whereas in Germany, another democracy, you are not. Sitting in Edmonds's kitchen we abuse democracy and use it to attack those who would strive to defend it from us. For good measure, the German adds some names of his own to the list; Holocaust denial is a crime in Germany.

How could I ever have doubted that the Holocaust – the systematic murder of millions of Jews, gypsies, homosexuals and trade unionists – happened? Simply, because I needed to. If you want to (dis)believe something enough, eventually you will. I was convinced that the film shot at the Nazi death camps was all made by Hollywood moviemakers, filming Russians in German uniforms murdering and hanging Jews. After all, why would the Germans have filmed this genocide themselves? There was a massive conspiracy to discredit National Socialism; the only people to benefit were the Jews who now controlled the world once more. Sit back, relax, think about it some more, and consider. Light a cigarette, go for a walk, and have a long wank. It's not very believable is it?

'Matthew, you will never get all of the things you want unless we demolish the Holocaust myth, first.'

Holocaust denial was the staple diet of the far right in the 1980s and 1990s and still is to a degree today. To make people believe that the Jews are evil, you must first convince them that they lie about the Holocaust. Because the party was so small, there were still massive temptations to prove your crankiness to others in the movement. At the time, nobody else was really listening to what was happening on the outer fringes of the political landscape in Britain, so we all just shouted like lunatics at each other. The sort of publicity Holocaust denial brought the BNP was remarkable. They even charged the BBC £50 for entry to their bookshop to film them at work. For the anti-Semites who sat on the NF's ruling body, it was almost too much to bear.

As I'd always had an inquisitive mind, and since my mother and father no longer loved each other, I decided Edmonds and Anderson would be my new parents – at least they still talked to each other. I thought I could fix them up at the social I was organising in my old local, The Swan, in Lee High Road. Of course, they'd known each other since the 1970s and had never liked each other, but I invited Edmonds, which made Anderson furious.

'That man is a fucking Nazi,' he ranted although Edmonds had politely declined the offer.

The social was to help raise funds to pay off fines – among them a £750 one for Terry Blackham – for the attempt to storm another Irish march, where we had managed to break through police lines, only to get battered by Red Action. Ten NF members were arrested for their efforts, even though they were all bruised and battered senseless by the time the police had arrested them.

The landlord sealed off the back of the pub and made sausage rolls, pineapple and cheese on sticks, and turkey sandwiches. He brushed his hair and greeted everyone as they arrived, formally shaking their hands and saying 'Call me Bill,' before getting on the phone to all his known friends exclaiming, 'They're here! The National Front are really here!' And indeed we really were. He charged us cost for the food, and we charged £5 to enter. In all, sixty fascists turned up. Ex-members, who had not been to a function in ten years, turned up and mingled with the new generation of kids trying to storm Parliament. Anderson arrived a little late and introduced himself as 'Ian Anderson, Chairman of the National Front,' at which Bill had to change his underwear due to his over-excitement. Out in the main bar, my old school friends stood, mouths aghast, as in poured a huge army of men and three women, in their Sunday bests for an evening of sausage rolls and lager with a Bruce Springsteen cassette playing in the background. Ian Anderson couldn't even attend a wedding without trying to flog his wares, so he sat in a corner with fifty books and 3,000 faulty NF stickers. While Anderson was trying to flog tapes of Ulster *Kick The Pope* marching bands, for twenty quid I knocked out copies of *Animal Farm*, and not the movie version of George Orwell's book, either.

At the end of the evening, after everything had gone so well, Blackham's brother walked into the main bar, grabbed the telephone from the barmaid and demanded a taxi. She refused and within minutes every pipe in every toilet was pulled from the wall, the toilet bowls cracked, mirrors smashed and stools broken. By midnight, piss and water were drenching the carpet, while Bill scratched his stupid head and barred me from the pub forever. We raised a healthy £500 for those members facing fines and Anderson was quite happy with his own sales, offering us five per cent of his sixty quid takings, although my suggestion to Anderson that we compensate Bill for his damaged pipework was met with a horrified scowl.

The money was normally sent to a Brighton-based football hooligan responsible for the 'Patriots Defence Fund', but this time, Anderson and Blackham tallied up the money in a different way. Richard White from Lambeth was given £150 to pay his fine because he was unemployed and had

absolutely no interest in ever getting a job. The remainder
was offered to Blackham but he refused. Instead, it was
funnelled into a separate bank account. I hoped I would be
offered fifty quid or so for my expenses for the revolution
but to no avail. The money went to a propaganda fund,
set up by Anderson for his printing services. I was to see
to it that we could drum up enough newsworthy stunts.
Already we had failed – like almost all other NF branches
in the country except Hull for some reason – to have an ad
placed in local newspapers on behalf of the local branch.
The solution was simple: we would have to make the news!

Meanwhile, the top members of the Croydon branch
were raided by the police, who were convinced that there
was some sort of paramilitary business afoot. Their houses
were searched and they were all suspended from the
Territorial Army, where the authorities thought they were
organising their paramilitary training. All of the leading
members on the committee went into hiding.

With the NF's annual conference approaching, Anderson
was desperate to show his diminishing membership that the
party was still active in London, despite the BNP's greater
numerical strength. Obviously the falling off in activities was
hurting his pocket, the greatest ideological driver he ever
had. At a hastily arranged strategy meeting in the Catford
home of a Scottish supporter who had previously hidden
the KKK Grand Wizard David Duke in his living room, a
small committee of six South London and Surrey members
sat around a kitchen table to draw up a battle plan. Ballard
was nervous, as he was now almost solely responsible for
the branch, organising leafleting and meetings. This left him
feeling uncomfortable and stressed, if not a little put out that
he had not been raided himself; without his own door being
kicked in, it looked as if he was the source of the information that had done for his colleagues. One of the Croydon
TA members had also refused to plead guilty to charges

arising from the anti-Irish confrontation and was being warned he could face a custodial sentence.

'What if he rolls over?' wailed Ballard.

In reality, there was nothing really to hide. Our TA members had not even been allowed to fire real guns yet, which, rather than placate Ballard, made him even more depressed.

For propaganda I suggested leafleting schools and printing a local information sheet for Bromley and Beckenham; what it was about wasn't important as long as it was newsworthy. We agreed I would take a long bout of sick leave following an accident playing soccer for Lewisham Police and would work on the South London campaign full-time, courtesy of civil service sick pay: full pay for six months.

The elderly Scotsman playing host to the meeting made weak tea and popped in every seventeen minutes (I timed him), to ask where all the money from the 1970s had gone. We decided to concentrate on Bromley, Eltham and Lewisham, drawing attention away from the Croydon branch. By Saturday, Anderson had earned the first of his money, printing a leaflet on the supposed removal of Beckenham's war memorial to make way for a new roundabout or something. He handed us 2,000 leaflets and asked us to arrange transport to Birmingham, where the national conference was to be held, for as many members as possible.

Blackham and I delivered the leaflets every night of the week bar Wednesday, and by Thursday we were front-page news. It hadn't been so difficult; we just made sure every newspaper office and British legion received a leaflet. I rang the local paper to pretend to be outraged that 'these Nazis' were so active in the area and they took the bait like a fresh salmon.

I liked Blackham, he wasn't difficult to get along with. He'd poke me in the ribs to make me rant and rave at people in the pubs who he knew but who didn't agree with our politics. His propensity for violence at the drop of a hat was legendary, but his ability to drop me home, while driving so pissed he could only keep one eye open, was appreciated. Still, we were getting a reputation for violence that was a little unsettling, even for people in the party.

CHAPTER 9

Our much-anticipated Beckenham leaflet accused the local council of 'expediency' – one word of many which neither Blackham or I knew the meaning of. The local press threw it right back at us. We decided not to wheel anybody into the press office to explain ourselves. The following week we did a press drop at all the local newspaper offices, enclosing a press release, appallingly typed on my mother's typewriter. I'd pored over its content for what seemed like hours, sighing to myself as I pretended the lives of thousands of people rested in my hands. These fantastic moments of self-aggrandisement amused the family tremendously. There I was, upstairs in my bedroom drafting long and important letters, stopping only for a wank and a cigarette. Our foray into the great public debate concerning the wretched war memorial may have brought no membership applications but, with the local press ranting and raving, we moved onto the streets of Beckenham more confident than ever before. We conducted furious and chaotic leafleting sessions followed by more equally committed drinking sessions where we tried to engage people with our anger and juvenile posturing. Others from across London came to join us, we were the only active NF group and we'd descend on the pubs in Penge and Beckenham in one large unkempt mess, whilst Blackham kept an ear open to make sure we didn't criticise the great leader, Ian Anderson.

The very few new younger members we had recruited were 100 per cent committed to a cause that they had no political or ideological understanding of. Most just wanted to drink and fight in the company of other angry white men. If they could be bothered to find out our policies, we simply made some up to suit. We adjusted our policies to their racism.

For a while we enjoyed celebrity status in Beckenham and Penge. The well-known former skinhead thug Blackham was making good with his politics, parading along the high street handing out leaflets and putting up stickers. On weekends, in the pubs around Penge and Beckenham, we would be sure to pop in and say hello, drink too much, leave some literature and go home. People we hardly knew would say hello, or stop and watch us, wondering what we were up to. Within two months we had distributed close on 100,000 pieces of literature, over five times a week. I set my bedroom up as an office and kept the membership files in the sort of order that the Germans would have despaired of. We bought 250 copies of *The Flag* per month and normally managed to sell about fifty. The unsold copies went under our beds, or were left on trains and station platforms. It really was a case of waiting for the great leap forwards, but our membership never grew as dramatically as we hoped and our PO Box was always empty. We had fifteen members in total.

One morning, Blackham left for work as usual and found a car parked outside his house. There'd been a bust-up over the weekend in one of the pubs, where an Irishman was punched to the floor and bar stools were thrown. Passing the car, Terry noticed 'IRA' scrawled in marker pen on the window, and called the police. For some reason I could not fathom, he actually believed this is the way the IRA planted car bombs. I liked him, but it was obvious he was not the most analytical of people. We all assumed the IRA wanted us dead – God knows why – but in even my strangest of paranoid states, even I would not suggest they'd bother to park a car outside my house and then pen 'IRA' on the window. But of course, by this same token we generally assumed that every Irish man and woman was a terrorist. These days the same line of thinking is applied to Muslims.

The police arrived at Blackham's house – for the first time ever, not to make an arrest – inspected the car, and called the experts. The experts arrived soon after and declared it all clear, Blackham blushed and carried on business as usual. What he had also done, however, was draw the entire Penge constabulary's attention to the fact that Beckenham and Penge's most notorious thug had stepped up a grade from racist yob and local Nazi organiser, to something increasingly more sinister, where even the graffiti of a drunk could draw him deeper into paranoia. In the intelligence office at Penge nick, where his picture was no doubt permanently pinned, there was probably yet another lunatic offering: Terror Suspect paranoiac.

On the back of the Croydon TA scandal this was not welcomed at all. The police were obviously desperate to get into Blackham's house for a look around. The Croydon organiser was pulling his hair out as he was visited again and asked if there was an internal dispute within the party. Blackham decided to make somebody pay for this and the Penge Irish community were top of his list. So as not to put any other temptations in his way, the colourful Barry Murphy retired from Nazi life again, muttering dark and sinister rumblings about fascists.

Throughout 1989 our thoughts had been firmly trained, not so much on the dangers of continued immigration, but more on the already present immigrants on our shores, changing the cultural make-up of our supposedly devout Christian country. The BNP had put northern communities with large Asian populations on the alert, with its deliberately provocative activities aimed at unsettling tense communities and using the inflamed situations as an excuse to accuse ethnic communities of being lawless. Like those in the East End of London, Asians in parts of the Midlands,

Lancashire and Yorkshire lived in fear of white youths fuelled by alcohol and hate-literature, rampaging through their towns. The BNP's provocative activities often deliberately brought the already untrusting ethnic communities into more confrontation with the police. This was another example of the BNP using democracy against the very people from whom it would remove democracy and its freedoms. At the time, the BNP and NF were heavily involved in campaigns against the rise of Islamic fundamentalism in the UK. It was just more traditional 'Paki-bashing' from the NF and BNP, but it tended to strike a cord with some white communities that shared areas with a large and visible ethnic population. The *fatwah* against Salman Rushdie and the often heated protests against the sale of his book, *The Satanic Verses*, seemed almost a godsend. Once more the question of race, and the intolerance of some not indigenous to the British Isles towards its 'freedoms', led to the creation of new branches for the BNP and NF in places like Nelson, Colne, Bradford and Batley. The Ayatollah himself was the greatest recruiter for the NF and BNP in those areas.

With the growth of the BNP already newsworthy, it was looking like there would be a summer of ongoing tensions in inner-city areas where fascists could deliberately target mosques for attacks. A vicious campaign of letter-writing and desecration, aimed at stirring up trouble between Muslims and Jews, started in the BNP, with branches in the north writing to their local papers to attack the power of Asian and Muslim identities, and the core of their religions, using Jewish aliases. In return, Jewish cemeteries were targeted for vandalism by BNP members, with the BNP blaming Asians, or even Jews themselves, for the attacks.

Some areas of south London, in particular Welling and some parts of Greenwich, were almost 'wog free'. Anderson had made it clear that to sink roots in local areas, the party shouldn't concentrate on race but on local issues. While the NF used Anderson's 'country policy' of campaigning in lower- middle-class areas on more local issues like the bloody war memorial, which we could not have cared less about, the BNP went into areas like Eltham, Greenwich, Woolwich and Bermondsey, where there were small pockets of ethnicity, and stirred the local whites into keeping their areas 'wog free'. Using the battle-hardened east London activists, the BNP poured huge amounts of energy into the areas surrounding its headquarters, almost as much as it did in the East End. The NF just could not compete with the BNP's endless resources and manpower, which came almost without cost as young men gave themselves self-lessly to saving the white race. This enabled the BNP to go into areas where some minor tensions existed and use them to their advantage. During the years the BNP was actively housed in the area, four young men were murdered. It is without doubt not a coincidence.

The NF's 'non-confrontation policy' provided few recruits nationally and only a few locally who were aware of the truth behind policy. Small-town newspaper editors didn't fall for it either, always reporting the presence of the NF in an over-the-top and derogatory manner. These smears actually suited those of us who did the real work and knew there was always an element of truth behind them, even if the editors did not know the facts for them-selves, but Anderson had hoped that his middle-class background and persuasive telephone manner would win us support in traditional Tory areas, even on the outskirts of large cities like London and Birmingham. The reality was convicted and drunken racists trawling across the gardens of Kent and Surrey, leaving the tower blocks to the persuasive physical presence of the BNP. The NF's policy was failing in the late 1980s and early 1990s, but the same ideas would later be employed by the BNP after its image change, more than a decade later. After all, Anderson and

Griffin had been comrades long enough to concur on
these necessities.

The NF annual conference was held in the Midlands,
but not everyone from London made it there. Having
missed the rendezvous at Watford Gap, one car-load
from Croydon went home, and another car didn't start.
Blackham was agitated for the whole journey because we
were running late and Anderson had given him a job to do.
Upon arrival, Anderson stormed up and asked us to start
laying the table with flags. The small team from Sheffield
congratulated us on the Welling Library job, which was, by
then, Nazi folklore, regardless of specific affiliation. Eddie
Whicker paced the back of the room dressed in a pink shirt
with braces as if the Mafia were meeting. Our seats were
reserved at the front of the hall and a surprisingly good
200 were seated in your average council hall-type building,
with a gallery overlooking proceedings. At the back of the
room, out of camera shot, skinheads sold their t-shirts and
records, while a large American dressed like a host from
Sesame Street put his arms around them and posed for
photographs. Unimportant people made themselves look
busy, while Steve Brady and his associate Tom Acton, the
two men behind the party's magazine *Vanguard*, roamed
the room, nodding at their small clique of friends from
the south coast who detested Anderson as much as them.
Hemel Hempstead-based John McAuley paraded around
the room in the company of some very fancily dressed Irish
friends, shaking hands and trying to look inconspicuous
among the proletariat.

There had been talk that the press would be coming
to the conference. The 'immoral' Channel 4, guaranteed as
they were unhindered access to the proceedings, did not
turn up, leaving the Birmingham branch official kicking his
heels in a pub some miles away. The absence of the press
created a mild panic because, for their benefit, Anderson

had pre-arranged with Martin Wingfield to debate the most controversial, and pointless, agenda since the reign of the Political Soldiers.

Wingfield proposed that the NF adopt a policy under which black OAPs would be allowed to stay in the country under an NF government. It was bitterly contested by the members, who thought they were playing a part in the democratic process. The NF firmly believed that, brown or black, they should go back, either to where they were from, or where they belonged. Anderson and Brady also spoke in favour of the motion, without much gusto. The object of the controversy was to attract press coverage to the NF's AGM, but without the press turning up, it all appeared rather hollow and contrived and not worth getting worked up about. Brady spoke about 'iron fists in a velvet glove,' but without the television cameras to show them at their best, the leadership were rather weak.

Twenty years before, such shallow desperation to grab even a few column inches in the paper would have seen such ideological opportunists lynched. Nobody from the party's executive spoke against the proposal. Instead it was left to a couple of skinheads and a man with learning diffi-culties from Brighton to raise their belief that genocide was more palatable then what was being suggested here. It went to a vote and that was when Blackham became important. The motion was passed amid huge furore and unpopular-ity, leaving Anderson, Wingfield and Brady looking very embarrassed that they had upset the core of the active membership for non-existent press coverage. Something like four votes got the resolution passed. Blackham was hissing at me 'vote for, vote for' and I was hissing back 'vote against, vote against'.

'We'll never actually do it,' he insisted, but it was too late. I took my chance and voted against the motion. Blackham was dumbfounded, the weight of democracy too much to bear. It would probably be nice to have someone left to be cruel to, once we'd repatriated all the young, strong and healthy.

Richard Barrett from the good ol' US of A addressed the conference. Barrett was an anglophile of the highest order, cuddling skinheads for photo opportunities and, on other occasions, waving his arms and generally behaving like a second-rate baseball coach. Dressed in baseball cap and dungarees, he implored us to continue the fight but without offering any substantial reasons to do so. Anderson looked uncomfortable as Barrett rattled on, shooting pained stares at Paul Nash who had organised the visit. It also transpired that a transatlantic pact had been sealed between the NF and Barrett's own American Nationalist Movement, which turned out to be little more than a gang of skinheads led by a fat old bloke who claimed to practise law.

After his speech, Barrett posed for more photos with his skinhead friends while Paul Nash hid from Anderson. Someone introduced me to him, so we exchanged addresses and posed for more photographs. His visit barely rated a mention in any of the NF coverage of the conference.

No sooner had Barrett returned to the USA than I received the largest envelope of ANM literature and flags imaginable. Barrett enclosed a copy of his *All The Way* journal, which was poorer quality than my own *Lewisham Patriot*. Inside were poor-quality photographs of Barrett and his skinhead friends from the Birmingham meeting and a copy of the transatlantic pact, which, when he read it, gave Anderson a huge migraine. *All The Way* also encouraged English Nazis to follow Barrett to America. The idea of living amongst Americans, and skinhead Americans at that, really did not appeal to me very much. I turned out to be right; some twenty years later, Barrett tried to put his hands down the pants of a black youth and was stabbed to death for his trouble.

We returned from Birmingham rather refreshed, despite the terrible resolution passed. At branch meetings, everyone informed their members of the good, high-quality turnout. Of course, it had been a highly stage-managed conference, that was clear to anyone with a brain, but these little opportunities to kid ourselves that we were actually a political party and not a hugely aggressive and incestuous drinking club were welcome relief.

Things in Croydon were also supposed to be settling down somewhat when, out of the blue, Ballard produced two former members of the Political Soldier wing of the (Official) NF, prepared to switch to our group and immediately take up roles on the committee. It may have relieved some of Ballard's stress but Anderson was furious; he had always distrusted him. He called Blackham and me to his living room/office-cum-bunker and started effing and blinding about things being unconstitutional over at Croydon NF, insisting that a vote was taken at the next branch meeting. Blackham and I would have to ship all possible members in to load the ballot if necessary and 'Batter the fucking life out of these fucking cunts.'

Of course there never was a ballot and nobody ever objected. At each committee in the country, people would just get together in the pub before the meeting and elect themselves. Every year they did the same thing and the members voted in favour once the meeting started. Without the ballot, the Croydon meeting went ahead as usual, though it was slightly more interesting than usual. Tom Acton addressed the meeting while the two new members sat at the back of the room looking rather embarrassed and Blackham paced the floor angrily with me behind him, cowering slightly. As John Merritt, one of the switchees explained afterwards, Anderson's real objection to he and Adrian Woods rejoining the party was that they were both friends of Cambridge law graduate Nick Griffin, who had allegedly pulled a shotgun on Anderson during the split. Anderson had also had his car blown up around the same time but the bombers were never caught, increasing his paranoia.

Merritt had once been used on NF recruitment posters in a revolutionary pose, looking rather angry and bullish, while in reality he was the manager of a supermarket and his wife was an animal-rights campaigner. Both Merritt and Adrian Woods returned to the NF, while what was left of Griffin's splinter NF was beginning to show signs of more internal differences, particularly after the virtual admission that their new ideologist Roberto Fiore, a man convicted in his absence in Italy for organising an armed fascist group, was a MI6 operative. Many of its other members had already upped and moved to France to live the agrarian life in electricity-free farmhouses, another reason for Merritt and Woods to rejoin the mainstream NF.

Croydon NF was now, on the face of it, in the hands of former members of the Political Soldier wing. No one from the Croydon branch was asked to fill the branch's place on the Directorate, the party's ruling body. The previous incumbents professed to being rather uncomfortable given the history between the two sides in Croydon, but accepted it. Blackham was never very friendly with either, which, following his appointment as London organiser, became one of the main reasons why the Croydon NF branch eventually switched to the BNP. The move also brought them back into contact with their old mentor Nick Griffin, who would later, through the Croydon NF/BNP, return to mainstream fascist politics as the BNP leader-in-waiting.

As was usual with Anderson, he asked Blackham and me to spy on the whole Croydon branch. Terry was spying on everyone it seemed, without one word of complaint or query about the ethics of it. And I didn't object as I still had the burning ambition that one day I would lead the party.

CHAPTER 10

We loved terrorists. Up at Brick Lane, Scottish Protestants in Rangers shirts would occasionally turn up looking for donations for their fellow patriots in Northern Ireland. Eddie Whicker and I knew a man who went to prison for gun-running and he too collected money for the UVF – the Ulster Volunteer Force. I care not that my family history is Irish, that my father is a Roman Catholic and so on. I never really hated the IRA until I joined the National Front, never cared for the people of Ulster who, like me, have apparently stood at the back of every queue, always accused and betrayed because of their loyalty by birthright. But once I'd joined the NF, every piece of news on the province was digested for further thought and discussion with Eddie. I was sure that the media was biased against the Unionists because of their loyalism. The countless documentaries on the BBC would always show Protestant children learning Catholic culture in the hope of peace. They had no politics and they didn't even really understand themselves what it was they wanted, other than for everyone else to fuck off and leave them alone. They always needed more guns and bullets and so we would empty our already empty pockets upon demand.

We had to hate the Irish more than any blacks. They were fighting back against our supposed oppression of them. At every opportunity, the Irish were to be attacked, which seemed to suit Terry Blackham very, very much. There was no point getting my knickers in a twist over his hatred of my own brethren. Not if I was gonna get that job at a university somewhere once we'd butchered them all. A good Saturday selling papers in Beckenham always ended the same; us bashing Irishmen in Penge before the drunken drive home at 100 miles per hour in Terry's car.

It was announced that Beckenham National Front would lay a wreath at the Beckenham war memorial on Remembrance Sunday. Back on went the Burton's suit, back into propaganda mode we went. The British Legion was outraged that we were planning to lay our wreath just after the fire brigade. Despite what the papers and the British Legion said, neither Terry nor I were being 'expedient' about the memories of British servicemen. Sure, we didn't really give a fuck where the war memorial went. But for working class lads of our generation, there was a real significance in the sacrifices of those men. As young boys, we had grown up reading comic annuals about flying aces and gallantry in the field of battle, making us as aware as anyone of the significance of their sacrifices. Politically, we felt they had been betrayed and that it was pointless for them to have fought Nazis and then come home to Britain to see the nation that they had fought to defend open its doors and hand out that nationality to Johnny Foreigner. That was why we were going to the war memorial.

Five of us attended the Beckenham service and stood at the very back of a three-deep circle of a couple of hundred of the great and the good. The weak November sun was shining and it was cool and peaceful. Everybody was looking at us in our natty suits and combed hair, standing respectfully with our heads bowed. The men from the fire brigade scowled at us, as did the scout leaders, the girl guides, local councillors and, you could almost imagine, the war dead. *Our* wreath was in memory of the fine soldiers of the white Commonwealth, South Africa, Rhodesia and Ulster! The NF had marched to the Cenotaph every Remembrance Sunday since the late 1960s, long after the war heroes had departed. It served as a reminder that even people from undemocratic and racist countries fought the Nazis in the Second World War. The war we felt we had lost.

During the silence, I felt my tummy rumble. Nothing major, a result of being the object of all that silent hostility. Then I felt a trickle as the wind passed down towards expulsion. Like a car travelling down a hill, it slammed on its brakes just before it fell out, passing through the back of my underpants. I clenched my buttocks – an expression I think I've read Jackie Collins use – but it was no use. I had to fart. It didn't matter what it would smell like, it just had to be silent. I stood perfectly straight, looked around me and prayed to God it wouldn't make a noise. Everyone was astonished. My fart ripped around the small circle of people, followed by a small aftershock of noise not expelled the first time around. The aftershock drew direct attention to me, though the British Legion's bugler did check his instrument to make sure he had not accidentally made the noise himself. Satisfied that he had the all-clear, he too shot me a dirty look. The firemen were wetting themselves, and one of my comrades rolled on the floor in hysterics. It was disgraceful. Blackham tossed his wreath on the memorial and stormed off; the entirety of Beckenham's well-to-do and respectable community had witnessed the NF fart their way into Beckenham folklore. He shot me an evil glance and brushed past me. I had embarrassed the branch.

On the main parade at Victoria three hours later, Steve Brady, a Gerry Adams lookalike, walked up and down the line of marchers, nodding approvingly. He only walked past the first 300, the remainder being skinheads and assorted football hooligans. The march was going to be massive! God only knows who most of the people were, but it was a tradition for this march to happen every year and people just had a habit of turning up for it. Blackham and I were head stewards, identified by our green armbands. Our job was to protect the front of the march: Anderson, Brady, Acton, Martin Wingfield, his wife Tina and the Flag Party. Just before the march was about to leave, Anderson had a panic attack and started abusing everybody.

A large group of reds were holed up behind police barricades, much to the disappointment of a small crew of Chelsea Headhunters – the notorious football hooligans, who turned up on the NF parade every year without fail. Police on horses, in vans and on foot circled the procession. As we marched off, a steady stream of abuse could be heard directed at us. Hundreds of long-haired, scruffy, unemployed types rushed at us, screaming abuse. One tried to grab the wreath from Anderson's hands and we gave him a karate chop to the throat. Whicker walked discreetly behind me, barking instructions: 'Watch this pillock in the green,' 'if that bird steps in front, smash her round the face.' The police could hardly keep the protesters on the pavement, so they concentrated on the back of the march, where it was more likely there would be retaliation. I puffed my chest out for bravado, did the Lewisham barrow-boy stride and headed, like a majorette, towards Whitehall, yelling 'Fuck off you queer cunts,' at all the protesters and tourists on the pavements. Blackham and I occasionally turned to the Flag Party, shouting 'Keep those flags high, keep smiling. Ignore these bastards,' but in reality, we hoped to God there would be a huge punch-up. I was just about to smash a small and defenceless-looking female photographer over the head, when Tom Mundy, the NF's only remaining ex-soldier, grabbed my arm.

'She's with the South African embassy,' he warned. 'She's friendly.' She smiled at me and continued taking my picture. I smiled broadly at her camera and wondered why or how Mundy knew her. Maybe she could arrange for me to join BOSS; maybe I'd become the Aryan pin-up of the week back in Jo'burg; maybe she worked for the

ANC. Maybe he was giving her one! She acknowledged my restraint. A startled Eddie Whicker muttered: 'Old meat like that is best kept in the fridge.'

The NF's bugler suffered from severe nerves, severe bouts of depression and an inferiority complex. He was a park keeper from Eastbourne and one of those miserable gits that always shut the park early in summer, a devout Christian, without any of the charisma of a modern-day evangelist. He later escaped a prison sentence for his part in a BNP bomb plot in 2006 on account of his age. Turned out, the cheeky bastard wasn't even born in Britain! He struggled through the last post as Anderson struggled through a prayer at the Cenotaph.

'Is that the best bugler the Aryan race has to offer?' shouted one protester, and even Anderson smiled.

I farted again during the minute's silence, though this time nobody heard. The protesters had lined up behind police barriers to cat-call and abuse us. A million cameras flashed and caught us in perfect symmetry, miming one of those obscure hymns that only an Oxford-educated wanker like Anderson knows the words to. The whole march there and trudge back took about an hour. The solemnity of the occasion was not lost on anyone. After the wreath-laying we relaxed. We threw off the shackles of solemnity. We had to practise our Cenotaph manoeuvres, because eventually the NF would be in government, standing next to the Queen in glorious sunshine at 11 a.m., not cold and lonely at 2.30 p.m. It must have kept Anderson awake for years, worrying how he'd ever get out of bed in time for a morning do at the Cenotaph.

Remembrance Sunday was one of only two days of the year the NF put on a public face. Many will surmise they hide at home in white hoods, up to no good, whereas all we really ever did was spend all year trying to get people to the national conference, trying to get marchers to the

Cenotaph, trying to persuade a tiny proportion of the entire electorate to vote for us. Men who paint swastikas on shed doors, men who dress in Nazi costumes in private, men who hate women, hate Jews, hate everyone, are hardly preparing for power. Come the revolution, most of them'll be manning the barricades trying to stop it from happening. That is the truth.

The after-march rally and collection for party funds was not a lively occasion. Those who were not paid-up members went home, or to find reds to attack at the train station. Some BNP members hung around to listen to Anderson, Brady and national organiser, John Hill, a portly, thuggish Brummie, address the 100-strong crowd. I stood at the back of the crowd, bored and lonely, watching Eddie Whicker posing with his fanclub of northern working-class fascists, who only ever read about him in *Searchlight*. There was so much we needed to do to save our nation that it started to dawn on me that attempting to be normal, to be acceptable, to be the 'iron fist in a velvet glove' when what we really had were dishpan hands, would not be the way. Later, Eddie and I conferred over the day's activities. Pleasant enough, but the speeches were boring. Brady geed up the crowd with a few tough words, only for Anderson to send it flat again. So close to Parliament, could we not storm the gates just this once?

The conversation turned to the plot to kill Ken Livingstone. Sometime in the past two years, word was all over the far right about the plot. One of the UVF members, who had a collection bucket with him, was discussing it again with me and Eddie.

'I'm getting the blame for it going tits up,' he sighed. He'd been under suspicion for a while, having been caught in Scotland as part of a potential gun-running gang, but escaping sentence had done his kudos no favours.

'Maybe it's your big mouth,' Eddie proffered.

There was a series of letters, which had been made available to the press by the UDA, of the NF's Steve Brady giving a rundown to former UDA boss Andy Tyrie of his connections with well-known Nazi paramilitary groups. You can imagine the surprise when, in an issue of *Vanguard,* the attempted 'hit' on Livingstone was mentioned. I only asked Brady about this once, during a minibus trip to a rally in Wigan. All he would do was confirm that he knew of it. It proved nothing apart from what we all already knew: that loyalists and Nazis both have big gobs. Future Milltown murderer Michael Stone, an 'independent', loyalist hitman, later owned up to being the proposed man on the job and, lo and behold, the gun was found hidden in Scotland. Stone was later imprisoned for murder and the English UVF man later wound up as a leading figure in C18.

The UVF had long been illegal and the UDA only more recently, partly because of its openly murderous campaign, carried out under the Ulster Freedom Fighters (UFF). The UDA had also been regarded as more susceptible to politicisation by the far right. Most loyalist terror groups only ever saw the British far right as an avenue for income, not something the NF or BNP had ever been very keen to donate to others. There was a keenness among anti-fascists to suggest that British fascists worked for the UDA/UFF on scouting missions, and that these organisations were offering paramilitary training to fascists in return. In reality, the training of drunken English and Scottish football hooligans was not in the loyalists' interests. Although there were plenty of willing volunteers to take part in training, the Brady experience and the Political Soldier NF's links to Gadaffi, left the Ulstermen wary of fascists. Loyalists, in comparison with their Republican counterparts, were embarrassingly lacking in modern weaponry and political analysis. In fact, it is fair to say the UDA had absolutely none; they were merely clinging on to the belief that they

would one day put their war to bed. But there are also strong
working-class convictions in the loyalist organisations. The
left seem to prefer to think of all Ulster Protestants as some
kind of land-owning gentry, when, in most cases I'm aware
of, they are, in fact, as bollock poor as their Catholic neighbours. Despite some political foundations in the 1970s and
1980s, the UDA was more reckless than any of the other
groups operating in the province.

Not only that, but even though they themselves were
made up of unscrupulous murderers and drug dealers,
most loyalist paramilitaries found the NF and BNP a less-
than-palatable political mouthpiece.

In 1980, Steve Brady concluded in his letters and discussions with the UDA, that the majority of European Nazis
were firmly in support of the Provisional IRA. On one 1980
fact-finding mission to the Nazis' annual international get-
together and beanfeast in Diksmuide, Belgium, two leading loyalists from the UVF attempted to buy weapons and
chemicals for use in Ulster. As a condition of the sale, the
Nazis demanded that Jewish targets in Northern Ireland
were attacked. Maybe this was to ease the conscience of
the Nazis, but the two loyalists steadfastly refused. At
another meeting a few years later, instigated this time by
a European far-right group which was down on its luck,
an indignant UVF deliberately sent along a negotiator
who was mixed race, ingeniously nicknamed 'Nigger' by
his comrades.

As for Livingstone's attempted murder, it probably
never really got off of the ground. The gun may have made
its way to Scotland where, by all accounts, it may still be
behind a wall somewhere, but it is unlikely that either the
UDA or the UVF would risk sending one of their only
decent hitmen on a high-profile murder on the London
Underground. Livingstone had trodden on a lot of delicate
toes in the 1980s, having aired claims made by a former

UDA grass, Albert Baker, that the security forces aided and abetted East Belfast UDA in the early 1970s. Livingstone used this information in his 1988 book and in speeches in parliament during the same period. It is possible that some people felt that Livingstone was inadvertently putting loyalists in danger, but the 'hit' on him is now, thanks to Stone, common knowledge. With the proposed hitman Stone now back inside for 600-plus years for an art stunt gone wrong, no one has ever seemed too bothered to look into the matter further.

CHAPTER 11

Still in my teens, I was gradually coming to realise that no matter what I believed in at a political level, at a person-to-person level it was not right. Don't get me wrong, I didn't have a sudden epiphany, although I had anonymously rung *Searchlight* after the Welling Library incident, which by now seemed like years ago. The 1990s were approaching; I was still a dedicated racist and fascist, but this ideology was not addressing the very things that I had begun to acknowledge had driven me into their hands. I had difficulties with the concept of victims, even faceless ones, and I knew deep down that, as ridiculous as it may sound, if we did come to power we were not going to be calling elections ever again. Sure, democracy wasn't really much of a friend of mine. It was a stupid and dangerous concept that allowed idiots to make choices about who governed them. I'd never seen or ever had a government that seemed to serve my needs. I couldn't even bend my needs or fears to fit in with their agenda. Class was certainly part of the problem, being working class. Surrounded as I was by other solid working class males, their obsessions were still overtly based on race.

I had friends now, as I always had done, but the nature of these new friendships meant that I would probably have to fight and die with or for them. That was not a party policy but a realisation that all the drinking and fighting and the endless confrontations were obviously going to lead to something getting out of hand. And why this overbearing obsession by our middle-class leadership with chasing the middle-class vote and a broader, middle-class membership? Were we not good enough or capable enough for government, or were we going to get butchered ourselves during the bloody revolution and race war we were striving for?

The membership began to dry up in the NF and at the Lane on Sunday mornings, more and more of my former colleagues would end up standing with the BNP because the constant politicking of Anderson was grinding down their will and passion to fight. Mine too it seemed. Sure, in a moment of coolness I could gently assure myself that I wanted a peaceful revolution where we just had to say goodbye to our black neighbours, but our politics and our literature were all about getting people angry and getting people to act. We *wanted* a bloody race-war, we felt it was inevitable and we would have to be the ones controlling the streets when it happened. We weren't the kind of blokes who could cry on each other's shoulders over loves gone-astray or bitter personal dissatisfactions. All of these friendships were built solely on our hatred and distrust of others. The class system, or what little I knew of it, was quite obviously separate to race. There were two ways of looking at it: downtrodden and ignored because we were either white or because we were also working class. The latter seemed most obvious to me but that attitude simply drew blank stares.

The BNP has itself continued this trend. More and more of their working-class activists have dropped off or fallen by the wayside. Whether it's desperation, frustration or, perhaps, their own sick concept of martyrdom, a large number of them can no longer conceal their pent-up frustrations and just end up trying to blow themselves or other people up. The BNP gently sweeps it under the carpet and points its fingers at the Muslim community.

1989: there was a flurry of circulars, the NF issuing one in response to a BNP letter which criticised the NF and

predicted its demise. The NF respondent (believed to be
Paul Nash) took issue with the BNP's attack on the Welling
Library meeting. Beginning with the most important prem-
ise that, 'nobody is going to argue about turning over a
red meeting,' the circular went on to criticise the BNP's
behaviour at the public meeting. Drawing obvious paral-
lels between the differing attitudes and ideologies of the
NF and the BNP, the NF-backed response claimed that the
BNP had wasted a unique opportunity to engage in debate
with the assorted women at the meeting and convince
them that nationalists have a right to office, 'an action
that would have won public sympathy.' Clearly, the writer
was echoing the new NF approach to dealing with people
opposed to nationalist views. What the NF hoped was that
the majority of the members on both sides who had read
the two circulars would see sense in the NF's approach to
mainstream politics, and disengage from acts of violence
against the enemy.

What the BNP realised was that newspapers ignored
our protests, or else people simply walked away when
the NF or BNP showed their faces. They revisited Martin
Webster's (part of the famous 1970s double act of Tyndall
and Webster) late 1960s belief that we would have to 'kick
their way into the headlines,' whereas Anderson didn't
want headlines, he wanted nice footnotes at the bottom
of the *Times*'s society columns. The question was, why
would we want to debate with these people when we could
simply crush them? The actions at Welling Library may
have landed many in hospital and in prison, but nobody
lost votes over the incident and all it rated were very small
column inches in a couple of the national newspapers.

And anyway, never in a million years were we capable
of entering into a reasoned debate with anybody. It was
because of this realisation that Anderson wanted the NF
to be perceived as 'racial democrats', in the hope that the

avenues of debate and exchange would not always remain closed to us so long as we worked on our image and glossed over our pasts. However, nobody was listening to either the NF or the BNP. Only controversial press releases gained publicity, not sound political comment on the events of the day from a nationalist perspective. As a result of the constant smearing, the BNP were as shy as they were cynical about standing at parliamentary elections. For 365 days of the year, the BNP also followed another Webster theory on the media: in nationalist politics, there is no such thing as bad publicity; the right had enough 'evidence' to declare to its members exactly who was responsible for the media campaign against it (the Jews). However, it did not seem prepared in the early 1990s to enter into parliamentary electioneering. The BNP could, however, run an excellent and forceful campaign in council wards, flooding areas with members and hoping to overwhelm the press with their own strength in numbers and propaganda. They were particularly good at this in the East End of London: 'Three pints of lager and an end to immigration please!'

I had always made a concerted effort to avoid old school friends. Our lives were very different now. Their lives were not taken over by the perils of Nazism; I acknowledged to myself that their lives had changed for the better. Whether I wanted their friendship or not didn't really matter anyway; they were shunning me. Their 'working class hero' was now an angry young man with ideas about justifiable genocide against an enemy he neither knew nor wished to understand. Our paths would cross occasionally, but the uncomfortable conversations would end abruptly because they did not want to listen to me ranting on and on. I could see it on their faces when we met.

I'd dug myself into that hole, but it was far easier to blame them for not understanding, for not believing in me and my politics. I did now realise that they would never be sorry for this in the way that I thought they would be before. All I could threaten them with now was violence.

Occasionally I'd be invited to a party, mainly so the old school crowd could gawk at me, or so I suspected. Of course, by now, I had a bit of a reputation as a foolish lunatic, involved in and with the most unpleasant activities and people. The NF had been considered dangerous and old hat for so long that I was judged to be a real lunatic for getting involved with them. I'd blown the opportunity to get a cushy little office job. I didn't go on interesting drink-fuelled holidays in the sun and finger girls from Slough. I was a static maniac who didn't want to grow up and didn't want to fit in. The smarter ones at these parties wanted to sharpen their claws and practice political debate, as they were more than likely heading off to university. There was no doubt I was good at debate, even if it was very difficult to keep my mind on it when so much of my time was spent with my hands down my trousers.

My contemporaries knew nothing of the policies the NF occasionally expressed belief in, and I knew similarly little about whatever internationalist and irrelevant shit the left was pushing on working-class kids that week. I copped to everything; yes, we did sell drugs at the BNP bookshop in Welling, upstairs we had a huge stockpile of firearms, and we were going to shoot any Commies or Jews that got in our way.

'Welling Library? Oh, you heard about that? Yeah, that was us, some heavies from Northern Ireland came over to help us out.'

My other party trick was to ask the host, 'So, who's the old slag at this do then?' And of course I still ended up at home alone, listening to Billy Bragg.

I could rant and rave about facism to anyone who'd even pretend to listen but I wasn't so good at hearing the opposing arguments. The only politics open to discussion were inter-party politics, and it seemed the more time I spent visiting Edmonds, the more Nazi I became.

One night I rang Anderson persuading him to call in to LBC radio, where they were debating racism. 'I am the Chairman of the National Front,' he began and I was asleep by the time he finished. We didn't know the names or identities of any of our lefty opponents, nor did we know what schisms they were going through among themselves. We were obsessed with their popularity, their worthiness and their confidence, but we never had the will or the confidence to sit down and tackle their arguments, even among ourselves. We were totally ignorant politically.

In an attempt to engage with the public, Terry Blackham and I went to visit a man in Eltham who was capable of shifting thirty copies a month of *The Flag*. Blackham saw it as an opportunity to become the top-selling branch; I saw it more as an opportunity to clear some space under my bed. There was no way I was willing for the branch to buy another thirty copies of the paper, even if we went top of *The Flag*'s 'Branch Efficiency Table'.

The house in Eltham was large, with those stone ornaments at the front of the path that tell you some working-class plonker lives there. Lions or bulldogs I do not remember, but Blackham patted their heads as we walked to the open front door. A startled child sat on the hall floor, burst into tears as we approached, and was scooped up by its mother. We asked for the man in the letter and she looked very confused. Surely we hadn't been deceived by yet another fake letter? As we prepared to leave, a man came to the door.

'Sorry, that's not my real name. Are you from *The Flag*?'

Blackham and I stopped dead in our tracks and looked at the bearded fellow before us, quite huge with a stupid grin on his face. 'Come in, come in,' he invited us excitedly. His house already had the uniform Nazi look about

it, newspapers and books on German militarism all over
the floor and Jim Davidson videos jockeying for position
on his overcrowded bookshelves. His wife immediately
left the room, taking the child with her, and our host shut
the door.

'How are you?' he asked in a deep whisper, stroking
his beard.

Blackham and I went through the usual routine of a
follow-up call: 'We're from the National Front, we received
your letter and thought we'd call around to see how you
are and if you wanted to purchase any literature, or if you
would be interested in coming to a meeting.'

Blackham pulled from his sports bag a dozen copies of
the paper and the magazine *Vanguard*. 'I like this magazine, I've already got it though,' he responded.

We stayed for over an hour and talked a lot of rubbish
about music and television, then suddenly I recognised him.

'My job is quite sensitive...' he began, getting very
nervous and blushing before I told him that mine was too.
Blackham almost had a heart attack as we were shoved up
the garden path.

'Who is he?' he growled.

'He's with the press!' I shouted as I tried desperately to
do up my seatbelt before we screeched off.

'You shouldn't have told him about the police,' whined
Blackham. 'You made him nervous.'

That afternoon I typed a new press release, proclaiming
that Beckenham NF would take back the schools from the
Marxist educators. It meant we'd actually have to leaflet
local schools, which made me slightly nervous given that
the last time I was in one, every other student was significantly bigger than me. The *Bromley Post* wanted to do an
interview. Anderson told the other local paper, the *Bromley
Times*, that we were 'redressing the balance', and that no
child under the age of fourteen would be given leaflets

because they were too young for membership. How do you tell who is and who is not fourteen? Anyone above a foot high and white classified in my book, so according to plan they all got leaflets.

We turned up unannounced at one of the local schools and dumped a couple of hundred leaflets, held in reserve by Anderson for such an occasion, on the laps of confused white kids in a very multiracial school. Terrified black schoolgirls ran inside to fetch a teacher, while the black boys took note of which white kids were accepting leaflets. They had no choice though; we thrust them at the children, trying to look appealing, although well aware that, without the promise of a free Big Mac, not much captures the interest of school-kids. The headmaster came to the gates to complain but the local paper had already said that there was no crime in what we were doing. I flashed the article under his nose. 'We are not interfering. No one is being obstructed. There is nothing you can do.' By the time the police arrived, there were three of us and half a dozen schoolteachers staring at each other on either side of the school gates. The helpful bobby reiterated what I had already told the headmaster, and warned us not to enter the school grounds – something Blackham had avoided even during his school years.

A week later I sat in the reception of the *Bromley Post* with my hair neatly gelled, holding an envelope of racist leaflets. An aggressive young woman came down to the reception with a note pad and began an argument that lasted a good half an hour. She used all the student chestnuts about multiracialism and I used all the racist arguments I'd practised many times in the pub. We shared a cigarette and paused for take breath. She didn't take many notes, but instead stared at me, confused by my age and my zealotry. I thought she was rather gorgeous, so I spent the rest of the time staring at the socks hanging out of my trainers and trying to act cool and aloof.

'I admire your front,' she said, and in reply I almost blurted out how much I admired her chest, but managed to bite my tongue. I never met women like this other than to argue with, but at least I was debating with her rather than just fantasising about her in my bedroom. Our conversation steered away from politics for a minute to her circumstances, something about her frustration at being a journalist on a small newspaper and a free one at that. She'd rather have been reporting on Thatcher going down the drain for *The Guardian*. We passed like ships in the night, and in the published article she spelled my name wrong. Some high-class broadsheet picked up the story, and I ended up on the same page as an article about failing education standards.

Anderson read over the press coverage and showed me a couple of thousand membership cards of the Newham Labour Party he had just printed. 'What bastards eh? Didn't even use a union printer,' he boasted. He'd sort of hoped that the local Labour Party knew who he was. One of the most outspoken leftie councillors even lived at the end of his road. Nobody knew Anderson and he couldn't bear it; he was more likely to be mistaken for Worzel Gummidge than recognised as the Chairman of the NF. However, there was more serious business to be dealing with. Anderson was organising a 'get to know you evening' with our Eltham inquirer. According to Anderson he was legit, we had just shocked him by turning up on his doorstep as we did. I would not be attending the evening, neither would Anderson. Anderson was not attending because of his high political profile, and I was not attending because I had half scared the bloke to death and, more importantly, I was too well known in the area where the meeting was taking place. Anderson wanted it made clear this new connection was too important to be blown. It seemed the NF's respectable image was finally getting him somewhere.

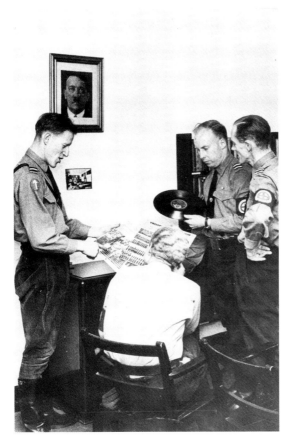

John Tyndall (holding the record) and friends in the 1960s. They didn't like disco much.

LEFT NF election meeting c. 1988. I should've taken that wine and found a good hairdresser.
RIGHT Me and Terry Blackham with a rare customer of the party paper. Beckenham c. 1988.

Charlie Sargent, leader of Combat 18, marching with the then BNP leader
John Tyndall in the early 1990s. Sargent went on to be sentenced for murdering
a political rival.

Eddie Whicker, London
c. 1989. Eddie models
his black shirt and
braces look.

Richard Edmonds, Bethnal Green 1991. On a 'Rights for Whites' demo after John Stoner's stabbing.

West Midlands 1990. Ian Anderson, John Hill and Eddie Whicker.

Eltham 1992. BNP members turn up to abuse the family of a murdered teenager, who were marching in protest.

Steve Brady, Ian Anderson, John McAuley and John Hill c. 1991.

The infamous battle of Waterloo station before a Skrewdriver gig in 1992.

Ian Stuart Donaldson, founder of the Blood and Honour network and singer in skinhead band Skrewdriver.

London UDA chief Frank Portinari (left) with a ceremonial sword and Eddie Whicker holding a pistol. Portanari went to prison for attempted gun smuggling in 1994.

LEFT Addressing the National Union of Students, Blackpool 2009. I was the first person to ever use the F word during the fraternal greeting. The students didn't seem to mind…

RIGHT Drinking the Bragg rider, London 2010.

Dagenham 2010. Billy Bragg confronts the BNP's Richard Barnbrook, making headlines around the world.

Police take action during a violent EDL demo in Newcastle, 2011.

An EDL rally in Leicester, 2010.

Nick Griffin
delivering his
own brand of
nationalist politics
over loudspeaker.

The EDL replace
the BNP on
the streets of
Dagenham, 2011.
Two Asian men
were hospitalised
by the racist gang.

Manchester Academy 2011. Introducing Bragg at a 'Hope Not Hate' gig.

Blackham was to attend on behalf of Anderson, together with the two Croydon members. Which meant that the meeting to prove what a decent bunch of people we were to our new high-profile friend, Mr X, would be attended by a man with a firearms conviction, a man who had MI6 investigating his movements and a crop-haired lunatic with more criminal convictions than *The Sun* had tits. I was a wee bit put out, but then the NF had always been about pulling rank. To lighten the blow, Anderson told me he wanted me to come onboard the NF full-time. I already was, I reminded him, but once the civil service sick leave ran out, he would have to foot the bill.

He agreed: 'I want you to be my right-hand man at the office, keep your mouth shut and your eyes open at all times.' The Directorate took a vote on it a couple of weeks later, and the job was mine.

Surprisingly, Anderson agreed to give me pretty much the same package as I had with the civil service so I took a week's holiday immediately.

I went and dug up as much information as I could on our new friend, just in case. It wasn't too hard given that the woman next door worked at the same place as him and knew my politics. She was black, too.

Having been screened by Blackham and the others Mr X requested another meeting, this time with Anderson. Anderson wanted me to go with him. He drove us there from east London, even though the pub was very near my south east London home. As usual, Anderson was too excitable for words. He was chattering on and on about what a big moment this was and how he was expecting it to be quite a nice little pub with a very conservative clientele, perhaps a dining area where we could have a nice bite to eat. He'd scrubbed his stained hands for hours in an attempt to get the ink off, but still wore a tatty, torn jacket and a pair of trousers splashed with paint. As we drove towards

our meeting place, I recognised it as one of the locality's
bigger shit holes, the sort of place where you'd wipe your
feet upon leaving, not entering. It faced a busy road and a
council estate, while another council estate sat behind it.
The pub was tiled green inside and out and the walls were
nicotine-stained as all good pubs should be. The carpet may
also have once been green, but had been so burnt by cigarettes and arson attempts by former landlords that it was
hard to tell. We took a table at the back of the empty room.

Anderson did most of the talking, attempting to be
charming and intellectual, at the same time realising that
Mr X was very down to earth, and a little naïve about
the NF. Mr X refused to become a member, not that we
expected him to, but he said he would be willing to help if
he could, on certain issues that he felt were deserving of the
sort of publicity publications like *The Flag* and *Vanguard*
couldn't get. The sneaky prick was probably just after
some new exclusives but Anderson was already beside
himself with anticipation. He was giddy with excitement,
strolling up to the bar and buying rounds whilst chattering on about his (unfinished) Oxford education. He could
see this friendship being the very thing the party needed.
I could see this was going to be a painful love affair with
a manic journalist who was far more of a whingeing Tory
than an angry working-class revolutionary, but Anderson
was excited by his new friend and began passing on interesting pieces of news that the NF would not be able to
make use of to Mr X. They were, in fact, little snippets
from local papers that our members sent in each week;
outrageous stories of loony left councils flying foreign flags
whilst banning our own, simple butcher's apron. The love
affair spread to encompass members around the country.
The idiots began cutting out Mr X's columns and sending
them to us, as well as sending him literature in the hope he
would join the party.

Mr X and I didn't hit it off however. I don't recall why, but it was most probably my fault. I thought he was a cunt from the moment I met him. Anderson had me at the newsagents every morning buying a copy of the stupid newspaper, scouring the articles to see if there was a hidden message for us in any of them. Mr X wrote under a couple of names other than his own so I even had to read the bloody limited financial columns in case there was something there. I just couldn't share in the excitement. Mr X had taken an unnerving dislike to me too. Every word I said to him seemed to make him uncomfortable or nervous. Perhaps I hadn't fallen flat at his feet and declared my love for him like so many others in the party immediately had, but I'd been to the House of fucking Lords so I wasn't going to be overly impressed by a right-wing guttersnipe. Word of the association leaked within weeks. Anderson treated this new supporter as his own personal conquest and sent Blackham to be Mr X's minder. If he wanted in on the NF, then he would have to get there with Terry by his side. What Mr X was not expecting was how eager the NF, and Anderson in particular, was to use their new friendship to further their own ends and, given any opportunity, to control his life. There was even some suggestion that members be parked outside Mr X's house as a 24-hour guard. I couldn't believe it.

By now, Anderson was in almost complete control of the party financially and physically, having siphoned off assets into side interests that he privately owned. Mr X was another asset and, although he allowed it to become one of the worst-kept secrets in history, Anderson refused to tell the rest of the puppet leadership about him. Mr X belonged to Anderson, or so we thought.

CHAPTER 12

Mr X was getting all hot under the collar about his new friends in the NF and I was getting a little browned off with them. Look at what they had done to me. I'd become an aggressive, unfriendly teenager with a flick knife in his coat pocket, copious amounts of unpalatable pornography under his bed and a permanently dark mood. It got so bad, that if we ever wanted light relief we would turn on a news programme showing starving black children in Africa. And even then, there was a terrible underlying fear that they would end up here, living next door to us.

Buoyed by his new acquaintance, Anderson was keen to produce a magazine of his own to challenge *Vanguard*'s extremism and promote himself. Despite being in support of the NF, *Vanguard* and *The Flag* were privately owned by their editors and *Vanguard* in particular was known to be more than a little unflattering towards Anderson's leadership. The new magazine would also be privately owned, by Anderson, and would be a cheaper way for him to advertise his book and sticker sales than having to pay Wingfield for space in *The Flag*.

The National Front as an organisation owned nothing, not even the Union Jacks carried by the Flag Party on marches. Everything was produced in support of the NF in case of another coup, so that the people in control of the party's structures could simply carry on regardless. In effect, despite its subheading – *The Newspaper of The National Front* – *The Flag* was actually owned by Martin Wingfield. Wingfield, Anderson, Brady and Acton were the chief contributors which thereby provided a forum for both sides of the internal power struggle: Anderson on one side and Brady and Acton on the other. As editor of the paper, Wingfield acted as a referee though he had no control over *Vanguard*. It was this talented editing that had helped keep Anderson, Brady and Acton together. Whereas *Vanguard* represented a small grouping of Strasserites and Conservatives, Anderson was not prepared to allow his magazine to be used as a think-tank or for anything even mildly interesting or informative. He wanted his magazine to represent one man and one vision.

The Nash brothers stepped back into writing for NF publications, independent of any cliques and nasty thoughts. Although Anderson absolutely abhorred the pair, they were in fact exactly the type of members he dreamed of, uncontroversial and without leadership dreams. But I was inclined to believe that the magazine would never have got off the ground if Mr X had not offered his services. He provided Anderson with his first major headline: 'The figures *The Sun* would not print', a rather dull and predictable story about *Sun* readers not wanting more immigration.

I became slightly concerned though, when the January edition of *Searchlight* mentioned the new NF publication in its far right round-up. Two months before Anderson's magazine, *Lionheart*, appeared, word was already out.

The entire magazine was printed in Anderson's garden shed, using cheap and nasty orange paper, probably left over from one of his other printing jobs. The first print run was for 500 copies, though there were only advance orders for thirty, all guillotined and stapled together by *moi*, who also had to remove the badly-printed copies and sheets printed upside down. The arrival of *Lionheart* coincided with a real change of affection and attitude on my part towards Anderson and the party. The more I delved into the NF, the more I felt like it was a big lie. The whole

charade of political persuasion and principles based on
class equality and freedom were little more than my own
dreams and rhetoric. The NF was ideologically and ethi-
cally empty and my illusions were being steadily shattered.
I thought we would be purer than the driven snow, more
committed than any champagne socialist crying into his
proletarian beer about the end of Communism; I thought
we would all live subservient lives in readiness for the great
white revolution. I had dreams of being championed for
the many sacrifices I'd made and of being occasionally
wanked-off by a nice housewife from Catford. This had
turned out not to be so.

Anderson became in my eyes, the most manipulative
and greedy man I had ever known. I sat in his dining room/
office surrounded by piles of filth, despatching books to
the back of beyond, accepting cash and cheques for things
we did not stock and putting up with temper tantrums
that would send most parents heading straight for the slip-
per. He was as shallow and petty as he was vile and dirty.
Nothing of any use came out of his foul mouth. His talent
had run dry, as had his bottles of cheap whisky. He was an
old romantic in many ways but it was only ever about him
making love to his own inflated ego, tossing the dreams
and lives and aspirations of his members and supporters
like dirty tissues into a bin. He actually cared for no one
and nothing except himself. The National Front was doing
appallingly. January's edition of *Searchlight* had put the
party's membership at 3–4,000 when, in fact, it was obvious from inside the NF that our national membership was
probably 800 at the most.

The NF was having great difficulty in getting membership renewals, because the vast majority of the committed
nationalists were looking to the BNP for results. Shortly
after our Rochdale debacle, the BNP had stormed into
the northern town of Dewsbury and sent the local ethnic

community onto the streets in violent confrontation with the police, gaining the BNP national press coverage and increased approval ratings from within the right. Most NF members by now preferred to stretch one NF member-ship fee out over two years, causing great stress to the party's resources as it continued to send members local and national newsletters for however long they wished to receive them. Despite this, Tina Wingfield managed to send me my cheque for forty quid a week without fail, while Anderson's empire of printing and his Freedom Books distribution network always came up short on a Friday, though he insisted I should still invoice him. They were rapidly making me as financially bankrupt as they were themselves morally bankrupt.

Blackham and I mailed out thirty bulletins a month, despite only having forty-five pounds in membership fees from our nine members. Even under the strained resources that the Front had to survive on, Anderson still charged them for all the printing and photocopying he did at his whim on behalf of the party. When branches needed new notepaper, it was Anderson who printed it for them. The National Front had no protection over the use of its name. Anderson printed stickers with the NF name on, and charged them three pounds for a bundle of 250. They never even stuck!

Searchlight had estimated the BNP's strength to be 'only a thousand' but it was the BNP that was more capable of and willing to distribute literature around the country free of charge, probably with the proceeds of whatever was left of Edmonds's payoff from Cable & Wireless. It was probably a fair estimate of the BNP's size. *Searchlight* may have been fooled, as were some far right members, by the NF's outward professionalism, and by some of the NF's educated leadership. For those of us close up, the leader-ship of the Front were only securing enough activity to

provide them with enough income to live off the movement full-time. Takings had fallen incredibly sharply in the
NF since the BNP had opened their shop, members were
dazzled by the sheer front of the BNP to do something so
brazen. The NF's inability to recruit *en masse* in London
was leaving the party crippled nationally, while the BNP's
high level of recruitment in London gave it the strength to
campaign nationwide, sometimes in areas where they were
even outnumbered, on paper at least, by NF members.

Nobody made a living out of the BNP. Edmonds owned
the BNP bookshop and took his earnings from the sales
of books and literature. Tyndall made his living from his
publication *Spearhead* and from his relationship with
his father-in-law, who had always secured a place in the
leadership of Tyndall's organisations by supporting his
daughter and grandchild. When I used to sit with Edmonds
in the BNP office, huge piles of cash and cheques would
be lying on tables and chairs and under newspapers. By
1990, it was impossible to imagine that the NF had ever
been bigger than the BNP. The 1989 circular defending the
NF from Tony Lecomber's and Eddy Butler's attack openly
admitted so: 'They claim to be stronger than the National
Front. Even if they were, what difference would it make?'

For some time, both National Fronts had been on the
lookout for bequests. A man of ninety pops his clogs, and
decides on his deathbed to leave all his money, or his property, to the National Front. Because the NF was not listed
in the phone book, senior members of both of the National
Fronts were always keen to unearth some recently dead
British Nazis. To this end, Patrick Harrington, who was
left holding onto the National Front name when the rest
of the Political Soldiers, including Nick Griffin, headed for
the hills, was said to be actively sending notices to solicitors' offices around the country advising that the name
National Front had been bestowed to him by an act in the

National Front's constitution. Even so, he still missed out in 1990.

An old racist popped his clogs somewhere in Wales in late 1989, cutting his sister out of his will and leaving his property to the National Front and British Movement. No one had ever heard of the old codger; he'd never been a member, had never even written the party a letter. The British Movement proper was long dead after *Searchlight* mole, Ray Hill, deliberately pitted leaders of the organisation against each other in the early 1980s in a sort of handbags and rags manoeuvre. Unable to cope with Hill's activities against him – he lost a leadership struggle… to a mole! – and unable to get the BM's membership to regroup behind him, Mike McLaughlin had disbanded the organisation in 1984 and gone to live in Wales, to run a survivalist business.

The BM had been started by Britain's post-war Nazi godfather Colin Jordan, a mentor to John Tyndall, Martin Webster and, for a short while, Andrew Brons, in 2011 one of the BNP's MEPs. After Tyndall and Webster left his organisation and started running the National Front, Jordan was caught stealing ladies' underwear from Tesco and stood down to let McLaughlin take over the leadership until such time as Jordan saw fit to return. McLaughlin refused to hand back the reins to Jordan and turned the BM into a profitable and violent street army of skinheads and absolutely dedicated, violent, racist Nazis. After its demise, many from the BM followed Hill into the BNP or grew their hair and got jobs. But the ideas and symbolism of the BM remained prominent in the 1980s and 1990s and there were many incarnations of it still active within the BNP and some, unsure whether there were legal complications, running twenty- or thirty-strong groups called BNM or BNSM.

This worried Anderson. He already as good as had his hands on half of the money, but the solicitors handling the estate were adamant that the British Movement, or its most legitimate incarnation, should get theirs. Who would that be? Colin Jordan its founder, by now on reasonably friendly terms with the BNP's Tyndall again, or even Ray Hill, the mole who finished off the British Movement, but was in effect its most popular choice for leader before its demise? The money had to go to the now politically inactive McLaughlin, Anderson insisted. Did Anderson know where McLaughlin was? Apparently he did. Anderson told me all that he felt I would need to know, for the sake of the party. He wouldn't even tell Blackham or the Directorate the exact details of the bequest in case any of them got their grubby mitts on the cash. During one of the afternoons when Anderson was not busy swearing and smashing up his printer in the shed, he took me to the pub to unburden his chest. The thought of up to £40,000 getting into the hands of anyone else scared him shitless and he was almost nauseous at the thought of it. We sat in an East Ham pub and he apologised for the stressful atmosphere that had developed in the office in the past few days, as the moment of collection came closer.

Anderson had thought about opening a bank account himself in the name of British Movement to collect all of the money, but had changed his mind almost immediately. I volunteered but he said it was too much trouble. They would want constitutions, referees, accounts, publications etc. One thing Anderson did have though, he said, was an old BM membership list he claimed to have bought from McLaughlin in 1984 when McLaughlin closed down. However, most of the names were out of date, or were skinheads already in the movement, or people they didn't want. If McLaughlin got his hands on £40,000, would he try to re-enter politics?

It was Martin Wingfield who apparently made the first contact with McLaughlin. Anderson was instructing the deal on the proviso that McLaughlin did not restart the BM or join the BNP. Now, this is where I concurred with people from the BM soon afterwards. Did Anderson receive any money, any finder's fee, from McLaughlin? After all, it was money for old rope for McLaughlin, and what was he still doing with an active British Movement bank account? When asked, Anderson claimed that McLaughlin did not offer the NF anything, not even a donation. I found it difficult, having known Anderson, that he would not have mentioned to McLaughlin the fact that there were many incarnations of the BM around, still relatively active even if only socially. One I was aware of was in Huddersfield, actually calling itself British Movement and there was one old-timers' group surviving among the BNP fringe in the Catford area. Anderson claimed that the NF even ended up short from the estate (a house that was left to the two organisations), after he offered the deceased's sister a small amount of cash to avoid any unpleasantness. McLaughlin apparently kept his word, though nobody has ever verified his deal with Anderson with him personally.

The large cash injection along with his new friend seemed to give Anderson a renewed faith in his own abilities with the turn of the decade in 1990. He regularly claimed the NF was Britain's Fastest Growing Political Party to anyone who cared to listen. By then, I had given up. The NF eventually ended up with about £35,000 and Anderson demanded that the party purchase two things: a computer and a minibus.

As I sat in the pub with him, Anderson spoke of a deal to purchase a computer for a grand that we could use in his 'office' (or as the BNP called it 'the home office') which would be of benefit to both him and the party. Although the Wingfields were running the administration, Anderson wanted the use of a computer to help him with his print-ing as he was still using Letraset and photocopier for his artwork and typesetting, a rather archaic way of doing business even back then. The minibus was to be kept by Anderson too, so that he could carry members around the country and make pickups of large quantities of paper for his printing enterprise as well as deliveries. Everything had fallen into place perfectly.

The day the computer was dropped off with a large thud on the doorstep, we both sat and stared at it for a good ten minutes before Anderson barked, 'Well, switch the fucking thing on then! Let's see what it can do!' Do? How was I supposed to know what it did or how to start the bloody thing? I looked at Anderson, then at the computer, before biting my lip for a second. 'I haven't a clue how these things work. It's just a keyboard and screen, it's a bloody terminal!'

Anderson switched it on and started writing on the screen. 'Where does it fucking print from then? How do I get a blank white screen with black writing? How do I do this…?'

No idea, either of us. He thought it should automatically start doing whatever you wanted, on command, but the thing was totally fucking useless.

'You should know, you should fucking well know how to make it work. Make the fucking thing work!!' By the end of the day, he was seething. I only went to a comprehensive you see, the computers had to be kept locked away from thugs and idiots like me. Over at the BNP meanwhile, Richard Edmonds had a degree in computing and Tyndall and Tony Lecomber were doing a computer course so that they could save on the cost of producing *Spearhead* by not using a typesetter. Anderson may as well have asked me to sail the Woolwich ferry. Even the work I had done in the civil service was still done with a trusty biro before being filed away somewhere dusty.

He kept stomping into the room and standing with his hands on hips and staring at me and then back to the computer before stomping out again. I heard him reaching for the whisky bottle as he crunched through the broken glass on the kitchen floor, beside himself with rage. He stormed off into the back garden and locked himself in his shed refusing to take calls, while he swore and stomped his feet around proclaiming, 'What fucking use is it then? What fucking use are *you?* Make it work! Tell it to work!' Working for the NF could be terribly like Fawlty Towers at times.

That afternoon, Anderson stormed in from the back garden and asked if I knew how to use a fax machine.

'Are you sure? You better be fucking sure 'cause if I get one and you don't, I'll expel you from the party.' Britain's fastest growing political party was having trouble keeping pace with modern technology.

Eventually I posed for a photograph for *Lionheart*, back-to-camera sitting at the computer, pretending I was using it to streamline the NF's wavering membership files. In reality, the computer ended up in Anderson's back cupboard never mentioned or used again. Funnily enough, in Griffin's publication *Attempted Murder* (a long-winded denouncement of Anderson, Brady and Wingfield) he too made much of Ian's difficulties with technology.

The first edition of *Lionheart* sold out. Most new publications do. This was due to good forward planning and someone possibly envisaging that the short-lived periodical would fetch a fiver on eBay twenty years later. Anderson took it all over the country in the party's new minibus on one of his literature runs that happened when the new publications came out each month. Up and down the country drove Anderson, distributing stickers and leaflets along with the party publications to the branches. It was described as a long drive from Exeter to Newcastle, when, in fact, it was down to Exeter on a Friday night to stay with a member down there, then, depending on how he

felt after that, a trip to the post office. From there he drove
to Birmingham. That was it. Those trusted branches then
distributed the bulk themselves. He would not go to Wigan
or Bolton because the NF's organiser there was a Steptoe
type who Anderson claimed smelled, and he only went to
Newcastle when we had an active branch there, which was
a month-on, month-off sort of arrangement. Leeds branch
had to hire a car and drive to a service station to meet
him but invariably failed to make it because they couldn't
be bothered and couldn't afford a car. One local wag
suggested we hand our papers to the BNP to drop off with
their publications in Yorkshire.

By the time Anderson returned, the entire country knew
that Mr X had given him his major exclusive. He just
couldn't help himself. Ninety-two per cent of *Sun* readers
had voted in a telephone poll against further immigration.
As far as I was concerned that was a rather low figure for
that particular newspaper and the reasons behind the readers' thinking are plainly obvious anyway. Still, Britain's
highest-selling newspaper had decided not to publish the
figures and Mr X had passed them on to Anderson, not
realising how important that would be to us. He didn't
realise it would end up in *Lionheart* as opposed to *The
Flag*. He had hoped it would be slotted in somewhere as
a piece of interest and began to panic when he got his
complimentary copy of the new magazine. On the Monday
night, Anderson and I drove around Fleet Street dropping
off our regular monthly press releases and publications and
waited for the phone to start ringing on Tuesday morning.
Not one call! Anderson told me not to leave the office, not
to even take a piss, in case the phone rang. It didn't ring all
week, except for business calls and a very worried Mr X.

Anderson told 'X' he would tell any caller interested
in the source of the story that he got it from ringing the
receptionist. 'X' begged him not to. All calls to the entire

Murdoch empire went through one switchboard. To placate him, Anderson took 'X' out for a curry over Wapping way. However I almost wet my pants when Anderson claimed it was a clandestine meeting, due to their equally high profiles. The word was out about 'X' within the movement. Anderson's carelessness had also given him a real fright. Nobody seemed willing to tell 'X' to be more careful, not even Blackham.

Everyone knew about Mr X and the NF and he was making no secret of it either, despite being quite easily scared when he thought he might be discovered among our number.

As for the minibus, instead of the usual comfortable fifteen-seater, Anderson chose one that would suit his printing company's needs better, one with stools along the side, leaving plenty of room for paper supplies up the middle. Eddie Whicker was furious, though as I recall it was so exciting for the vast majority of activists that they didn't seem to care. They all came around one Friday afternoon and sat in the back as if it was the new minibus that was going to win them votes. They literally lined up outside Anderson's house, climbed in the back of the vehicle and sat there. The minibus was going nowhere, rather like the party.

CHAPTER 13

Anderson insisted that I take the printing side of my job more seriously, but being still young and attempting to be radical, there was nothing I despised more than watching the supposed future leader of the white revolution crawling and sucking around his black and Asian clients, all to make a few more pounds for his retirement. Anderson had a classic business-first attitude towards his life as Chairman of the NF and, as absolutely no money from his private business made its way into the NF, nobody ever needed to have a crisis of confidence over such double standards.

Though I was falling out of love with being involved in the NF, I quite enjoyed being the full-time Nazi about town. It gave me plenty of opportunity to take calls from the very few newspapers that rang, most of whom wanted to speak to the BNP anyway. The more Anderson was away, the better the job became. Occasionally I'd just curl up to sleep for a few hours, or read old copies of *National Front News* or *Nationalism Today*. Occasionally, I would ring *Searchlight* from Anderson's phone, not always speaking but sometimes I would tell them something very minor, if only to make it worth reading the next time it came out.

I was constantly probing what happened with the NF and BNP merger talks. During negotiations in 1987, after the Flag group formed out of the warring NF, Richard Edmonds, speaking on behalf of the BNP, insisted Tyndall be Chairman of any merged party or, as he would be known without internal democracy, 'Leader'. He was merely laughed at. For his efforts, Edmonds was seen as a dangerous psychopath by the NF leadership, who viewed his renditions of the *Horst Wessell* sung at an East London market on a Sunday morning as embarrassing. Nobody ever minded Edmonds being a Nazi, but did he have to be so open about it? When he was arrested for attacking the South Bank statue of Nelson Mandela in the mid-1980s, Edmonds refused to answer the arresting officers in English and spoke to them only in German. While locked up in his cell, he sang the *Horst Wessell* continuously for three hours until the Superintendent came to see him with a glass of water, remarking, 'Your throat must be sore. Would you like to see a doctor?'

In early 1990, I was voted onto the National Directorate of the National Front, one of the youngest people to be so in the history of the party. Paul Ballard told me excitably that it could be my first step towards becoming leader of the party. I was not allowed to vote on the Directorate as I was a party employee and employees had to serve the party. If I wanted to become a voting member of the some-time thirteen- to seventeen-strong ruling body, I would have to stand for election at the next AGM. My stock had risen even higher with the appointment. I realised that with my full-time employment and position on the Directorate I was capable of wielding some respect among Nazi circles. At the South London meetings of the BNP that I continued to attend, Edmonds would address me from the top table in search of approval or perhaps support and, no matter what Edmonds ever said or did, he would always have my support because of his selflessness to the cause.

The likes of Phil 'the thug' Edwards and Barry Roberts, old-time NF and BM activists from south London, would sit next to me at the meetings and ask me questions after-wards. Roberts had been one of the first people I had met on joining the NF. A skilled worker in his late thirties, he was a thoughtful and secretive man in a difficult marriage to a younger woman that I felt made him appear emotionally bankrupt. It was he who first introduced me to Edmonds and drove me to all the weird meetings as I was being slowly introduced to that world. Roberts was involved in anything that could be considered mildly interesting to the Nazi cause. His old mate, Phil Edwards, was roughly the same age, perhaps slightly younger, equally thoughtful and fair as Roberts, though better known because of his active and violent past.

Edwards was selfless, honest and committed to nationalism, with an ability to turn on the violence when necessary, though not beyond reasonable debate either. Neither Roberts nor Edwards liked Anderson. They were both committed National Socialists, absolutely disgusted by the things I told them about working over at the NF. Like many National Socialists who progressed through the ranks of the early NF and British Movement and all the hundreds of offshoots and discussion circles, Roberts and Edwards were staunch anti-Semites, maddeningly so in fact. Both managed, however, to live relatively normal lives, popping in and out of the movement when it suited them, mixing with old Mosleyites in the East End or going to meetings of the League of St George. Their hatred of Communism was virulent in a throwback to the 1960s. It was people like Roberts and Edwards who made Nazi life interesting.

Edwards often gave me a rundown on the history of the punk movement, the Bromley scene as it had been known. Edwards was very unhappy about the involvement of Mr X, who he called 'that red' in the National Front. Some people felt 'X' deserved a good kicking, not our undivided attention. The fact that he was a former SWP activist and anti-fascist, gave the NF the impression we were making inroads into mainstream life and gave the realists very uncomfortable feelings that we were in fact deviating from our ideological distrust of the mainstream.

Was the far right going to be hijacked by the Tories again? Anderson certainly appeared to be sending feelers out in that direction, courting a Conservative Party member and old Tory friends on some church council from Oxfordshire over dinner, pouring the man's wife drinks while another senior member almost raped her! The more dedicated racialists were deserting the NF in light of its apparently growing liberal afflictions. Anderson felt more comfortable in the company of Tories; actually most far-right leaders, including Tyndall, felt very comfortable in the company of Tories. The highly influential Tory rightist, Adrian Davies, cultivated friendships with members of the far right, myself included, to support his myriad, bizarre right-wing organisations. It was he who invited me to all the meetings in the House of Lords, and Tory constituency meetings. A balding Cambridge graduate with a plum so strong you would have thought him an equerry to the Queen, Davies had flirted with the BNP in the early 1980s and ruined his chances of ever being selected as a parliamentary candidate, despite his solid right-wing Tory credentials. He was one of a few Tories moving around behind the scenes of organisations, pulling out 'good' members for discussions on topics of mutual interest.

His was the sort of company that Anderson aspired to keep, though Davies thought Anderson terribly low class and lacking in backbone. Knowing of my friendship with Davies, Anderson had instructed me to keep on good terms with him and the Tory right, though it slightly perplexed him that he had not yet been approached. Davies, too, sounded warnings about Mr X, claiming that it was near improper to allow someone of his ilk to exercise influence, particularly on the Chair of the NF. Davies had waited and waited for years for the NF or the BNP to grow up and appeared at the time to be busying himself with grabbing members with potential for some future project.

For the life of him, Anderson could not understand why a fellow Oxbridge type like Davies would rather spend time with people like Roberts and me than with him.

When the anti-federalist movements began in earnest in Britain in the early 1990s, Mark Cotterill was one of the first to break from the NF and form his own, essentially Conservative right aligned organisation, The Patriotic Forum. His affiliation to the Conservative Party was immediately approved. Brady and Acton also straddled some of those organisations through their friendships with members of the Conservative right. Davies was cultivating members of the far right who he felt capable of running small independent organisations able to challenge mainstream Conservative Party thinking and possibly able to persuade certain constituencies to appoint a member of their caucus as a prospective parliamentary candidate.

Mr X's protestations that the NF should have as much right to television time as the Communist Party certainly struck a cord with Anderson. To protect the name National Front he decided to register it with Companies House in Wales as a limited company. I went up to East Ham Library for him and dug up as much information as possible, and rang as many branch activists as I could to get them to send proof that the NF was actually national, an apparent prerequisite. The six NF branches that had achieved local notoriety in the past year sent us cuttings from their local papers for us to present to Companies House to prove we were indeed national. Upon opening the NF's application, a civil servant apparently became so distressed that they called on their union representative to take action. Companies House went on strike over having to handle local newspaper cuttings bearing the name NF, even if said cuttings mostly carried headlines along the lines of 'Local NF member convicted of indecent exposure'.

Within hours of the strike, BBC Wales were on the

phone to the office wanting a televised interview. Anderson was so excited he cut himself shaving before racing up to the BBC for his interview via satellite. It was terribly exciting stuff, but it was also unlikely that we had any members left in Wales to video his appearance. When Anderson returned, he acted with the sort of airs and graces that would make you think Melvyn Bragg had taken him to dinner and fondled his loins under the table. Anderson lay back on his couch, not caring that his arse touched the floor and the crotch in his pants was ripped, and folded his legs. He was a natural, they'd loved him. 'I had to wear make-up, obviously,' he said. 'But I think it's fair to say I nailed the interview perfectly, like a natural. You know I'm very good on television.' Then he told me how as a teenager he nearly dated the spunky former *Tiswas* presenter, Sally James.

Ian Anderson and Martin Wingfield became the proprietors of National Front Printers Limited, at a cost of one thousand pounds to the party's rapidly plummeting funds. If the company didn't trade within one year, it would become null and void. It becomes particularly null and void when a private printer does all the printing for the company for his own benefit and not the party's. As the NF no longer had a business side to it, we counted that as £1,000 spent on getting Ian onto television.

At the same time, the BNP continued to turn the East End into a racial minefield throughout 1990. Weavers School played host to two violent and noisy public meetings in support of BNP local election candidates. Phil Edwards turned up at one meeting, belting demonstrators on the way in, before sitting peacefully at the back to listen to the speeches. The NF's John McAuley was turned away and attacked at the second meeting, by both BNP and anti-fascist demonstrators. At the same meeting, a skinhead asked from the back of the room what was to be done

about the American guest who had just touched his willy
in the toilets and all hell broke lose.

That year, an East London schoolboy named John
Stoner was involved in a fracas with an Asian student and
was stabbed, becoming a martyr to the BNP and acting as
'proof' that the traditional East Ender was under attack
from the Asian invasion. One of Stoner's cousins was
Conrad Happe, an overweight and obnoxious fascist. He
was so moronic he was dangerous, with a silly bumfluff
beard. Because he knew Stoner, the BNP elevated Happe to
be some sort of authority on the situation. Stoner remained
silent on the issue of the stabbing, but his grandfather and
Conrad were both helpful to the BNP. Grandpa spoke at
one Rights for Whites march used to stir up the Stoner
issue, and all he could do was complain, 'Things ain't 'ow
they used ta be 'round 'ere.' Jewish graves in the East End
were desecrated, including one where a BNP activist was
the caretaker. The BNP stepped up distribution of copies of
its hate sheet denying the Holocaust, and the NF struggled
to keep itself together.

As a sort of distraction, Eddie and I went to Trafalgar
Square for the release of Nelson Mandela early in 1990
to see how the left was getting on with their stuff. Tony
Benn reckoned they were the most emotional scenes since
the end of the war and, rather like we would have acted
on that day forty or so years before, Whicker and I were
abusive to all and sundry. We jumped on a Peace Bus that
was circling the area and had a conversation with the
driver that went something like: 'What the fuck are you
doing? Do you wanna smack in the mouth? Drop us at
the square.'

Once at the square, we mingled with the throng outside
the very embassy where, for years, NF members had bared
their fists at anti-apartheid demonstrators and smashed
placards and heads against the pavements. Apartheid had

meant there were always plenty of reds to slap around when one was in the city and feeling frisky. Once the NF had stood over a Troops Out picket outside an army recruitment office at Charing Cross and the organisers of that picket went to get help from the 24-hour picket outside the embassy. Upon the arrival of London ANC, Eddie piped up, 'You needn't have bothered coming here, we were just about to come and see you.' I remember the embassy picketers being rather relaxed about the whole thing. They knew that every Saturday somebody was coming to attack them.

In amongst the throng, Whicker and I screamed loudly, 'Hang Nelson Mandela!' and the crowd blew their whistles in approval, shook our hands and hugged us in the sort of hyped-up hysteria that makes television evangelists rich. 'Mandela is a black bastard,' I shouted loudly for all to hear, but they wouldn't acknowledge it, so Whicker and I got carried away with the emotional crowd until there was a slight crush. I put my boot into the chest of a Paul Weller lookalike and Eddie appeared to grope the breast of every woman on the square. Squeezed against each other amongst all the tears, we could not help but admire the resolve of our enemies who for years had maintained a non-stop picket outside the South African Embassy, in the face of daily violence and intimidation. To make our point, however, whatever exactly it was, we punched a man selling copies of the *Militant* newspaper to the ground and I stamped on his fingers. No doubt they put this down to some left-wing sectarianism. That evening we relayed the whole story, right down to the feel of hard nipples on Eddy's coarse hands, during another well-organised piss-up.

I went to my first Directorate meeting straight after the influx of new funds, at a King's Cross Hotel close to where the Director of Public Prosecutions was later found kerb crawling. Before leaving for the hotel (in the new minibus!) Steve Brady called in for a cup of tea over at Ian's. While Anderson bathed upstairs, Brady asked me for Mr X's number. I didn't have it. Upon Anderson's reappearance, an uncomfortable negotiation took place. 'X' had tried making contact with Brady over the Armagh [UDR] Four, a sort of Protestant equivalent of the Guildford Four or Birmingham Six. Anderson was furious on the inside that Mr X had tried to go direct to Brady and not through him.

In exchange for Mr X's number, Anderson decided that Brady would have to back him up at the meeting. I stirred the tea in disbelief as Anderson told Brady to say nothing and go along with whatever he would declare at the meeting. 'You too. You say absolutely nothing,' Anderson demanded of me. Number exchanged for favour, we set off for King's Cross.

It's funny to see men who have long criminal records and are mainly illiterate, don glasses and behave as if they were running the government. My new title was Secretary to the Executive Directorate of the National Front, and men whom I had got drunk with until we'd fallen over, politely nodded in my direction as if we were merely acquaintances sharing mutual political respect for each other. This was supposedly our future cabinet. Once the handshaking was over, some stuck their large hands into bowls of complimentary mints, filling their pockets. Others filled up on sugar lumps and tea bags, stole pens and note pads, looking for anything that was not nailed down.

Before the Directorate's meeting, the five-person Executive met in private, as in all nationalist 'democratic' organisations, to stitch up the meeting beforehand. Halfway through the boring proceedings of reading the minutes from the previous meeting (these were held quarterly) and the regional reports ('Birmingham and West Midlands branch have initiated a move to remove all pint glasses

from the Union Jack at branch meetings!'), Anderson
grimaced and announced he was in financial trouble and
needed to borrow a sum of money. Then he coughed.
My mouth fell open in surprise and everyone present –
most regional centres bar Leeds & Yorkshire, where the
regional organiser was always excused – looked towards
Steve Brady for an outburst. Brady nodded in agreement
with Anderson.

'Steve's seen the papers the bank has sent me. I need
£8,000 to help with my mortgage, otherwise I cannot
continue to be Chair of the party.' There was a silence,
until Brady finally found himself and spoke up: 'Yes, I've
seen the papers, I saw them this morning at Ian's house, it's
very up-front.' This must have been a code for Tom Acton
(another editor of *Vanguard*) to explode: '£8,000? The
party can't afford that.' Anderson was unmoved. 'Look,'
he said. 'It's a very tough job being Chairman, and I very
rarely bill the party for all the hours I do. I will sign a document if you wish, binding me to pay it back.'

Things got very uncomfortable with Acton, a former
accountant, absolutely furious about what he told me a
year later was blind theft. Nash gritted his teeth but stayed
silent, while the financially-strapped Wingfields went along
with the plan uncomfortably. Acton suggested that a solicitor be consulted to draw up an agreement but Anderson
refused, saying that it would cost the party money it couldn't
afford. He said that he would draft an agreement at home
that Acton could check if he wished. The money was his
and there was nothing anybody was going to do about it.
For me, it was like the final kiss of death to everything I
believed in the National Front. I sank into my chair, the
members would be furious when they found out, but the
party's ruling body had just sat there and said nothing on
their behalf. I didn't know whether it was true or not about
Anderson's financial difficulties but money was leaking out

of the organisation on harebrained schemes already and nobody could give a toss by the looks of it.

When we finally moved onto business, there was some sharp criticism of a recent lull in national activities. The party had buried itself lately. In particular the Birmingham branch membership had been complaining at not having had the opportunity to smash up pubs in and around London for what felt like an eternity. Anderson agreed to a series of rallies around the country to allow the members to respond to their BNP counterparts. There was no doubting that NF rallies were easier on the eye than those of the BNP and less likely to cause pained embarrassment should someone cast an eye over the proceedings.

Since the events at Welling Library I had rung *Searchlight* maybe five or six times, always speaking to the same Geordie voice who would quietly note down what I said and say thanks very much in return. I knew other people in the party were obviously passing information to them and I suspected someone else on the Directorate was too. Would Anderson's borrowing of £8,000 from the party's coffers make it on to their pages, or would I do the decent thing and just break the confidentiality of the meeting and run screaming to the members instead?

I lay in bed and thought about it. This party was not going to achieve even the very tiniest of the things that it offered. It couldn't even be a safety valve. Where did I stand, now that I had seen it sink to its lowest ebb? The BNP excited me as much as it terrified and worried me. It wanted to crush everything before it and in an opposite direction to that the NF took. Even when it was being openly Nazi, the BNP was still far more dangerous than anyone would ever know. I still believed in my race, still believed I was the victim of being born my colour and my class. Nobody else had yet managed to speak for us. And yet in three years moving between the NF, the BNP and all the small satellites where I was allowed to relay my fears and even, at times, encouraged to attempt to critique them, could I honestly say that the far right really spoke for me at all?

I needed this to work for me somehow. I needed men like Richard Edmonds and the psychopaths with heavy chains and flick knives in their pockets to prove themselves to me. How long could I wait, and what exactly was I waiting for? Did I really want electoral success, knowing that we would merely fill council chambers with drunken incompetents? My colleagues tended to view campaigning as a way to recruit others like themselves to strengthen the drinking club. Everything we believed was defended violently and angrily and every campaign was fought bitterly between visits to the pub and the police cells. If we were so ideologically secure, why did we have to have it explained to us why we opposed the things we campaigned against?

A St George's Day rally was fixed for Bromley, and a huge turnout was required from all regional centres. It was definitely going to be a tough rally to pull off, given that Beckenham NF shared Bromley with a fairly old BNP grouping; though they were largely inactive, except when Edmonds held his meetings above a pub there or at an old football ground. For some reason, the local council permitted us use of the Civic Centre on the proviso it would be a public meeting. Anderson had privately hoped that the council would refuse a meeting, allowing us to stir up controversy over freedom of speech before the NF sidestepped Bromley to go to a hotel somewhere else, like Orpington. He was furious that the Tory council wanted the meeting to go ahead. 'What now, another bloody pitched battle in Bromley High Street?' he asked furiously.

The few activists in London and the south east got very excited in anticipation of a potential riot. For Terry and me it was a win-win situation. Lots of BNP members were bound to travel over to Bromley on the Sunday afternoon, ruck with the reds we knew would be outside the meeting and then somehow, marvel at the brilliance of a professional NF rally. We put rather imaginative figures on it, expecting that there was no way we could not get 3–400 people along. St George's Day was our day after all, a two-fingered response to all the ethnic nonsense of Notting Hill Carnival, St Patrick's Day and Gay Pride; a day when we could remember that we did have a culture, a history and something to celebrate. There was no way I was going to do any fucking Morris dancing or nonsense like that, but it would be a great day to get pissed and have a fight in the name of England's first migrant worker.

I replaced the unknown Geoff Burnett as the guest speaker at the Croydon branch meeting that month and drew a good crowd. I was afforded the usual guest speaker privileges of free alcohol and travel expenses. I advised all members to be at the rally later that month and gave some waffling explanation about the NF's transport policy that went down like the proverbial fart in a spacesuit. What was I thinking of? I also had to flog, on Anderson's behalf, half a dozen packs of stickers and books. Barry Roberts drove me home in silence while I told him of my growing concerns about the NF leader. He was not impressed by my speech very much either, wondering what all the nonsense about trains and canals had to do with the evil Zionist conspiracy I should have been addressing. I begged him to bring some activists over from south London to help promote the rally and he grudgingly agreed. It seemed like as good a time as any to tell Roberts about the BM monies. His slim, flat features began to distort. He ran his hand over his bald head and then down over his mouth. 'That's not good,' he said quietly to himself.

The proposed Bromley rally made few column inches in the local press. 'Why on earth did they give the rally the go ahead?' wailed Anderson again, throwing the local paper down with all of the other newspapers on his impromptu fourth estate shagpile. Neither the local press nor excited members were ringing. He began to panic that we would get turned over and there would be nobody there to witness it. I suggested that perhaps we had burnt our bridges with regard to casual nationalist muscle. 'I mean, imagine if they did turn up, only to find that there was no chance to dance with the reds and we had done our usual and gone off to a hotel somewhere?' I waited expectantly for his manic explosion, but he was back in the kitchen dipping into his favourite tipple again.

Terry Blackham drove over on the Monday before the rally to convince Anderson that it should go ahead. Ian was slightly more upbeat, though on the day before at the Brick Lane paper sale, Blackham and I hadn't had much luck persuading people to show an interest in travelling over to Bromley the next week. 'Too far to go, it's Kent, not London,' complained one BNP member. We did press drops that night around Bromley and I carefully raised my concerns over Anderson's leadership with Terry for the first time. 'What would you prefer Maff, a Nazi like Edmonds or Tyndall?' He laughed to himself. 'I fucking hate reds, niggers and Pakis the lot of them, but I don't get the Jew business. I see Ian as someone I can take home to my mum who would seem normal. And we want our mums to vote NF, don't we?' The answer for me was surprisingly, 'no'. The thought of my dear old Mum falling for Ian's bullshit was appalling. Fuck me, was I becoming a snob? Was the NF all of a sudden not good enough for my mum? The conversation ended as quickly as it had started. I shot Terry a quick glance. Did he really think anything that we ever did was the sort of thing to make our mothers proud of us?

On the following Tuesday, a new Newham NF member who lived around the corner from Anderson came to see me. He lent me some money and bought me a packet of cigarettes. He was only a year older than me and covered in tattoos, incapable of walking to the shop without an involuntary outburst of violence. He took me to the pub, and I poured my heart out to him but he didn't really understand. He was just a racist thug, overjoyed at being able to go to the house of the Chairman of the NF every night and drink tea in his living room. To take my mind off events, he regaled me with stories about beating up Asians outside the tube station and a shooting at the ski club in Becton in which he claimed he was involved. This complete fucking idiot had two birds on the go and was enjoying as many blowjobs, hand-jobs, gobbles, nobbing and shagging as he wanted. He told me to get a tattoo to impress the birds and start shagging to take my mind off my predicaments. He also advised I get a bigger knife for travelling home at night. 'In case I get jumped?' I asked. 'No, to knife some Paki,' he scorned.

On the Wednesday, Anderson printed some leaflets advertising the march and billed the NF for them. I went out on a pre-arranged date with a student whom someone had assured me – rightly as it turned out – would definitely shag me.

On the Thursday, I went to work feeling nauseous. Anderson looked rather pained by the whole episode.

On the Friday, I finished work early and went to lunch with Blackham and Anderson. Blackham and his brother would organise a dozen Palace supporters to provide security, though we are disappointed there has been no commitment by reds to protest at the meeting.

On the Saturday I was picked up by Blackham and we joined two car-loads of NF activists. We were going to meet outside the Churchill Theatre in Bromley to hand out leaflets about the Sunday rally. Anderson met us there with two large Union Jacks on poles. Thirty of us (the entire active NF membership for London and the south east) handed out leaflets advertising tomorrow's St George's Day rally and tried to sell newspapers. The public were hardly interested in what we had to offer or say on the subjects that really mattered to them.

On the way to get coffee I passed my old maths teacher selling SWP papers and we exchanged strained pleasantries. The SWP were having about as much luck as we were. Because no traffic passed through the shopping mall, I stood in the middle of the road handing out leaflets to uninterested shoppers. The press weren't interested either and we hadn't achieved any additional press coverage since the tiny announcement a few weeks before. Just as I was about to give up the ghost, a huge man took a leaflet. 'What's all this?' he screamed, like a prom queen, pointing and shaking his fist at me. 'Suck my cock you faggot,' I began, before I was knocked flat on my face. I bit right through my lip and could feel the blood covering my face and neck. My nose exploded, my eyes closed and I couldn't stand up. By the time I did, Barry Roberts was holding him bent backwards over some railings, while Anderson and Blackham and a dozen others piled into him with kicks and punches.

I was covered in blood, staring at this bastard and the lads beckoned me over. 'Finish the cunt off, just finish him,' Blackham urged me. The man screamed for help in agony as I stood, dazed and bewildered in the middle of a motionless high street, dazzled by the sun and the warmth of my own blood. The SWP came running but didn't intervene as the NF crew turned to face them with their hands making beckoning motions. 'Let's fucking 'ave you too.' They stood watching, motionless as NF members with shoes covered in blood left their victim battered on the floor to rot. Blackham walked towards me saying furiously: 'Get over there and stamp on that cunt's head,' pointing behind him to the mess on the floor that still hadn't moved.

A brave woman shopper went to the injured man's aid while Anderson quickly started packing away. A dozen NF were now confronting the SWP who were moving away too, backing out of the area. Terry's brother grabbed my arm and took me into the toilet to wash my face while laughing in it all of the way. 'What a fucking punch, you mug; he fucking let you have it, didn't he?' Outside, shoppers were berating the NF, little old ladies and women with children pointing and gesturing at them, calling them bullies. Terry came into the toilet and looked at my face. 'They've led him into the park. Clean up and let's go kill the cunt.'

I should have gone to hospital for stitches; even today my lip will split right down the middle for no apparent reason and remain painfully cut for weeks at a time. Instead, the NF members chased the man through the park until they could run no more and decided to buy me a few drinks instead. It takes only minutes for something like this to become folklore and the subject of much banter. The poor guy never saw the rest of us and could be forgiven for thinking there would be only a handful of others there with me. By 6 p.m., a headhunt for reds in pubs was organised. 'We'll start at the Star and Garter,' one tells me, 'and we won't let up till we find the bastards.' I was touched. My faith in the brotherhood of man was renewed. We were planning to trawl middle-class Bromley on a Sunday night and smash glasses into the faces of anyone even remotely progressive, or with glasses or, worse still, a ponytail.

Overnight the story snowballed to the point where we had apparently fought hundreds of reds with knives and iron bars and people heard how I had been jumped, not by a burly gay man but by a gang of blacks. That night, the Ayran jungle drums were alive and active, and revenge was exacted on two innocent men, held down in an alley in Bromley and having their heads and limbs stamped on.

My teeth ached all night. My lips stuck to the pillow, even though I wasn't trying to fuck it for once. In the morning a tooth fell out as I painfully and slowly brushed my teeth. I could not even open my mouth wide enough to brush. The stupid knife that had stayed in my pocket while I was punched the day before was replaced by a bigger one. After a night's agony, I was convinced that today I would actually have to stab someone to get back my pride. I was so hungover, I could barely move or think straight. I felt so fucking ugly, staring miserably into the mirror at a pitiful teenager with stupid, broken dreams and crying like a girl.

Still Welling Library played on my mind. Those ladies would be celebrating my facial agonies and broken teeth if they knew what had happened in Bromley. At least I'd had my revenge taken care of for me by my comrades. Did we really attack a meeting of women and gleefully report and celebrate it?

The Bromley rally was more than peaceful. Filled mostly by long hard coughs and whispers, the hall was four times too big for the 110 people who made it to the rally, which included not a single member of the general public. A dozen east London BNP toured the area disappointed that there was not one red to be found, called us 'wankers' and went home. In those days there was no Sunday opening, so to be in or around Bromley Civic Centre on the day of the rally, you would have had to be attending the meeting. The Palace football crew did not show up which also annoyed the BNP mob who would have gladly done battle with them instead. Some people were out and about, just happening to be walking their dogs, hoping for a glimpse of some aggro, but none materialised. I sat at the very back of the hall manning the bookstall with my eyes black and my lip scabbed and disgusting, trying to hold a conversation with a man from Brighton who was trying to flog a couple of hundred dirty magazines to me.

Anderson paid tribute from the front of the room to
members hurt in the line of duty, and I got a 'Hear! Hear!'
from the crowd. I blushed and smiled until my lip split
again and spilt blood onto the newly printed constitution.
We recorded the rally on a small portable stereo but it was
a pointless exercise without a background of anti-fascists
screaming abuse. Like during school assembly, my mind
drifted while the various teachers plodded through their
speeches, occasionally raising titters, but mostly, in school
tradition, simply exhorting people to do more work for
their future, put more money in the collection, etc. If we
had all worked a little harder at school, we would hardly
want to be there, would we?

It was during the Bromley meeting that Anderson did
the most disgusting thing he had surely ever done. He
turned his attention to AIDS, the scourge of fornicators,
homosexuals and drug users and declared it a 'bloody good
thing', in almost Lutheran rhetoric, to solid cheers from
men who hide their small willies while using the end cubi-
cle in public toilets. This 'bloody good thing' had recently
taken one of our members from Leeds, a haemophiliac.
The member had donated £1,000 from his small compen-
sation to the NF before his impending death because he
had no one else to give it to. Anderson knew this, and *The
Flag* described the member as having suffered an industrial
injury, just to make sure that none of us could be tainted by
the gay plague. The thought of Tina and Martin Wingfield
handling the generous donation with rubber gloves is
very unpleasant. No wonder most of the other letters they
received contained human excrement.

My old friend Murph also turned up to the rally, though
this time in the company of a very attractive young lady
he had met through Adrian Woods, one of the Political
Soldiers now running Croydon NF. She was very sexy, as I
remarked to her, upon which she looked at me like I was a

lunatic. I burped 'Bollocks', hoping that would attract her but it didn't. Murph had a woman and I did not. She was lodging with Woods and was a devout racist and trainee policewoman. She was not impressed by my position in the Front though.

Tina Wingfield lied, claiming the rally had collected over £1,000. It was in fact just over £300 and we still had to pay a cancellation fee on the other hotel we had kept on standby. After the rally, Blackham and I stood in the doorway and bade farewell to our friends from Birmingham and the Midlands sauntering off to their cars, feeling downtrodden by the weight of failure resting on their collective shoulders, because they had driven all the way to Kent for little more than an exercise in boredom. Anderson gave me a lift home and asked if I had spoken to Mr X recently, which I had not. 'Leave him to Terry and me, you concentrate more on the Conservatives,' he warned. He also raised a smile by mentioning that Blackham and his girlfriend were babysitting 'X's' children. 'It's a terrifying thought isn't it?'

Nash, Murphy and I met above the Golden Lion in Waterloo, went upstairs to the pool room and racked up the balls. Nash had a large file, the 'Anderson Files', a series of records Nash was keeping on Anderson's betrayal of the party. The file was no secret, but to Anderson it was a joke, something he felt did not physically exist other than in Nash's mind. Murph and I chatted about the torrid love affair he and the policewoman were engaging in in the room she rented from Adrian Woods and his wife. By all accounts it was all hot and sweaty, while downstairs Woods and his wife would fight bitterly over the sound of a screaming child and the barks of a large and aggressive Rottweiler.

Nash suggested a whole list of ways we could manoeuvre against Anderson and push the party back into the hands of the members. Who was going to help us do that? Nash could not think of anyone willing enough to help. So it was left to me, the party employee and supposedly Anderson's right-hand man, Paul Nash, an energetic but uncharismatic Directorate member and, for some reason, Barry Murphy to do it. Nash reeled off ten party officials who he knew wanted Anderson removed. Nash was terrified that the BNP was going to make a breakthrough before we did. In the twenty-three years that the NF had been going it had not had one single elected official on even a Parish Council. I thought about Nash's energy and enthusiasm for saving the NF, whilst it seemed that Murph had been to the meeting only to boast about shagging.

Through Adrian Davies, I spread the word to Cotterill of the growing dissatisfaction at Anderson's leadership among London members. Cotterill phoned me at home and asked discreetly if I would be willing to go to Torquay one weekend and possibly take Blackham with me. It was difficult to say clearly, but I intimated that Blackham would not be in favour of any anti-Anderson ideas that Cotterill might be shaping. Halfway through the phone call I stopped listening completely and was overcome with an enormous wave of despair. The idea was to get influential street soldiers like Whicker on side, very discreetly and while doing all of this, maintain my position in south London NF and at the party office.

I realised that I did not want any of this, I didn't want to save the NF. It felt as if my stomach had been ripped out, I was empty. I really couldn't give a toss about saving the NF or the BNP. What was going on? I put the phone down as it suddenly felt as if my world had turned in on itself. Violence fucking hurt, I could see my battered face in the mirror but that was not bothering me too much. It had certainly been the best punch to connect with me in over three years, but this was hardly my first black eye or split lip. There and then nothing about the NF or even the BNP seemed to matter. I had been ringing *Searchlight* occasionally, every time I had these pangs of guilt, which had started immediately after the Welling incident, but I had also been struggling with how blasé I was at times about how easy and enjoyable it would be for me to put certain people onto lorries or trains heading off 'east'. Not that we openly said there would be death camps for one moment but it was fucking obvious. I steadied myself in front of the mirror. 'I am still a National Socialist, I am still a white Aryan, part of the master race,' I assured myself, then went to bed and had a wank.

The party was fighting the mid-Staffs by-election that year, when the first seeds of dissent started to show. There were three market towns in the constituency of mid-Staffs and we had a separate active team to cover each. In one town I spent three solid hours on the loudhailer breaking race relations laws and exhorting middle-class shoppers to vote NF. Towards the end I was shouting into the microphone: 'If you want a nigger neighbour, vote Labour,' while smoking Woodbines and whistling to young girls. 'Show us yer tits love, and vote National Front!' It may have accounted for our incredibly low vote, but it did give me a chance to suss out the situation in the Midlands, and surprisingly I found the regional membership was split down the middle.

People like John Hill, the legendary thug who ran the region and in whose house the party's national information phone line was kept, had lately taken to punching members in the face for dissenting or, worse still, attending BNP meetings. I stood in Litchfield market with my loudhailer wrapped over my shoulder telling him how 'The NF's fucked. Anderson is fucked, the whole party is fucked.' I think I'd finally managed deadpan. He stood face to face with me, his large flat nose up close to my more Aryan model. 'I'm gonna talk to John about this,' he whined, 'John can fix it up,' to which another Birmingham NF member quipped, 'No he can't. He doesn't give a toss.' This dissenter, who would stand in Torquay with Cotterill as his election agent, was later attacked by Hill at the annual conference when the party was heading for its demise.

For the rest of the campaign I trailed up hills to small housing estates with new Fords parked in the driveways, accompanied by a dozen Birmingham members kicking over milk bottles and trampling through daisies, handing out leaflets and barking, 'Hello love, Vote NF' to the inhabitants of middle England.

Whicker defected to the Corrective Party, and followed their candidate, Lindi St Claire, around the market, asking her questions about her past as Miss Whiplash. This was more her constituency than ours anyway. Whicker stood in the town square with his large hands thrust deep into his pockets giggling to himself when not handing out her leaflets, while we sat in the pub watching him. Perhaps Eddie was forming a Whiplash/Sledgehammer Alliance along the lines of the LibDem Alliance of the time. She beat us, but was quite gracious about it, even when we stormed the church hall to protest at not being invited to address the electors at hustings. Perhaps she could sense that we were half-hearted about the whole affair. It had cost the NF something like £3 per vote and our newly-founded local branches folded soon after.

Still I traipsed over to east London every day with my head down, wondering what it was that I believed in. I hated blacks and Asians, but I didn't actually know any. They were everywhere and it offended my eyes just to see them. The way they walked and the way they spoke to each other. They were so ignorant, they had absolutely no manners and they had as good as polluted the East End of London with their foreign sounds and smells, their aggressive manner-isms, shit music and a total lack of respect for real local people and their cultures. What did they want from us, what had we left to give them that they didn't just take when they felt like it? And what about us, the great, maligned white working class? Where were our middle-class knights from the councils in shining armour, coming to impress upon us the beauty of the things *we* said and thought, sang and fought for? Why was integration a case of us accommodat-ing people who did not even want to learn our language? I was a long way, a very long way from boldly shaking hands with these invaders and throwing down the welcoming prayer mat for them. I had an idea about an England I had never actually known, but had heard about. In this England our front doors were left open and we borrowed cups of sugar and minded each other's children. We worked hard and played hard in our small industrial nation and married the first girl who let us put our hands up her skirt. No, these cunts could never be a part of it.

Cotterill had been charged with scheming to remove Anderson, but was found out very quickly. A system of spying on colleagues in order to curry favour in the upper echelons of the cult was a sickness that affected the move-ment from top to bottom. People who would back you up in a fight and break every unbroken pint glass to defend your back, would quite as easily stick a knife in it if they thought you were thinking something you shouldn't be, or in some cases, thinking about thinking about something you shouldn't.

One day at work, not long after the mid-Staffordshire by-election, Anderson rounded on me. 'What do you know about Mark Cotterill? Is he with the BNP now?'

'Not that I'm aware of,' I replied.

'If you hear anything about Cotterill, I want to know about it.'

And almost immediately Anderson began plotting against Cotterill. He summoned me into the living room and sat back on his arse-less couch and pursed his lips. 'You may need to go down to Torquay and do some digging on Mark Cotterill. I have another man there already doing the same thing so it will be good if you two can meet up and exchange notes.' He was having a laugh, surely? Whenever he was uptight or confused, Anderson started talking nonsense. 'At this juncture we cannot afford to have someone in the party who is potentially going to cause problems.'

He was actually digging, not on Cotterill, but to see if there was anyone else plotting against him who he could buy off, or so I suspected. The trip never happened because I demanded the train fare and some extra beer tokens up -front. Like my wages that week, and most others, it never materialised. Anderson was offended. Business was picking up though. I was also drunkenly promoted to sub-editor of the second issue of *Lionheart*, but was removed from the job because I did not realise notwithstanding was one word.

One of our new bits of business, in a classic example of Anderson's double standards, was a job for the Sri Lankan community, printing a book that he was incapable of doing on his limited machinery and technology. It was an attack on the Tamil Tigers written by a neurotic Essex GP. She kept Anderson pinned in the living room for hours at a time explaining her beliefs, and continually changing the text and artwork. For the first fifteen visits Anderson kept his cool surprisingly well, bending over backwards and being charming, until, on the sixteenth visit, he went ballistic. I was in the back room staring and swearing at the blank computer screen when I heard Anderson explode. The Sri Lankan woman started screaming back and as I flew out of the back room he was trying to remove her from his house, with some difficulty.

'You cannot do this. You cannot do this,' she cried. I picked up her handbag and threw it over both of them as they struggled in the doorway. It landed and spilled its entire contents into the road. Then we pushed her into the front garden and then through the broken gate as she punched, kicked and bit the pair of us.

'I'll do what I want. Fuck off you Paki,' he retorted and we turned and walked back into the house.

She pushed her lips through the letter box and shouted, 'I want my money back, bastard,' in answer to which Anderson threw open the door and screamed, 'You haven't even paid me you fucking witch,' and began chasing her up the street while she made noises like an impaled pig. I made myself busy stamping on her handbag's contents, but I couldn't find her purse. Anderson returned to stand at his broken front gate swearing at her car as it shot off. He then stood with hands on hips, master of his own domain. 'That's the last time,' he swore as he pushed past me. 'No more Pakis. This fucking poll tax will see me right.'

The poll tax dispute was a godsend. We churned out thousands of leaflets for the unsuspecting autonomous community groups, whilst simultaneously mailing out stickers and leaflets to racists who hoped the poll tax would lead to some form of ethnic cleansing. Officially we were against poll tax, although in reality we loved it. All, of course, except for those of us who could not afford to pay it.

For a while, Anderson thought about giving up the printing for good. Mr X reckoned he would get £5,000 for a story about him printing the Labour memberships but of course it was not enough. Plus, the assorted incarnations of the British Movement were hot on the trail of their money now and it became the subject of intense scrutiny. Ian started to refuse to go to the Lane on a Sunday in case they were there.

Mr X submitted some articles on music and eating faggots or something, which I thought was very unfashionable. 'X' was another exponent of the idea of the English being cultureless fools living in old England as a nation of shopkeepers, doffing our caps and squaring up to our opponents under the Queensberry Rules. Maybe it was his SWP past, but he had very defined ideas about class; that we should actually like the screaming uselessness of Oi! music and the blandness of English fare. As a matter of course, however, 'X' felt it appropriate to search out the best Indian tucker at the same time in a column for his official employers.

Mr X attended the Beckenham branch meetings, as a result of which almost the entire party hierarchy began going there too, giving their full attention to his searching questions from the floor. He was struggling hard to find out what the NF's policies actually were. Any racist could be a supporter, but what were the policies of the party? I could have told him the minute he started asking questions: make them up as you go along. There aren't any.

Almost as if to pay a compliment to Mr X, London NF planned a day at the seaside in Bournemouth, all cockles and whelks and kiss-me-quick hats, traditional English *Beano*-style. In honour of *Only Fools and Horses* we christened it the jolly boys' outing. Now my aunties used go to Eastbourne every year for a bit of r 'n' r and a dry sherry, until they were ninety-one and eighty-three. My old school friends, on the other hand, used to go to Spain, drink half the national debt and have sex with girls called Alison. A poxy day trip to the south coast looked like being my great adventure. Even the geriatric aunties could do better than that!

We go to Bournemouth, without a hint of sex in the air, and trail from pub to pub in the pissing rain, spending the proceeds of the Beckenham branch meetings' collections on Fosters and Woodbines. We started drinking at eleven, while Mr X and his family headed to the beach with Blackham and his girlfriend, for one of those family days with bucket and spade. When we bumped into them, 'X' grinned and passed quietly by, as if the damage had not already been done. It was not by being seen with us in pissing Bournemouth that he would be found out, but by attending dinners held to remember Sir Oswald Mosley in London with Blackham. The two men dined together as Lady Mosley recalled her late, black-shirted husband. Lecomber and other Nazis at the dinner could not believe their eyes that he was there. John McAuley almost choked on his meal in horror. One or two people at the dinner even considered attacking him, recalling his staunch lefty credentials.

The Bournemouth trip was an endless afternoon of drunken punch-ups between thirty NF members. Eventually the police rescue one of our mob stuck on top of a steep hill, while we all stand at the bottom baring our arses at bemused holiday-makers. The beauty of drunkenness is that you can never piss your pants because you know you can relieve yourself anywhere you feel comfortable. And comfort is so easily found. While the police coax the man in the Tranmere shirt down from the hill, we all take a piss on the footpath, trying hard not to look at each other's willies.

Later we fought a running battle with some locals in a pub, throwing glasses and balls off the pool table. I caught one of the locals smack in the face with the eight ball, before being weighed down by an ashtray planted smack on the back of my head. The fighting came to a halt as one of our number pulled a large knife from his carrier bag and began waving it at the horrified locals. 'D'you know who the fuck we are?' he screamed at them, backing off. 'D'you fucking want some of this? You're out of your depth, cunts.' The barmaid was crying her eyes out and the locals were trying to placate the knife-wielding Nazi. 'Leave it out lads, come on,' began one, but the knife was thrust at him again. We easily outnumbered them, but not one of us told our comrade to put his knife away.

The barmaid was hysterical, 'I'm calling the police,' she wailed and the locals began jumping up and down telling her not to. Casually the knife was returned to the carrier bag and we walked out slowly, breaking everything that we could on the way. The barmaid quickly slammed and locked the door behind us. Outside the pub, Murph was running his hands through the WPC's hair while they sat on the bench in the, apparently romantic, drizzle. 'Thanks for your help, you Irish cunt,' he's told as we shuffle past looking for another pub. They sat next to each other on the coach trip home and things got very fruity between them. The old organiser sulked in a seat next to me while everyone sang along to a Diana Ross song on the radio. 'X's' youngest walked the aisles, giving Nazi salutes before resting happily on Blackham's knee. I couldn't help thinking that this was the best and most terrifying group of friends a man could want.

CHAPTER 14

In 1990, the IRA bombed Eltham, not at all far from where I was living and, by now, drinking heavily with all of the other white trash. Unlike us, the BNP could not produce an immediate response, while within hours we had bundles of Paddy-baiting leaflets ripe for dispersing in this part of south London. Eltham was ripe. The pub culture was underage and aggressive, very working class and right wing, in a Nikes and Ford Escort sort of way. A couple of times we clashed with some blacks in McDonald's and held a stormy paper sale in Eltham High Street, driving up and down with a mobile unit to pick out trouble makers in the area. It was the most profitable paper sale I ever went on with the NF, other than at Stamford Bridge or Brick Lane. We camped out in the area on and off for a couple of weeks, but clearly these were not the sort of people Anderson wanted in the party. People actually gave us the Nazi salute as a sign of approval. Because he lived there, Mr X invited a few people around to his house for a private get-together. Blackham drove himself and another member over to 'X's' house, where Ian Anderson was to address a private meeting, outlining his vision for a new Britain.

By now, the UDA magazine *Ulster* was part and parcel of the NF and BNP's literature. The BNP bought their copies in bulk from Belfast, while NF members procured theirs from agents on the mainland for a ten pence discount. There was something quite exciting about clasping the new copy of *Ulster*. Who were the men that printed it? Had my copy been stuffed into an envelope by a killer, licked and taken to the post office by him? It was a tame publication, light on rhetoric, deep on history and tradition and cartoons. The pages of offerings were always crying foul about some betrayal against them but the UDA seemed almost incapable of any deep political comment, simply because they were not sure how they should stand politically; the UDA seemed marginalised and lacking a direction, constantly under fire from within its own community.

The one thing the UDA did now want, however, was English members. Having undergone a leadership change in the late 1980s, the UDA was now under younger and even less responsible leadership. They no longer cared that their supporters on the mainland were a bunch of perverts, dreamers and grasses. Their illegal alter ego – the UFF – had been trying to match the IRA bullet for bullet and was constantly cap-in-hand for money and support from mainland sympathisers. In England they experienced some support in Liverpool and the West Midlands, though their active campaigning was almost solely on the back of the NF and BNP, who sided with the grossly outnumbered loyalist activists in Britain.

It was not unusual for UDA members in Britain to be lumped in with fascist supporters of those organisations. A UVF structure did exist in Glasgow, as did a UDA one, though in England and in particular London, a few long-time Nazis had switched over to the loyalist cause, solely as a means of increasing their street credibility once the ballot box strategies of the NF had failed and multicultural Britain had embraced its black sports stars.

After months of long and secretive phone calls, Eddie Whicker decided that he and I should come to Ulster's aid. In his opinion, it was a way of furthering the street war in London against the reds. He'd been on and on at others for a couple of years about becoming properly organised but had always struggled with our internal sectarianism.

Blackham for instance, loved smacking up Paddys but would never stand with the BNP. 'We'll do it without him,' he told me excitedly on the phone.

Eddie answered an advertisement on our behalves for people to join the UDA. The ad insisted that people willing to join should not be Walter Mittys. The ad was directed at members of fascist organisations who were keen anti-Republicans. The Walter Mitty reference was said to be directed towards the likes of Steve Brady, who it was felt had damaged the loyalist cause by his lack of discretion as well as to the fact that many other people were passing themselves off as representatives of the UDA on the mainland. The main offenders were Scotsmen who had ingratiated themselves in London fascist circles, but were in fact just hard-drinking Protestants from Govan or Paisley. Ian Anderson's attitude towards the UDA was a cautious one; Anderson's Freedom Books had a minor business agreement with them for merchandising and he had attempted to make other business contacts with them for his printing services and enamel badge pressing, although the UDA were notorious for not paying their bills on time – and who was going to argue with them? Someone at the UDA office in Belfast had shown initial interest in what Anderson had to offer, and had sent their London commander to see Anderson at Brick Lane in 1988. He was a former street fighter in the far right during the early 1980s, who had fallen into obscurity when changes were made in Belfast. The impression that Anderson had given him was that he wanted a business relationship with the UDA that would also offer him some kudos, but that he wanted no part of his NF to be directly involved with the UDA, or any constitutional organisation the UDA may have attempted to form. Though their violence was understandable to us all, in 1990, the UDA's *Ulster* magazine served notice to loyalist residents in Belfast that it would not tolerate the continued harassment of Chinese restaurateurs in the city. The NF was welcome, but not its racism.

The UDA's response to our letter of application was swift. Full credit to Her Majesty's postal service and the, no doubt, first-class office management of the UDA headquarters, as within one week, Whicker had received a letter, postmarked north London, inviting him and me to a meeting. We discussed this over the telephone with baited breath; what does one wear to an informal get-together with the UDA? I checked my wardrobe for something conservative and serious, while Whicker had picked out a nice green tie to wear with a yellow shirt for our six o'clock meeting at Waterloo. Strolling along the concourse with Eddie at my side looking all perverse and menacing, I had what Blur would call an 'enormous sense of well-being'. I felt dangerous. Would I have to hide a pistol in my pants?

Like me, Whicker arrived everywhere early so we stood under the big clock looking inconspicuous, while I smoked another fag and passed comment on the probable sexual orientation of Londoners going on their merry way home to miserable lives, walking their dogs while their wives cried bitterly into the ravioli about the lack of excitement in their mundane existences. There we stood, the last exciting and dangerous men in the free world, Whicker as Clint Eastwood and me as Charlie Sheen, the rookie. Apparently, according to Whicker anyway, men in prison draw an outline of a woman on their foam mattresses, dig a hole between the crayoned legs and get a little fruity. Would I ever know, would I ever feel the shame? A fat Italian in a shell-suit passed us twice, and we became convinced that Special Branch have followed us, whispering into their radios that 'Whicker is wearing the yellow shirt.'

Our instructions were to walk into a specific pub, approach the barman and ask for Billy. We headed towards the pub with a confident stroll. The fat Italian appeared outside the door in the company of others and I immediately suspected foul play. I was ready to do an about turn, shouting to Eddie, 'Dump the tampons, it's the gabbers!' (I always got a little cockney in Eddie's company) when the fat Italian held out his hand and said, 'I'm Billy. Come inside.'

We headed over to a table where some other men were sitting, and our host bought us drinks. The fat bearded man at the table held out his hand to us and said 'I am the commander. You are Eddie Whicker,' then proceeded to dump onto the table a huge collection of press cuttings on Whicker dating back a good seven or eight years. The fat Italian returned with our drinks and held up his favourite picture of Whicker from *Searchlight*, December 1988. The humour was splendid. I felt like I was on the set of *Peter's Friends*, resembling Stephen Fry at his awkward worst, while four UDA men all chuckled and asked Eddie to recount tales from his past. We were in.

The commander was obviously a fan of Whicker's and had collected enough press cuttings on him to hand over to Michael Aspel for a large presentation of the big red book. While we were sitting there around a table in London, talking like we were on Belfast's Shankill Road, I couldn't help but think about Whicker, my friend and closest ally, being the centre of such adoration. Surely we, and especially Whicker, should have been the ones to hand out the compliments and drink cards, not receive them. And while Eddie retold the story of our lacklustre leader's rather swallowing pockets and I added extra useful titbits out of spite, I realised uneasily that I was losing my friend to something that, should it ever eventuate, I could not play any part in. What made us all, some of whom were definitely Catholic, want to murder and maim or contribute to the deaths of men and women they would never know or meet, I wondered.

In July, Eddie announced that he was going to Ulster for the 300th Twelfth of July Protestant celebration. Politely, I declined to accompany him. It tends to be for the English and Scottish voyeurs who attend an aggressive orgy of relentless violence fuelled by patriotic alcohol abuse. Blackham surprisingly offered to go with Whicker in my absence.

On a weekly basis we were encouraged to send Protestant 'prisoners of war' postcards with pictures of the Queen or something similarly pathetic and unmistakably British. I was probably the only one who bothered; the thought of some heavily tattooed prisoners admiring my handwriting on the back of a picture of Her Majesty in her resplendent and pompous best, going to sleep at night with them posted next to their pillows was highly amusing, if a little disconcerting to me. What did Her Majesty offer those poor souls? A sense of identity, perhaps? I had to admit, the Ulster loyalists had a better idea of what it meant to be British than I did. They also had a better idea of what it meant to be working class too. So why did it make sense to them to run out into the streets and shoot other working class people just because of their religion? I knew the stated reasons, but was confused that they really did not seem to care what their victims thought about any of the issues they themselves purported to be killing for. But sadly we still admired them. They came from the same sort of council estates we did, shared our language and our fears, so that we too demonised the Irish Catholic community in our hearts and minds as the aggressive invaders of the six counties.

To cash in on the reaction to the IRA bombing, I decided to hold a march in Eltham. Instead of running it past Anderson, I suggested that Blackham organise it, with my help. Ballard and Nash also agreed that it would be a good idea to have a London march, particularly in south London, where we were struggling so much against the BNP. I suggested an anti-IRA march to Anderson that week, and that it should be in Eltham, where people would still feel a sense of outrage so would be ripe for a bit of anti-Irish fervour.

'It's a bit too south London, isn't it?' he suggested. 'I don't want any more repeats of Lewisham.'

'Ian, I went to school around there, the BNP is active there, there's good groundswell and not many blacks, but plenty of reds,' I retorted. 'For God's sake, they're still carrying out regular racist pogroms in Eltham, why *not* have a march there?'

It was a startling idea. Anderson said he'd think it over.

'North London,' he said, two days later. 'We'll have the march on Nash's patch.'

The march took place in Enfield. Anderson had bought some second-hand drums off an abandoned Boys' Brigade outfit in Rochdale as he wanted to reform the NF marching band and I had spent much of my spare time practising marching with five others on Streatham Common. Anderson had rung round all the branch organisers to get a show of hands of who would be attending. We would be lucky to get 200 people; it was August, the football season was over and the water in Majorca was being urinated in by just about every football thug who might have wanted to come. Two members agree to postpone a weekend in Sudbury.

As was becoming usual, the march was an utter humiliation. The drum corps struggled to walk, think and drum at the same time. Every time we got together there were fewer and fewer of us, like depressing family reunions. This time we managed sixty-four marchers. I could take it no longer; I felt tearful and lonely on the way home so I took a slice of the collection and headed for the pub with me old mates from school.

Iraq had just invaded Kuwait. Mrs Thatcher was on the television, so was George Bush. We had a new enemy; no longer Moscow, it was now Mecca where the guns were aiming.

'We always have to have an enemy don't we? Why don't we pick on the Americans?' I blurted out.

The others looked a little stunned. 'I thought you guys liked war?' they asked. I wasn't really sure if we did or not.

Back home, my brother who did love war was in his room, polishing our grandfather's old army boots. A huge amount of military hardware was starting to appear once more in his bedroom, plus *Jane's Defence Weekly* and *Soldier of Fortune*. The combat jacket and trousers were neatly pressed and an NBC (nuclear biological chemical) suit appeared on the washing line. In a moment of fear I asked my mother if Iraq was close enough to invade us. She said probably not. It was clear then: my brother must be an Iraqi agent. Bloody Mossad would now want to kill the two of us!

CHAPTER 15

One of the most relieving things about not being a Nazi anymore is regaining a sense of decency and sensitivity. For years inside the far right, nothing got me upset. Sure, there were the usual minor juvenile emotional upheavals, but horror stories and tragedies were like some sort of cherished good news to us. Every shocking, vile incident, every disgusting news story was welcomed as it would prove we were right about whatever it was we could to use it to suit us for. This included floods, rapes, murders, terrorism – everything. The world was so evil that we could immunise ourselves to its apparent nature. Or perhaps, we could revel in it as if nothing could hurt us. Occasionally I'd catch a stark glimpse of myself, without a smile and seemingly without a care. I'd talked, bullied and convinced the life out of myself and consumed my thoughts and emotions with hatred. This way, nothing could harm me. I don't know whether this was because we were genuinely evil or just misguided. We were certainly emotionally damaged, victims of our own bullshit-posturing. Perhaps deep down, for everyone, it was a charade. But I had switched off, and without much difficulty.

In the middle of my little drama, Martin Wingfield announced that he was withdrawing from the NF to move up north to Barrow. Barrow, the tiny non-League football team that for some reason *The Flag* had been following the fortunes of. Anderson decided to open the administrative PO Box in East Ham because nobody would want to join a National Front based in Barrow. Wingfield declared he would continue to put the newspaper together, only because Anderson refused to buy it from him on behalf of the party.

Anderson went all northern and admitted to being 'chuffed to pieces' that it would no longer be printed on the south coast. A printer was found over Barking way, who turned out to be Jewish. Initially, Wingfield didn't even go to live up north, which made the situation all the more strange.

The Directorate meeting to discuss the forthcoming annual conference had to be shifted to a hotel after people refused to have the meeting in Anderson's living room. With no vacuum cleaner in the house, I had been on my hands and knees with a dustpan and brush, sweeping up old glass, bogeys and god knows what else from under the sofa. Anderson got more than a little defensive about people's refusal to hold the meeting in his house. Why couldn't a dozen or so people cram into his living room and drink tea out of his two (filthy) mugs? I pretended to be as perplexed as him, but was very grateful when he threw all the newspapers back on the floor.

On the agenda for the meeting was what the NF should and should not discuss at the conference. There were the usual non-controversial motions like 'hang all child molesters', a staple NF policy, and 'hang all rapists', which would probably have to be mitigated by 'as long as they're not NF members'. The whole boring process of stitching up the conference was done with a knowing glow of satisfaction by those present. We were all so very important. Fuck the members.

Tina Wingfield was also voted a pay rise on the basis that she would not be holidaying in Spain that year. Opening my big trap, I suggested the new Deputy Chair, Steve Brady, should take her on holiday instead. To make sure there was a clear definition between 'Movement' and 'Party', the NF decided before the conference to ratify its decision to stand fifty candidates at the next general election, guaranteeing the NF television time by way of an election broadcast. Possibly this is where the idea for Tellytubbies was devised.

None of us could decide where we stood on the issue of the Iraqi troops in Kuwait; the country was in recession and Thatcher was unpopular but none of these issues were up for discussion. Instead, second on Anderson's agenda was the proscribing of the BNP. Everyone on the Directorate agreed to the motion being put forward, which meant it would be passed at conference. It was hoped that this would kill off the increasingly successful rival party. 'The BNP is damaging our chances and our name,' said Anderson. I then relayed this to Edmonds, over tea at the BNP office, prompting him to respond that 'the NF is damaging the good name of National Socialism.' To lighten proceedings, Anderson and I announce that we will be holding an election seminar on how to deal with the press, and how to run an election campaign. 'If they want a party, the NF should have a picnic,' suggested Edmonds.

The IRA blew up Ian Gow, the MP for Eastbourne, just before the national conference took place. I felt a little sad and remorseful for him, mainly because my comrades took so much joy from it. Gow was a firm friend of Thatcher but resigned from the Front Bench over the Anglo-Irish Agreement in the 1980s. The press reported that some women from the SWP were shouting sickening slogans about his death at Hammersmith tube station so during the week, Blackham, a couple of others and I went looking for some of them as they were putting up posters, jumped out of the car and battered them to the ground. We would've done it anyway, but we felt that if we were caught this time, the police would have been sympathetic to our reasoning.

There was no way the Tories were ever going to lose his seat, so it would have been pointless for us to fight it although Anderson declared that we should, in memory of Gow and to remind everyone that it was his party's policies that killed him. Mr X then rang the office, asking whether the NF were going to stand in Eastbourne. Apparently the other parties were considering it despite the circumstances surrounding the MP's death.

'Definitely,' I said.

'Can I quote you on that?' asked 'X' to which I again responded, 'Definitely.'

It made the front page of *The Sun* on the Saturday, though thankfully Mr X did not use his name on the story. I met Blackham in Beckenham High Street and we both bought a dozen copies for posterity, though I knew I could never take mine home now. Mr X even attributed a rather articulate quote to me that, in reality, I had never made. Anderson denied ever having sanctioned a decision to stand and made me feel very small. 'We'll have to fight it now, though, won't we?' said he with his shaking hands on hips.

That year's AGM took place in central London. I got to sit in a room behind the conference room under strict instructions to sell as many stickers, books, videos and magazines as I could. All through the day's proceedings people popped in to stretch their legs. When the conference room was full, I counted ninety people in attendance, which *The Flag* later reported to be 100 'delegates'.

The man with the UVF connections popped in to check on me. 'Have you and Eddie joined the UDA?' he asked, casually reading the back cover of a book.

'I think so,' was the best I could offer. He nodded appreciatively, then came in closer.

'You know it's not secure? They've got all kinds of silly bollocks going on. I don't want to say too much, if you know what I mean...'

I took notice, after all he did get locked up for his previous actions, plus he was a bit of a plonker with a nasty temper.

A few others came in during the day to complain and bitch about things that barely interested me at the best of times. Their lives got so caught up with the most minor details about the most minor of things; their lives were so empty they had nothing else to do but concoct conspiracy theories. Someone left a copy of *Searchlight* on the table and I read that instead of listening to the awfully banal business of being a full-time anal Nazi.

The NF candidates chosen so far were paraded before the audience. Eddie got the biggest cheer, as he would expect. Afterwards I told him that his address was displayed at Birmingham Town Hall so people could see where the candidate lived and who had signed their nomination papers. He was not the least bit interested. 'I got the biggest cheer Maff. Who in all honesty is gonna come knocking on my door late at night when the candidate for law and order is in the house holding a pistol?' Indeed.

Three people abstained from voting on the resolution to proscribe the BNP but twenty more came in to complain about it, even though they had voted in favour. There was not one vote against the motion. I voted in favour of everything; why argue?

After the conference there was the usual piss-up and a bit of a discussion as to whether it was worth travelling to some train stations to pick off some football hooligan gang that we could all agree none of us liked. Instead we ended up fighting with the staff and patrons in an Irish pub. It started with someone in the toilet tearing down an anti-Irish sticker and ended with two men laying comatose in the toilet and the bar staff hiding, as stools and glasses were hurled at them. Some of the northern lads did a runner but most others just walked to another pub and watched the police and ambulances turn up. A great afternoon was had by all. We took a seat by the window and watched while football hooligan gangs added to the confusion. I didn't feel uncomfortable. Sure I had days where I was wracked by guilt and self-pity, but this is what I did and this is what I was part of. I know it was wrong, but there really didn't seem to be anything else and my head was buzzing with the thrill of being a pimply politician for one half of my day and part of a vicious gang of thugs the next.

Most of the conversations had been about the rise of the BNP and how ineffectual the party was in countering them. A lot of people were moving across, not because they were avowed ideological Nazis themselves, but because the BNP was saying and doing what we wanted to hear. So what if Tyndall dressed up as a Nazi? If we could go Paki-bashing while he admired himself in his bedroom mirror, who gave a fuck? By eight o'clock, as one after the other my comrades had departed to their homes, I was the last one in the pub, wishing that I had enough money to hire a hooker.

The NF media conference was booked by me under the name of Anderson's print company at the Clarendon Hotel, Blackheath. I told Anderson it was central to trains from the south coast, but it wasn't. I booked it purely because it was a ten-minute walk from my home. The media conference fell flat when only eight of the thirty people we had been expecting turned up. Anderson was the only person in the room who had actually been interviewed on television in the last ten years, and you may recall how he had 'nailed it' perfectly. He sat in the tiny room we had hired, crossed his legs and actually interviewed himself in front of the other seven of us. He started off politely asking himself questions, which he answered perfectly, before turning on himself with tough, nasty questions, which he also deflected perfectly too. The seven of us just sat and stared at him.

After our own, rather flat AGM, Anderson and I rang around all the London hotels, trying to find where the BNP would be holding theirs. Edmonds had been badgering me to attend but I didn't feel as if I could. Eventually we found the Great Western had a booking by the so-called Chesterton Society, and called to tell them it was really the BNP. They had four times more people than we had at our own rally and they did not take a vote on anything once.

I spent the afternoon before the election address was posted, at the Hancock printing empire with Tom Acton, printing the bloody things and cursing Anderson. Acton was a poor printer and, according to Anderson, a poor accountant too. During the Eastbourne election campaign, Anderson claimed Acton was having a nervous breakdown, but during my time with Acton the only thing he seemed interested in breaking was Anderson's neck. I did not mention any of the various plots I was involved in, or knew that Acton was involved in. Given Brady's recent elevation to Deputy Chairman, it was possible that things were already afoot. Acton announced that he and the Nashes had recently approached Andrew Brons, a lecturer in politics and former Chairman of the party, to rejoin, a move which would almost certainly lead to Anderson's demise. Joe Pearce and Roger Denny were also keen to make a comeback now that Wingfield was gone, or at least going.

Hancock's premises were on an Uckfield industrial estate and brimming to the roof with bomb manuals, copies of Hitler's *Mein Kampf*, KKK manuals and pornographic calendars. Just about every piece of Nazi literature in the world passed through the premises, most of it making ours look timid in comparison. I took literature instead of payment, knowing that on the far right the cheque is always in the mail. I sent a dozen postcards with Adolf Hitler on the front to a dozen unsuspecting recipients, and put a Danish Waffen SS poster on my bedroom wall. The calendars with German women and farmyard animals were not for giving away.

The southern branches of the NF went to work on the Eastbourne by-election full-time. A couple of young skinheads were living in Cambridge, young and in love and they came across an NF sticker with the Worthing PO Box number on it. The next day, they packed their bags and moved to Worthing, certain it was the centre of NF activity. It wasn't, so they moved to Eastbourne and worked full-time on the Eastbourne election for the NF, courtesy of the dole. The NF had more than a dozen people active in Eastbourne every day during the election. This was more of an indictment of Thatcher's employment policy than an example of people's commitment to the party, but I enjoyed the break and any time I managed to spend alone down there. It was rumoured that the deposit for the campaign was donated by a landlord of an Irish pub in south London, after he was visited by a family demanding protection money on our behalf. There certainly did seem to be a lot of cash flying about as we drank dry pub after pub.

There were quite a few young people down in Eastbourne, on weekends anyway, so it was inevitable that Eddie Whicker would end up throwing somebody through a bus shelter. Inevitable, I suppose, that we would harass the local Labour Party, damage someone's car and exchange blows with student types outside the front of a pub. We got resoundingly beaten at the polls by the Liberal Democrat alliance. They all beat us, so we put in a contingency plan to give Lord Sutch a good kicking should we ever meet him. Though I do remember he applauded one of our candidates at one election, one where we also came last, obviously.

Eddie had been going to more and more UDA meetings whilst acting as a driver for Frank, which was 'Billy's' real name. A senior UDA figure also came over to the mainland for a series of supposedly clandestine meetings. Sectarian murder, for which the UDA was now better known, was on the increase. The UDA were planning to use 'cell' structures, to counter the success of the police and military infiltrating them.

'You're still on the team Maff,' said Eddie. 'Frank's very impressed with you.'

My only thought was, 'has nobody noticed that Frank is a Catholic?'

CHAPTER 16

When a man you've never met before gives you flowers, that's romance. When a man you've never met before approaches you with the names and addresses of members of the Troops Out Movement, that's the UDA. There I was, downing the dregs of a pint of XXXX, slight beginnings of a beer gut chaffing at my belt, when I was approached by a man. Not *that* way.

I could often be found on Borough High Street, listening to the rancid tones of a cockney larrikin pianist. I spent my time in the corner with me mates, drinking, acting stupid and ignoring the skinheads, right up until *Land of Hope and Glory* at ten to eleven, when even my mates would give Nazi salutes and clamour for a touch of the Union flag doing the rounds.

'It's Matthew, isn't it?' said the bloke. Could be a trick question I decided, so pretended I didn't hear. If he was less confident next time he asked, I'd trust him; too confident, I'd run, worried he could be *Searchlight*, the IRA, anybody. He held out an envelope for me and I took a peek, why not? Just names and addresses and some tatty old envelopes addressed to Troops Out's PO Box number. I looked at him in admiration. They'd not been tampered with, at least not after the point at which they were removed from their proper place.

'I'm the Postman,' he said. 'Could you pass these on to the proper people?'

By this he obviously does not mean the addressees; it's one of those Nazi references meaning someone like us; someone silly, some sexually frustrated bloke, either of these would have done just as well.

A young lady from Leicester describing herself as 'radical,' wanted to know if there was a coach in her area bringing people to London for a march. Maybe she could form her own branch?

Why? Why would a woman in Leicester want to form a branch of Troops Out, in Leicester? Did this sort of thing happen outside of London and Belfast? Another letter was more personal, a complaint about some-one else. Joan Ruddock MP sent her apologies that she couldn't attend their next march in person though gave them all her best wishes. There were an awful lot of women's names on the list. I realised I should have joined Troops Out.

Eddie and I sifted through the mail, then he asked me the strangest question yet. 'Have you ever sent someone a turd in the mail, Maff?' Gordon Bennett, think I, imagine asking my mother to post a turd on her way to work one morning. Apparently, the expert turd-sender backs one out onto a newspaper and leaves it to go a little solid for a couple of hours or days even, before popping it into an envelope at a later date. It becomes solid though still a little soft, like a melted Mars Bar, and you can even flatten it. No I've never sent a turd in an envelope, though the more I think about it the more I cannot help admiring people with the time to perform such a delicate process. Do they lay four or five turds before choosing their favourite? Is there a quality control process for texture, colour and general all-round content? Imagine sending one with a little bit of baked bean poking out. You're just exposing yourself and your poor nutrition. For a terrible moment I had a picture in my head of me holding open a jiffy envelope while Eddie Whicker cupped his saggy, greying testicles with his spare hand, spread his arse cheeks with his other and backed out an angry Aryan turd for me to post for him. Instead, he says the UDA will keep the lists and letters for future reference and who knows, I may have contributed some good to the cause. 'Frank is really gonna like this, Maff, this is good work.'

I gave the letter from Ruddock to Ian Anderson and he issued an immediate press release 'exposing' her as an IRA supporter, but it failed to make the newspapers, even *The Sun*. Thinking I'd passed the first test for the UDA, happiness abounded. I could now threaten to have people shot with greater authority.

On one of the few normal nights out I had during my teenage years I went to the old Hammersmith Odeon to see the Beautiful South. Me and three old school chums in the cheap seats up top, quaffing lager, wearing the t-shirts we bought in the foyer, and eyeing up girls we could never possibly get to. In the toilets before the band hit the stage, a young man in a suit asked if I was a Communist. 'No,' I said. 'I'm a fucking Nazi.' He looked at me quite surprised, shook his penis and said, 'Right on!'

I decided that night that I should change my life. During the encore of *You Keep it All In*, the South's laconic front man, Paul Heaton, turned to the crowd and asked if anybody had a problem they kept bottled up. Everyone around me raised their arms. Not me though. That's none of his fucking business, thought I. We went back to a friend's house and played The Jam loudly, and they pointed at me during *Down In the Tube Station at Midnight*, when the guy yawns, 'Too many right-wing meetings'. My heart was as empty as my life, my pockets were full of lint and my jeans ironed with creases down the middle.

'Who's Jackson Browne?' asks Anderson, all concerned.

'Where does he live?' I say suspiciously.

'On Radio 2. I just heard this song that goes, "I am neither capitalist or Communist", or something, by Jackson Browne.'

There was not much disco action in any far right cupboards. Everyone was terrified in case they ended up tapping their white toes to a black artist.

'What's good to listen to these days, you know, youth culture-wise?' he continued. How the hell would I know?

'The Beautiful South?' I suggested, then hummed *A Little Time* because Radio 2 loved it. He shrugged his shoulders, so I played him a tape.

'I love this song!' he said, 'any blacks in the band?'

'No, they're all white, Ian.'

'Do a piece on them for one of the mags, make it good.'

He trudged out of the room in the direction of the bottle of booze.

Then I remembered. 'Ian... er... one Irish chick and about five lefties.' But he didn't hear. He'd shot off upstairs to go rummaging under his bed for a copy of the old *Bulldog* magazine.

So, I wrote an article about pop music for Anderson. I was going to end it with 'not bad for a bunch of Marxists' but thought better of it. Any good nationalist music reviewer must include an attack on black musicians, so we added in something about 'negro rhythms'.

This was the first instalment in Anderson's next project. No doubt he thought we were going to corner the *Smash Hits* market and get Kylie Minogue around to his grotty back room for a provocative photo shoot and questions like 'Mandela: Shoot or swing?'

CHAPTER 17

The end of 1990 approached along with my political career. I leaned across to Blackham and muttered, 'If I'm still here next year, I'll slit my fucking wrists.'

He looked at me with surprise and said, 'If you're still here next year, I'll slit your fucking *neck*.'

I could not have been further removed from reality, from my family, former friends and from society. I hated the far right. I felt like a big man in a tiny jar with the lid sealed.

Our commitment to stand fifty candidates at the next election stalled somewhere around the twelve to eighteen candidate mark. Thank God I wasn't twenty-one, otherwise the black neighbours would have received a leaflet with my photograph on stating: 'Matthew Collins has lived in south London all his life. He believes that Britain deserves the best not just from, but for, its people.' Then there would follow a small paragraph about me that would have been almost identical to that of Eddie Whicker standing in Birmingham and every other stupid candidate we could rustle up. It should have read, 'Matthew Collins. It will drop off if you don't stop that.'

I began to think I was growing up and actually had no politics or political inclinations whatsoever. Back in the office I could hear Anderson in the shed in his back garden smashing his print machine to pieces and swearing loudly. He came in, grabbed his bottle of scotch and headed back out for round two with the poor dilapidated machine. I stared at the telephone that never rang. I had nobody to talk to.

My life was in review. In 1990, the far right became larger and more active, so confident, not in its own abilities but in the uselessness of society, that it stood up and shouted violently. It impressed itself with its violence. I hadn't suddenly become an anti-fascist, not even an anti-racist. I was just a badly let-down teenager who blamed everyone else for his failings. I was certainly not perfect. All the violence, all the racism, the paranoia and endless amounts of wanking and dreaming of some stupid foreign notion of my own identity had suddenly taken its toll. But it was the fascists I hated, not myself. My own mates and comrades. My only friends were all fucking mad. Mad, bad and very, very dangerous.

I didn't get out of bed for a week, and Anderson rang me daily to abuse me.

'The Remembrance Sunday march is coming, we need you in the office, not home in bed.'

I went leafleting with Blackham during the week before Remembrance Sunday and I told him that the NF was fucked.

'What can we achieve here, Terry? We can't achieve anything. All is lost, let's give up and go to the pub!'

He took my leaflets out of my hand with a pained expression.

'I could see this coming. Go home. I know it's over. It's better you go now before I really do slit your throat.'

I gladly left him at the pub door. Perhaps it would be as easy as this.

Like Terry had, Anderson thought I was voicing disapproval at the way the NF was run politically. Perhaps I was. It was hardly energising any more, maybe that was the real cause of my lethargy? But it couldn't be just that. It just was not right to walk around for the rest of one's life thinking stupid and wicked thoughts all of the time. It's quite possible that I had got it wrong, not them, but why did they sicken me so much? Any if not all the affection I held for these people had gone and been replaced by a cynicism that had now articulated itself into a need to get laid, make (new) friends and ditch the old ones completely. I was, after all, still a teenager.

So, was I out of a job?

'God no, take a rest after the march and decide what you want to do. But please, stop upsetting Terry.'

The future of the party revolved around a man who flared up more regularly than Anderson's haemorrhoids. Who controlled whom now?

Mr X was now writing the Beckenham branch bulletin instead of me. I didn't get told I was being replaced but the sarcasm rather than the spelling mistakes of my last bulletin had obviously been a last straw. Mr X made a few digs at Irish members. The dirty fucker was making me feel like a Paddy. He even said I could earn the branch some extra money by being the Guy on bonfire night. The Irish thing had come back to haunt me, but this time it did not bother me in the slightest. I knew full well it was being done to hurt me. In fact, it gave me strength as it set me apart from them. One thing I knew for certain was that I would make Mr X pay for it. I was the only bastard he had not invited to his lavish Christmas party. Well, me and Murph.

The 1990 Remembrance Sunday parade passed without incident or, in fact, many marchers. Leeds NF made it to Victoria but not out of the pub and there was a huge panic two minutes before marching time because there was hardly anybody at the assembly point. A few football casuals hung around, unwilling to join us. The scene was desolate. The BNP had not turned up to bulk the march up, and once we'd given out the flags and formed the drum corps, there were perhaps only 100 people behind us.

As the wind blows up Bressenden Place all you could smell was stale beer, last night's vindaloo and defeat. This used to fill me with such anticipation, such excitement. It was the camaraderie of idiots. He with the tattooed head would play the bass drum to his own tune, we'd just try to accompany him the best we could. Instead of our usual parade, it became an embarrassing shuffle past busy roads with tourists on the London winter cheap. A black girl came out of McDonald's in her uniform and screamed 'Oh my god! NF? Niggers Forever!' The one remaining wit shouted back, 'Get back in the kitchens and cook your burgers, woman!'

As Christmas got closer, I drifted in and out of political (Nazi) consciousness. Thatcher was gone before the end of the month. I watched her leave No. 10 and was stunned. Change *could* happen. Mrs Thatcher took a large chunk of my memories of childhood from No. 10. Poverty, mass unemployment, the Falklands War, milk for school children, the miners' strike, even The Housemartins and Billy Bragg. But the Tories were still in, with a new grey man, without a degree or any dress sense. Anderson must have found some comfort in that.

To celebrate the festive season, Terry Blackham went on a drinking spree in Penge. Half of Ireland were apparently celebrating the break-up for Christmas too, all of them in Penge, all of them in the Dew Drop Inn pub. Now I don't know what really happened, I only have the word of the one-eyed witness which goes something like this:

Terry decided to bury the hatchet, and popped into what was (in his opinion) a pro-IRA boozer off Penge High Street. As Terry entered the establishment, the barman recognised him and decided that the pub would not serve a patriot of such high standing in the community. After a bit of tutting, Terry decided to stand up and be counted, and leant across the bar to remonstrate with the bar-fellow. There were some cross words, and Terry reminded the barman that he was, after all, only Irish and could be spending his

Christmas hols elsewhere if he so chose. The barkeeper offered Terrence an entire crate of empty pale ale bottles to take home on his head, but Terrence refused the kind offer on the grounds he would not be able to balance the entire crate on his head alone. He dropped the crate, and accidentally managed to connect with the barkeeper, causing some bruising. Terrence, realising the spirit of Christmas cheer could easily run dry in such circumstances, returned to the family home to unburden his woes to his elder and equally cheery brother who had, himself, an indefinable love of our Celtic brethren.

Accompanied by another man, the elder Blackham decided that he would drop into the Dew Drop himself, but first of all he would purchase a large carving knife in case he needed to, for instance, cut up a turkey. The man in the shop selling the knives obliged with the 'biggest fucking knife' he had and Blackham Snr and his accomplice were now all set for a pleasant evening's drinking. What happened next is conjecture but there was an awful lot of blood in an interval that, before the ambulances arrived, allowed Blackham Snr and his friend to return the knives to the shop they came from, with the cheery Christmas observation, 'We won't be needing these any more, we've finished.' This left the shopkeeper with two choices: resell the knives as shop-soiled seconds, or let them become Her Majesty's evidence. Blackham Snr was sentenced in the New Year.

CHAPTER 18

A man from *Searchlight* and I shared an overpriced cup of tea in a museum in town. This was a peculiarly surreal moment by any standards. What was his agenda? I knew what mine was, but what was his obsession with people like me? Further, were we going to become friends or was he going to try and stick his cock up my arse, like all lefties do?

I had my newspaper laid out on the table, as per my instructions. I had also ordered myself a lemon meringue pie, in an attempt to look a little sophisticated while I awaited his arrival. Upon his almost magician-like appearance in front of me, the man from *Searchlight* eyed me suspiciously, as if I could have been there to shoot him. It didn't even cross my mind as I sat there broken-hearted. What would be the point, for a start?

He asked me if I knew of the last time I had been photographed by anti-fascists.

'All the fucking time,' I told him.

'I know who you are anyway,' he said and then we parted.

I had to leave first, no doubt so some fucker could take my photograph. I stuck my hands in my pockets, bowed my head, stuck my collars up and ran for the Underground. I went home to bed cursing my stupidity.

After the meeting, I felt a bit numb. I also had to ask myself honestly what my motivation had been for doing it. It hadn't been financial, as not even my meringue had been paid for. *Searchlight* was a sinister magazine that nosed in and out of the rubbish bags of far-right activists, published the details of their findings and humiliated the decent law-abiding patriots that it exposed. It harassed us, tormented us and even scared us. This magazine was totally dedicated to fighting everything I had for so long thought I stood for. Who read it, and what for? People who were even *suspected* of helping them were often left in a pool of blood and piss. *Searchlight*'s mere existence cast a huge shadow over everyone's confidence. Even in meetings attended by very few people there was a suspicion that even among our closest and most trusted comrades one of us was 'selling out'.

The truth was, I was changing. Why take two steps forward, followed by three back? I didn't enjoy the company of fascists, perverts, thugs and incompetents. The 'movement' was a guarded place where you couldn't breathe or blink differently, show compassion, have other friends or other interests. Sure, the grass is always greener on the other side of the fence, but the fence was long and high where we lived.

The same week I met *Searchlight*, I met Adrian Davies in a Lewisham pub because he wanted to talk. It struck me, as we sat in the pub, that I had friends in the far right with £100,000-a-year jobs and about eight educated years of difference between us. Davies wanted to offer me his tutelage. He knew I was low and confused, had got my fingers burnt and had a permanent look of hopelessness on my face. He talked about his disasters at Cambridge University over a woman, his political aspirations – 'If I thought there could be a nationalist government tomorrow, I'd vote for it, then get the first boat out!' – but his concern for me was genuine, although misguided in many ways.

Davies was such a Tory. He was short, bald, portly and *incredibly* posh. He was always flitting in and out of the far right with little success. Adrian said I should prepare myself for all the rumours now I was in limbo. The word was out that the young Nazi about town had fallen out with the NF leadership. The rumours would be sexual, financial, religious, racial, everything.

As if a light had been turned on somewhere inside his obviously overworked head he'd decided that what I needed was go to university, and 'literally fuck every woman that you ever speak to. Forget politics, forget the NF and the BNP, that's all finishing. The political landscape on the right is changing so much that you know nothing and can do nothing unless you go to university, get a good job and contribute to your own well-being.' I noticed that Davies kept all his money in a small purse and paid for all his drinks in small change.

He was right. The first rumour came out of the Anderson faction in Croydon NF. The guys at *Searchlight* had already heard it. Anderson had set me up in a small flat in Barking on the NF's funds and I was biting his pillow. The police (of course I was a police spy) had taken me off the job and I was now moving to the BNP. My old man had apparently been released from Long Kesh and had persuaded me to join the INLA (Irish National Liberation Army). Eddie relayed them to me daily over the telephone, as Anderson despatched rumour after rumour – except, I'm sure, for the one about the flat in Barking – all over London via Blackham. The idea was to scupper any plans I had to join the BNP. Anderson also called to remind me, in a friendly manner, that I was still a party employee and was still a member, so not to do anything to damage its interests. Not that I'd signed any confidentiality agreements, but I understood.

Anderson, Blackham and I still rang each other almost daily. Even for them it was difficult to lose comrades and friends I suppose. Terry and I could barely be in the same room as each other but we still needed to talk to each other because we both had shared a hatred of black people and there did not seem to be enough other people who thought the same way to just let another lone traveller simply pass you by. I had stopped leafleting and selling papers with Blackham and the rest of south London NF and instead spent my evenings watching the never-ending pieces about the BNP on the local evening news. It was an almost daily event. Richard Edmonds would always be filmed throwing open the doors to the BNP shop and welcoming whichever news team it was inside. He even refused entry to a black reporter 'and that's my right', he told me.

Searchlight wanted another meeting and the mix of curiosity, and fear as to what trouble this would get me into, was too tempting to turn down. I knew they'd think I was just another workingclass, clueless and uncultured idiot. The meeting lasted an entire afternoon and it was long and painful. The security was enormous and involved changing cars, short cab rides and very nearly a paper bag over my head. The trip was made in silence except for the grunted instructions given to the taxi driver as to when to move on. I don't know if the drivers were in on the job or not but they took instructions that seemed to be sending us around in circles and down one-way streets back the way we had just come. Eventually we ended up at the back of a shabby London hotel. With my collar up, I entered, accompanied on either side by my two 'friends', and walked straight to the elevator.

This was it then. My legs were like lead jelly and my stomach was screaming in terror. The room was small, with a net-curtained window and a small single bed with brown bedding. Perhaps he was going to try and stick his cock in me.

The meeting began. Since our last meeting, he'd been away to do his research. They showed me photographs of myself with the friends and foes I had nurtured since I was fifteen. I had to name every one of them. Having made a habit of sticking my fingers up at photographers I was now seeing the results. Even in a photographic still you can tell when someone's shouting 'cunt' at the photographer. I'd been on a lot of marches, paper sales and provocative meetings in my short life, that much was obvious. Quite clearly, so had *Searchlight*.

Towards the end of the interview, as the rain pissed down outside the window and the cheap bulb was casting a dim, golden light, the tables turned against me. Photographs of Eddie and me in Birmingham photographing Irish marchers, photographs of me and other known UDA men, photographs of me with people I'd said I'd never met, at places I'd never been were produced. They knew these were dangerous times, they knew what I was loosely associated with. They knew more about my relationship with Mr X than I'd ever known.

Suddenly, for the first time ever, I was really scared. What the fuck had I been doing? I could easily get myself killed. But my biggest fear was of myself, having been with these people who, when described aloud for the benefit of the tape, were not just the peculiar misfits I had known and associated with, but dangerous monsters. Everyone I described as being an 'alright, good bloke' had 'gets pissed and smashes things up' and 'wants to blow up a synagogue' following afterwards. Men with no lives, no compassion, who could have crushed me at any moment had they chosen to. Men who would go on to murder people, plant bombs, attack innocent women, drive cars loaded with guns, give support to cold-blooded killers, fight as mercenaries in foreign wars. Men who would cover up for each other if one of them killed me now. They were not going to go away, I would know these people for the rest of my life and, from this day on, live in fear of them. How could I not realise this awful mess around me?

I gulped for a long breathless period and went to the

toilet for a loud and embarrassing dump while the two people from *Searchlight* whispered in hushed breaths outside in the room. The whole hotel seemed to be full of people that were there for the meeting. People loafing in reception, people waiting outside the room, people I have never seen since.

The meeting finished quite abruptly. I had a few tears which, when I brushed them, only made it worse. The man offered me an apple to take home. The woman didn't say a word. There were no smiles, no arms around the shoulder. They just repeated the magic act of seemingly disappearing into thin air, picking up as they went, the large amount of security that came with them.

All the way home I cursed myself for what a fucking idiot I had been. The rain in London only brings out strangers and raincoats, passing you by with anonymous heads bowed, not stopping to ask your name as you pass against them. If meeting *Searchlight* had been an attempt to unburden myself, it was not having the desired effect. It was a dreadful, intimidating meeting. To them I was obviously still a, very confused, Nazi fanatic with an irritable bowel. I obsessed about what I had said to them and what they would do with the information. No arrangements had been made to meet again and neither of them had ventured a hanky for my tears. Why were they trying to break an already broken man further?

Terry Blackham needed a bit of help at the office. Things were getting done in a strange way. Cheques were being cashed, but there was no stock. He didn't know how to do things.

'Come over, we'd love to see you. Ian thinks you feel a little bit surplus, but this is all your own doing Matthew. You've alienated us.'

Ian must have been whispering this speech in his ear, because Terry couldn't have read it and there were *at least* two words that were not part of his limited, gruff vocabulary. Panic set in, so I immediately obeyed and caught the train into London. What if it was like the plot in Chesterton's *The Man Who Was Thursday* and Ian Anderson and Terry Blackham were also passing info to *Searchlight*? It wasn't that much of a weird idea. Someone, somewhere inside the party had been keeping an eye on me and had been passing info to *Searchlight*.

We took a little lunch in a pub in East Ham, where all formalities stopped when a stripper came in and, well, stripped for a group of laddish builders in the middle of a freezing pub. Some bald guy was getting his head stuffed between two tits covered in shaving foam while his mates made lewd comments with their hands in their pockets. We lost Terry and, probably sensing that this would be a weak moment for me too, Anderson began the spiel I'd been waiting for.

'We don't want you to join the BNP. I know that it is a possibility, but we think the breakthrough for the NF will come when the Tories make their move. We know that you're in with the Tories through Adrian [Davies] and we think there is potential there, for you and us.'

I would have given anything to have had my head between those sagging, tattooed cockney knockers as opposed to having to sit with this far less appealing pair of tits.

'Let's go back to the office,' said Anderson.

Back at the office which was, if possible, even dirtier than when I left it, Terry was overcome with his importance and showed me pictures of Mr X and himself at a London UVF function just before Christmas, with men in balaclavas and other loyalist regalia. Anderson somehow sensed this was not a good idea and coughed 'put those away now, come on', and Terry snapped to attention. I had my chance.

'That's not very clever of him is it, getting himself photographed like that?'

Ian agreed. 'His carelessness has cost us all dearly.' He too was looking at the awful state of the office and Terry's appalling administrative skills. Not only did he not clear up after Anderson, Terry actually doubled the mess.

'It keeps me off the building sites working here,' said Terry glumly. 'The fucking reds have got the word out about me. If I go onto a building site in London some Irish cunt's gonna either drop something on my head or push me off the scaffolding.'

He scrunched his nose up, he hated the idea of having to take a low profile, particularly when he enjoyed the work on site and it obviously paid much better than the NF.

We didn't mention Mr X again for the rest of the afternoon. Ian went out to the printing machine in his back garden while I showed Terry how to fiddle the mail order records in case the Jews at the tax office were ever going to be even mildly interested. Terry even asked me what he was 'supposed to do all day… I mean there's nothing to do. The phone hardly ever rings, Ian won't let me near the printing side, I'm as bored as hell.' In a moment of madness, I promised him I'd come back the next day and we'd go leafleting together in streets where BNP members lived. For a whole day I was not one bit scared of the lunatic. He seemed quite helpless. I did the best I could, but I could not make stock appear magically out of my arse. Terry drove me home, in almost complete silence. I wish I had asked him to teach me how to drive.

Searchlight picked me up in a car the next day. The man was insistent I cancel all of my plans – so out went leafleting with Terry – and join him instead. He parked his car just off the estate and told me to get into the back. Another, enormous, man came from nowhere to get in beside me. The new man was much more chatty, almost friendly. He was built like a brick shithouse and looked like the sort of bloke who worked out in front of his bedroom mirror with his cock in his hand. He fancied himself.

'You're a bit of a character Matthew – I can call you Matthew can't I? I've just been reading *The Flag*. The NF's got exactly the same line on the Gulf as *The Guardian*,' which he was also holding.

I grunted. I didn't know what *The Guardian* was saying so I took his word for it. Our new friend gave directions to our destination.

'Cheer up,' he said, leaning over to push the lock button down on my door, 'We'll be there in a minute.'

He kept tapping his shoulder so I got the message that he was carrying a gun. An hour later we are sat in a flat that wasn't furnished any better than the cheap hotel room. We spent three hours going over everything we had done only a few days previously and Blackham and Anderson were furious I missed leafleting. Apparently Terry had sat indoors all day waiting for me to arrive.

1991 started with a letter from Anderson and a pay cheque, effectively paying me off after I'd told him that I would prefer life on the dole, to taking a pay cut to accommodate Terry. He told me he was hurt and I told him that I was skint. Neither of us gave a fuck about the other's predicament.

One Monday morning in February, *Searchlight* hit the stands with 'Gotcha: Front's Chum on *The Sun*' emblazoned across its front page. Fucking hell!! I hadn't been warned and had not seen the article. My phone call came sometime after eight that morning. I was being ordered over to east London, by Angry Anderson.

'Get over here now, we have a major problem!'

I refused outright. 'What is it? I've got a job interview today.'

He exploded. I could hear the phone being hammered

on the bottom stair, by the front door where he took and made his calls.

'You get the fuck over here now, TODAY!'

The life drained out of me immediately. The fucking Jews at *Searchlight* probably didn't roll into work until sometime after midday. I slumped on the living room couch. The phone rang again. This time it was Whicker.

'They didn't keep that secret very long, did they?' he said, chuckling to himself. He read the entire article about Mr X to me. Apparently, Blackham had even posed alongside Mr X in *The Sun*, masquerading as a homeless person for a feature on homelessness. I hadn't seen it or even known about it. Other things I had known were thrown in there, but it was the work of four or five other parties as well.

'He's going to sue, so if you're the source you'll be in court facing him, and me,' shouted Blackham furiously down the phone when he rang a few minutes later.

Anderson and Blackham quickly drew up a list of possible informers that started with ten names and grew to over a dozen, then thirty. They had to start with the Directorate, then slowly move through all the people who had seen Mr X with the NF or Blackham, at meetings or functions. The list grew longer until even Anderson was under suspicion from himself. Then it was Brady and Acton, Nash, Murphy, Adrian Woods, everyone. But the fact was, it was *Searchlight* that had the story and only my commitment to the NF was under the spotlight.

'Everyone in the NF has a huge fucking mouth,' I told Anderson when I called him back in genuine shock at the story. It was now a quarter to ten. In little under two hours the NF had almost imploded. Ian sounded distraught but I felt nothing for him, not an ounce of sympathy and, funnily enough, not an ounce of regret. They'd already had the chance to speak to Mr X, who had obviously told them of the story himself. *Searchlight* had not contacted him for a comment so he was suffering in the shock of it too. No one in the NF had actually seen the article except for Anderson, Blackham and Whicker, who subscribed to the magazine under a different name. They had relented somewhat by mid-morning, given that there was stuff in there that just could not have come from me.

'When we find the cunt that's done this to us, we'll fucking bury him, no questions asked,' said Terry and I did not doubt that for a moment.

During all of this, I could not help wondering when I was going to be getting a magical financial windfall. If the Anderson story about printing Labour Party memberships was potentially worth five grand, surely this was worth *at least* the same? I had to get into the little car with the man from *Searchlight* again, but this time I was to make '*absolutely certain*' I was not being followed. We'd arranged signals to give each other as I approached the car in case either one of us sensed danger. I was handsomely paid with record and book tokens.

The Mr X scandal dragged on for the next few days. There was nothing in the papers, though the *Daily Mirror* had now begun to doorstep NF members that I had mentioneded to *Searchlight*. By all accounts the *Mirror* decided not to doorstep Blackham after they assessed the situation as too dangerous. Whicker's place of residence was impossible to gain access to and the *Mirror* also put him on the too dangerous list. Poor old Murph had stood frozen to his doorstep, speechless, whereas other members confirmed the story from behind closed doors, not wanting to get involved. One particular member allegedly offered them more information for ten grand. The *Mirror* refused.

On Sunday, copies of *Searchlight* were handed out at Brick Lane by the BNP. BNP members usually stole copies from a leftist bookstall on the market, but they had actually gone out and bought them during the week to photocopy and distribute and the entire fascist community of London read the story aghast.

I stood with the renegade members of Croydon NF, the rest of the London party having gone into hiding on Anderson's instructions. By now I knew the article word for word, but nobody was overly surprised that the story was now out. Tony Lecomber enjoyed rubbing it in but commented loud enough for the rest of my comrades to hear, 'You never said anything about this, Matthew.'

We took the traditional Brick Lane Sunday drink with the BNP that day, watching strippers and eating a selection of mussels and whelks off the bar. I opted for a lift home with Edmonds that afternoon, and nobody seemed to care.

'It's time you joined the BNP, Matthew,' proclaimed Edmonds over his driving shoulder. 'The NF cannot protect anything or anyone.'

It was like being given the answer to a simple mathematical equation. Was I blind? Was I too scared to go to prison with these guys?

'We're off to Portsmouth next weekend, come down with us. It'll be a bit of a wind up, there's loads of Jews down there.' A week later the local paper in Portsmouth reported a series of desecrations of Jewish graves.

CHAPTER 19

When meltdowns happen, they happen immediately. In such a small organisation everyone gets to feel the heat. The whole of the NF leadership seemed to have gone into hiding to avoid an inquisitive and nervous membership. The *Searchlight* story dominated every branch meeting and leafleting session across the country. Phone calls were made up and down the country and the organisers and members began attacking each other in a spectacular case of Chinese Whispers. My bitterness helped me stir the pot without a problem. I launched into a series of tirades about party corruption. Barry Roberts, perhaps at the behest of Davies, dragged me for a drink with some other nationalists, telling me it would be a good opportunity for me to kick Anderson 'while he's down'. Hopefully this would help keep *Searchlight* off my back too.

Anderson had very quickly lost control of a party he, I and a few others, mistakenly thought he ruled with an iron rod. His and Blackham's outbursts quickly alienated people who were already sceptical of the NF's future potential. The party membership had already plummeted dramatically over the last year or so, to the benefit of the BNP. The now-damaging relationship with Mr X had been held up as proof by Anderson that his and the NF's ideological shifts were working, and that the departure of the party's hardcore was no long-term loss. Certainly there were those who rallied around him, in particular those he had favoured for their unquestionable obedience. But others, tired of the NF's lack of confrontational ambition, attacked the leadership for its weakness over the leak. The worst of the attacks came from the experienced backbone of the party, who had watched it disintegrate too many times before. The NF was, said Ballard, 'almost totally without ideological purpose,' encouraging the Croydon branch's former Political Soldiers, trained by Nick Griffin, to remove the previous officials permanently. No wonder that, after engineering an initial witch hunt, Anderson's phone remained off the hook as he took to his bed with a bottle of own-brand scotch.

Copies of *Spearhead* were mailed to every NF branch, folded perfectly so that the recipient saw page five of the December 1990 edition first. Over four pages were given to the previously unheard of Graham Miles and his article 'The National Front: The Writing on the Wall'. When it had originally been published, like most BNP attacks on the NF, it was ignored. It attacked the NF's election strategies as well as the previous AGM, quoting an 'inside source', obviously my big gob over tea and biscuits at the BNP office. A whole page was given over to the leadership split in 1980, something that still rankled with Tyndall, and by the end of the article, it was meant to become clear to the reader that Tyndall had always been right.

Tyndall and the BNP thought their time was now. Although there had been no way of knowing at the time that the article was penned, that the NF was about to lurch headfirst into another crisis only a month or so later, the plebs who manned and staffed the organisation obviously believed that the article had been penned by some Nazi oracle. Both Eddie Whicker and I received copies through the post. Eddie studied his thoroughly before deciding what to do.

He travelled over to Anderson's with the article in his back pocket, to watch Anderson, drunk and hysterical, and Blackham, brainstorming furiously and planning Stalinesque purges of the suspected traitors. Rather like my own, Blackham's rise had been meteoric. His obedience and violent streak made him a perfect minder and pocket gimp for Anderson. He rang around, issued threats and kept up a menacing presence in the minds of people up and down the country. Distance had never been an obstacle for Terry when it came to carrying out threats.

This was a major security leak but one couldn't help feeling (as one sat nervously shitting oneself), that this was a slight overreaction. The deal should have been to brush it off. If we were really part of the established political environment and ostensibly a proper political party, shouldn't we take this in our stride like all the Tories caught with their pants down? According to Whicker I was top of the purge list, but, telephone threats aside, I knew that if they really thought I was behind the leak, I would have been taken out long before Anderson's paranoia had gripped him.

In fact, Terry had good reason for almost *knowing* that I could not be the leak. Aside from the lax moment he showed me the pics of him and Mr X at the UVF social, he had kept his gob impressively shut, to me anyway. He must have somewhere deep down realised, that Anderson had been appallingly indiscreet, as had Mr X himself. To him, I was just a former comrade, kicking his leader while he was down.

Anderson's poor handling of the Mr X leak, coupled with his inability to maintain control during what was, after all, another appalling security lapse, infuriated Whicker. Having travelled over to east London to offer advice on internal security matters, Eddie looked around the back room office, and was horrified by the mess and the filth the party was being administrated from. He lost what little faith he had in Anderson on the spot. 'Worst of all Maff, they've got the party Union Jacks lying on the floor covered in shit.' As for Terry, Eddie 'despaired' that Ian was 'sending a good man bad.'

Searchlight was mildly surprised that Terry and Eddie were charged with internal security; 'They're doormen at best,' I was told, 'not people with the brains to run a proper internal investigation'. Mr X announced that he was going to sue. Could *Searchlight* afford this? Could they keep me out of the spotlight? We had a meeting where I got pissed and distraught to such an extent I threw up and the man from *Searchlight* just sat tapping his fingers on his knees, while we went through the story again. I was driven to visit a libel solicitor. Despite my absolute horror at how quickly my life was plunging into an abyss and the possibility of me having to go to court, I still managed to somehow maintain a cheery disposition at the solicitor's office. The man from *Searchlight* assumed I had somehow got over my little drama earlier and was actually looking forward to going to court.

'Are you mad?' I asked. 'Or do you think it's me that's mad? I'm not going to court, no way, not ever.'

He agreed that it was not a good idea. If I could just ride this through I thought, I'd be out of all of this in no time and start afresh.

With twenty quid from the man from *Searchlight* I spent the rest of the day in the pub. *Ne Me Quitte Pas* by Nina Simone was on the jukebox, and, although I didn't know what the words meant, I felt them. The NF was lurching headfirst towards disaster. When I had loved it, things had looked so much brighter.

With a potential show-stopping court case in the air and my amour for *Searchlight* fading, I next made my way to Welling and stumbled upon a meeting while the absent Edmonds was at the Co-Op buying tea bags. Lecomber and Eddy Butler, the BNP's East End election specialist, were sorting through the administrative nightmare piled up on the kitchen table when Lecomber abruptly turned to me and said, 'It's Richard Edmonds that's becoming the

stumbling block for the BNP. Lovely guy, but look at this.'
He held up a dozen letters with cash, and more cheques
still uncashed, and groaned.

Butler commented that the bookshop needed someone
with real quality to run it. Neither Butler nor Lecomber
appeared to have full-time jobs. The two faux intellectuals, both notorious for waffling, were competitively
vying to replace dear Richard in the very bookshop that
he owned! Both of them hated Anderson, Lecomber for
the previous slights against him, Butler for more personal
reasons. We drank tea and chatted, gossiped and told
jokes barricaded inside the tiny back room for most of
the afternoon. Round-faced, balding and now wearing
glasses, most people thought Lecomber was a terrible bore.
He was not without a modicum of charm and, in a way,
possibly because he had spent so much time in prison for
his bombing convictions, he could be a little distant and
naïve too. Butler was taller and thinner. Like Lecomber,
he was stretching his limited intellect in the hope of playing an emerging role in the growing BNP. To do this, they
both had to be especially nice to the BNP leader John
Tyndall, and throughout the afternoon they praised him
endlessly, like he was the second coming of Christ. Both
of them were eventually going to stab the 'great man' in
the back.

Back at home, I emptied my entire life into the rubbish
bin while my mother looked on bemused. Something inside
me told me to throw all of this Nazi and fascist shit into
the bin, to put it out of temptation's way. I felt surprisingly little sentiment. I kept nothing. The pages and pages
of nonsense, the CDs of Nazi rock bands that I had bought
out of a sense of loyalty, not musical appreciation, all went.
I threw out bulletins, newspapers, flags, magazines and
home-made weapons and then locked myself away. As if
sensing a tragedy was in the making, the family ignored me

while I trudged around the house confused and depressed, smoking cigarette after cigarette in torment.

I met *Searchlight* for tea and sympathy. I was to meet the chatty, large bloke from now on. I must have moved onto the 'safe' list of Nazis, but I never asked the exact reason.

'This is your unique opportunity,' he told me. 'If you want to go, you can.' Solicitors were meeting over the libel writ and my friend was confident I would be in the clear. 'Go back to school, go on holiday, read a book, make something better for yourself.'

In order to drum up some new support, Anderson sent himself on a speaking tour to address back rooms of pubs, promoting and firing people as he went from empty room to empty room, discovering that the party was hopelessly lifeless and split. My branch's bulletins began to arrive at the house again for the first time in months. The spelling and grammar had deteriorated so badly that it was obvious that Terry was operating on his own again.

In mid-April there was a surprise guest at my next *Searchlight* rendezvous. The great Gerry Gable entered the London hotel wearing a ridiculous ponytail. He ordered me a large brandy and positioned himself comfortably beside me. So this was *the* Gerry Gable, the 'baby eating, burgling, Jewish-Communist'. For a man in his early fifties, he had already amassed a legendary status. He was the first person we had been taught to hate in the movement and I had always sort of assumed he would walk around in a black cloak and a red neck scarf, not a ponytail and Italian suit. He was friendly enough and straight away began telling me how well he had heard I was doing in the party. 'You've got a lot of friends,' he said, raising his eyebrows as he spoke. 'Better still, you're driving the NF mad,' he chuckled to himself.

The NF's financial mismanagement, backstabbing and lacklustre leadership were my selling points. 'I'm out of favour in the party for all the right reasons,' I told listeners in an East End pub. 'They've taken money out of the cause and furnished their private lifestyles. Money that was not theirs to squander, but ours, the membership's, to make our lives easier, to finance bigger actions and operations, not buy new couches and business transport.' There had almost been a lynch party formed there and then. Gable had heard all about it. The word to *Searchlight* was that I was trusted by the BNP and my friends in the NF, who relayed to *Searchlight* the immense dissatisfaction that the NF leadership had in my new-found liberty. 'They'll probably ask you to come back into the fold,' Gable said. Edmonds and Lecomber had already been onto me to run a Lewisham BNP.

Gable had business on his mind. He leaned forward to speak quietly into my ear. Mr X was being pushed to sue *Searchlight* over the story by the NF, he told me. The stupid fool was seeking counsel from the NF's leadership, desperate to find the mole in its ranks. As Blackham relayed to Whicker that April, Anderson was convinced that *Searchlight* would be forced to reveal their source in court and then he'd 'have the bastard'.

'A good journalist does not reveal his sources, ever!' Gable told me, sitting back with a smile on his face. Apparently, Gable thought he was a good journalist so case closed. But he did have to ask, *would* I go to court for him, to front the story up?

'Look Mattie, I stand by you, I stand by the story. I'm asking you to face X in court. We're at a critical stage and they're pushing to send the magazine under, not even on a decent matter of principle.'

So *Searchlight* couldn't afford it. How could they? Like the NF, they probably only had a couple of thousand members. The traditional left had not been at all interested in the far right after 1979, and back then in 1991, we had no idea of the monster the BNP would have become fifteen years later. I could barely raise a squeak. The brandy had been for the shock, obviously. I became uncontrollable at the nightmare of facing the future murderers, gun-runners, drug dealers and bombers of the NF and the BNP.

'Have you ever been to Portugal?' I heard Gable ask through the panicked screams in my head. Everything had come to fruition. The predictable doom and violence of my future was now being planned in my very presence.

'They'll kill me,' I mumbled pathetically in response.

'Who, the Portuguese?' asked the other man.

There was absolutely no way I was going to come out in front of those fucking nutters. No way, there was no way. I could name ten people who would not hesitate to kill me.

'Spain it is then,' Gable confirmed.

The scene had now been set. The rival solicitors were going to go into battle and I was to go burn myself under foreign sun, find myself, and consider that upon my return if an agreement could not be reached, I would be news-worthy as the man who named names and would have to walk into a London court, face my former friends and tell the world about the Front's chum on *The Sun*. I sat dazed for what felt like hours as Gable chatted away. 'Nothing's concrete,' he said, 'but I think you'll get away with it.'

This man was supposed to be a monster, if not *the* monster behind all of the great conspiracies, and here he was with me, chatting away like he was my Dad about holidays in the sun. I still did not believe him, how could I? 'What we'll do is, we'll buy some books for you to read and we'll ring you every day,' he said, rather proudly. He could fuck his books. I wanted beer tokens and some Spanish Fly.

'It's a deal. Today is Monday, you're leaving on Thursday.' Then he leaned right into my face. 'No getting pissed, no mistakes. Make your leaving good and make it convincing. You haven't got long to get this right.' And he was serious: if I fucked this up, they'd dump me in a hole without a trace.

Adrian Davies agreed to be my alibi and tell people that a 'friend of ours' was sending me to Spain to look after a property. He thought it was a 'splendid idea' even if it would mean I'd miss a Bow and Poplar Tory Party meeting, where the great Norman Tebbit was to speak, having only recently stolen Anderson's own line on the great 'cricket debate' as to being able to tell someone's true loyalty to a country over who they'd support over a game of fucking cricket.

Over at NF HQ, Anderson and Blackham were surprisingly sympathetic and incredibly downbeat. It was good that I was entrusted to look after a property in Spain belonging to someone in the Tory Party, and I got a little teary that things had become such a mess over the Mr X debacle. Maybe my mouth was too big, maybe I'd said too much. After all, the BNP was full of moles. Both readily agreed, and for a moment I thought Anderson was going to give me back some of the tax he had deducted on my behalf but had not paid. But he did not. 'When you get back, it will all be sorted out,' said Anderson, which is exactly the same thing Gable had told me. Terry just stood there with his hands on his hips in deep thought, before adding: 'When it's sorted, we'll have the cunt and all the loose tongues will stop. We'll have that cunt and then we'll have those BNP cunts too. You'll need to make your fucking mind up which of us you're with while you're away.'

A one-year passport was issued on Wednesday morning by my local post office, and on Thursday morning I was heading to Gran Cranaria.

It was my first ever time on a plane. Like everything else since the leak, it seemed to be happening to somebody else and I was just going along for the ride. The plane took off and landed on time, I was shoved on a coach and dumped in a half-finished holiday resort.

For the first time in my life I had real freedom. At the back of my mind at all times was, of course, the goings-on in the epic libel battle and every day I went to reception to take a call from London, but I was my own man. I discovered I was almost totally incapable of feeding myself or doing the washing, so I was grateful for the endless supply of summer holiday clothes someone in the *Searchlight* office had purchased for me, right down to flip flops and a stylish baseball cap.

On my last planned day I got into a bit of a panic when there had been no phone call. I tried to reverse the charges to the *Searchlight* office, but the number was permanently engaged. An awful panic set in as I paced the floor of a half-finished marbled lobby, begging to try the number in England again. There was no way I'd be going back if I had to face the NF. I'd rather stay in Spain, I could handle the loneliness easily.

Late in the afternoon as I worked myself into a state, *Searchlight* finally rang.

'Come home,' said the voice.

Mr X had accepted a very minor payment (£1,009) in court from *Searchlight*, without a single word of apology from them. They had stood by their story. It had cost *Searchlight* seven grand in legal fees and Mr X apparently much more. Why had he climbed down? Was it the video of him and Blackham at the Mosley dinner that his lawyer knew about? Was it because he knew how leaky the far right were, or was it because of some letters written to Gable years before that might have shaken his loyalist credibility?

I travelled back to London, knowing that I would be back on the firm again. Mr X's capitulation no matter how he tried to dress it up in public had infuriated Anderson. It also turned out that Mr X had made a number of visits to the BNP bookshop where Edmonds had remained blissfully unaware as to who he was. I pointed out to Blackham that the mole could have come from inside the BNP so he stepped up his aggression towards them.

To regain some much-needed face in the long run-up to the forthcoming election, Anderson conceded that the NF's failure to campaign in London had lost them most numbers. He decided the NF should concentrate their efforts on the capital again, partly as a result of being decimated elsewhere. The plan to stand fifty candidates was quickly forgotten. East London was completely lost to the BNP on one side and hordes of Asian immigrants on the other. The NF was stronger south of the river and, despite the uncertainty surrounding the stability of the Croydon branch, the NF was focussing attention on Bermondsey, as it was their last great hope for London. The local MP, a Liberal Democrat named Simon Hughes, had been getting up the nose of everyone on the far right. For the NF, it was by being a liberal, for the BNP it was by being a democrat.

I was now back in the fold, but the bond of trust had been shaken between Anderson and I, even though he kept saying that I was welcome.

'He just wants the membership money,' Gable laughed aloud.

Blackham was in a permanent sulk, driven by paranoia and suspicion. I was now to meet Gable weekly, if at all possible. Spain had been good for me. It had put me in my place and given me some perspective. I was a young man after all, an irresponsible teenager who couldn't even do his own washing. And that was good. There was no reason to grow up just yet, I just had to learn to show respect to myself. Gable tested me, gave me book and record tokens and took an interest. He loved hearing stories about Eddie. Like the other man from *Searchlight* who occasionally came to our meetings too, they had a grudging admiration for him. They backed up what I'd heard of the legend of Eddie at Stockport Station in the mid-1980s.

'I was there,' said Gable's mate. 'We couldn't believe it.'

The NF leadership at the time, Griffin and co., were running for the first train out of town and Eddie, bringing up the rear, was stranded.

'He turned to face five hundred anti-fascists, and took the station to pieces, smashing all the doors and windows. It was mainly so he could attract the police to his plight, but no one wanted to be the first inside to challenge him from our side. Later, we came across him on the London Underground when we'd been scouting an NF meeting and he got on the tube with us and just stared at us, didn't blink and didn't flinch.'

The BNP began standing in council elections in earnest that year. As a party it had grown enormously in strength and confidence. Its actual paid-up membership was still very small but they fought council elections both in the east of London and in the south. Anti-fascists became more militant too, stepping up their activities. Steve Tyler and the BNP defended Bermondsey and their patch there ferociously. At a local council election where Tyler had stood, I sat in the back of his getaway van in which we were to ferry him out of the area after the election count. The police got him out of the back of the hall, we opened the back door for him to get in, and the gobsmacked officer in charge stood with his mouth open at the sight of grown men huddling there with iron bars. Tyler got in, shut the door, and off we drove, leaving the foot soldiers to tackle the anti-fascist demonstration.

Steve Tyler was going to stand in Bermondsey for the BNP and Terry Blackham was going to stand for the NF. There had been no negotiations between the two parties. Anderson had apparently refused even to return their calls. Edmonds summoned me to the bookshop in Welling to discuss it. Anderson gave me his tacit approval to 'tell them to fuck off'. Lecomber was becoming a regular at the shop, perhaps he was working there for a salary, I didn't know. The place had certainly begun to improve; it was noticeable how much the party had grown and how many people were there day in day out, drinking cups of tea and listening to Edmonds delivering blistering speeches while Lecomber plodded through the mail and the book orders.

Both parties were preparing for a clash in Bermondsey. The BNP were working the area in their usual boot-boy ways. Unlike the professional operation they try to run now, they had no ward maps or any idea where their vote would be stronger by way of canvassing an area. The area was simply covered with stickers and posters during evenings when Edmonds drove a minibus-load of activists into the area while the pubs filled up with BNP heavies. Blackham ran small leafleting drops by a handful of NF members. I had the NF, the BNP and *Searchlight* all on my back to get involved in the campaign.

'I want both of their leaflets and I want to know what they're up to,' Gable told me.

Bermondsey, part of the London Borough of Southwark, tips south east London into the Thames. It's also a little bit Lambeth and a tiny bit Lewisham in its identity. A former dock area, it's been immortalised by both Samuel Pepys and Charles Dickens in stories of the great white working class of yesteryear. Its train station became Surrey Quays, replacing Surrey Docks some time during the late 1980s or early 1990s. Few of the locals seemed able to pronounce the new station properly, even fewer cared to. It was a maze of council estates and dimly-lit pubs, surrounded by back alleys and disused tunnels covered in graffiti honouring the local football team. Only one team was openly supported here; whether you went to the games or not, your team was Millwall. The actual suburb of Millwall is in east London, little more than a spectacularly-thrown brick across the

Thames. And believe me, if the locals could aim one into east London, the locals would.

Here in this part of London strangers were rarely welcomed, rarely tolerated. What I would later come to understand as regeneration in New Labour parlance, had started in earnest during this period. Former places of work were being converted into yuppie penthouses, squeezing and dwarfing the working-class community there. If, unlike the people living in Millwall, the people in Bermondsey didn't live on an actual island, in their minds they did. Being a white visitor you were just about tolerated.

On the first Saturday morning of the campaign I stood between the two parties at the Blue Market, a rather below-par market that sold nothing of any use or value. The NF had half a dozen members, few of whom were old enough to vote, and the BNP had a dozen or so meat-heads. I walked between the two groups, much to Blackham's chagrin, just chatting, picking up bits of gossip. A Canadian television crew were there to do a piece on the strange case of two equally small and insignificant Nazi parties fighting the same seat. It must have seemed very *Life of Brian* to them. Edmonds spoke on behalf of the BNP, angry and articulate, pointing at the interviewer while ranting about blacks and crime. Blackham insisted I speak on behalf of the NF and when I spoke, Edmonds stood next to me agreeing wholeheartedly. 'That's right Matthew, yes, yes, absolutely correct. RIGHTS FOR WHITES!' The polite Canadian interviewer thanked us while her English crew looked rather shocked. Everyone in Canada would hate us by teatime.

Ten minutes later, excitable kids came running up the road being followed by a slow-moving open-top bus adorned with balloons, carrying the Lib Dem candidate Simon Hughes talking through a loudhailer. The bus was attacked. The young children fled in panic as the doors were kicked and windows showered with bottles. Then I heard 'Duck!' as thick batteries were thrown at the group on top of the bus. The driver panicked and stalled the bus as, like animals, groups of fascists tried to force their way on. I don't know what it was that Simon Hughes had said to the local papers, but he had really wound this lot up. The whole market came to a standstill as the attack continued. Cars behind the bus had their doors kicked in too.

'Not so big now are you, Hughsie?' they screamed as he and his terrified supporters hid from a hail of stones and batteries. The locals on the market were not overly impressed. A large chant of 'Rights for Whites' went up as finally the bus took off as fast as it could.

In 2007 I addressed a fringe meeting at the Lib Dems' conference in Brighton. I'd been struggling with my fifteen-minute speech all the way down there on the train. Before my meeting I went to see *Searchlight*'s current editor Nick Lowles, speaking at a meeting attended by Hughes. My speech was now set. As I went into my meeting and began my speech about that day, a startled-looking Simon Hughes stood up to roars of laughter and said, 'My God, do I remember that day! It was absolutely terrifying!' Lembit Opik later bought me a pint in the bar, telling me, 'It was surreal.'

CHAPTER 20

After some hefty persuasion by both *Searchlight* and Ian Anderson, I agreed to join a national turnout for the next big weekend of campaigning in Bermondsey. A dozen leading Anderson loyalists, including two from Birmingham, were also in town. After four hours I realised I was on a pub crawl. We ended the evening near the Elephant and Castle. Looking out of the window, I stared at my favourite Indian eatery with a watery mouth and commented to John Hill, the national organiser of the NF and a parliamentary candidate for law and order, that they did the finest Vindaloo in London. 'Really? I fucking love a good curry, me. Who's up for a curry then?' he asked, rubbing his large hands together.

Well, obviously I was. But something did not bode right about the situation. We'd spent the whole day coming to terms with the BNP saturation of Bermondsey, and our own unease about having to face them again, plus Terry was very drunk which normally meant agitated. Hill was already on licence over a fight in a pub in Birmingham where he had led a small group of NF activists into an attack on a group of Socialists. So I refused, thank God. Most of the others would not eat curry because 'Pakis cooked it' but John, a stocky street fighter, managed to persuade five of them to go get a curry, including, strangely, Terry Blackham, who I didn't think had ever eaten something so daring as a prawn cracker before in his life. I waited in the pub with Anderson for his taxi to turn up.

'We need you back on the team for good Matthew,' he said, putting another pint in front of me. 'The party's going through some transitions at the moment but we have to stick to our guns.'

I was so pissed that I actually thought for a moment about telling him it was me who had fucked the party over. I was absolutely terrified of getting caught, but also immensely proud that I had got away with it and wanted to rub his nose in it. The words were even on my tongue as he got up for his taxi, but I knew that would ruin everything. He'd have to find out later, from somebody else.

Five large and aggressive fascists walked into the Indian restaurant, already the worse for wear, and demanded five pints and some popadoms. The fascists sat down for their meals and began their usual charming witty banter about 'Pakis, poofs and coons' when an incredulous customer asked them to tone down the language, in particular the racist remarks. It took them less than two minutes to destroy the restaurant and its magnificent fish tank. I watched the police piling out of the station and into the restaurant as the riot spilled out onto the pavement. The street filled with passersby stopping to stare as horrified diners fled into the traffic. The NF was taking the restaurant to bits.

As my taxi passed the restaurant I could see Hill through the broken window face down on the table, with two coppers holding him down. The fighting was continuing and the police were struggling to contain these well-rehearsed vandals and hooligans.

'Not a smart place to start a fight is it?' said the driver. Was there ever?

Still without a number for *Searchlight*'s Gerry Gable and with it being the weekend and the office being closed, I took it upon myself to make inquiries the next morning. Blackham's mother confirmed he was still in the cells and also let slip that Terry had not been 'coping too well' with the break-up of his relationship with his long-term girlfriend. 'Go and see if he's alright won't you?' she asked.

A local member drove me to the police station so that I could make my inquiries. The desk officer smiled broadly. 'We've got five of them here helping us with our inquiries and we're not letting them out together.'

Later, in Eddie Whicker's living room, we laughed long and hard about the curry house incident. It was good to see him again, it had been a while. It was tempting to feed his ego and tell him what the left thought of his hard-man heroics, after all there was nothing wrong with confirming what he already assumed. Whicker had been notable by his recent public absence and *Searchlight* had touched on it with me briefly. But Eddie Whicker was my friend, a good friend. I'd fumbled and skirted around the issue when *Searchlight* had asked but now, having to think clearly, it was obvious that he was dangerous, like having a pit-bull around young children; no matter how friendly it is, you know that deep down inside it wouldn't mind ripping into their necks. You didn't get tattoos or vernacular like his by just looking hard and menacing. For so long, that had been his attraction as some kind of pocket monster at my disposal but now that I had crossed over to the other side, those hands of his would strangle me without thinking twice.

Out of the blue, he pulled a video camera from behind his couch.

He'd been doing some more filming, this time of what looked like an ordinary suburban house with ordinary-looking suburban people coming and going. He grinned so widely, his tiny pencil moustache creased under his nose. 'This is the home of a fucking red who does stuff for the IRA,' he spat, his facial expression turning to revulsion. The videotape had already recorded a dozen or so Republican sympathisers, none of whom were known to us, going into a house that he would not tell me anything else about. On Hitler's birthday, 20 April, the UDA were

going to film people attending a Republican meeting at
Islington Town Hall. He brought up the possibility of
putting UDA activists unknown to the left on the coaches
or buses coming into town. The plan was to use the lists of
names I had given him via the Postman. Or, he said, 'Just
plant a fucking bomb on them.'

Was he serious? 'You watch the TV, Maff. You know
the score. There's blood on the streets in Belfast almost
every day. The fight is on. I've told Frank I want you on the
team 'cause I trust you. You've got principals.' Yes I did.
And a lot of Irish relatives too.

Rolan Adams was murdered in 1991, almost exactly
two years after the BNP shop opened to the public. It was
not entirely a surprise. While the BNP had been concentrating its main efforts on the East End, where it had traditions, overt racism in the borough of Greenwich, which
had never been a secret, seemed to be exploding from the
confidence the huge white population gained from having
the BNP in close proximity. Edmonds had stood in his
office in April of that year, telling the BBC's *Panorama*
program that the hate sheet *Holocaust News* for which he
was so proudly responsible, 'was a wonderful statement
of truth.'

I always thought of racism as acts done without the
knowledge of the victim: silent, snide comments, refusal
by a cab to pick up, turned down for a job in favour of
someone better 'suited'. But it was not just politicised
Nazis who went out and attacked people because of
their colour. The youth culture of knives and violence
that remained, for the most part, outside the school gates
when I was there, was finding its way in through a hole
in the fence. The youth centres were closed, the community vanishing. During my entire life on a council estate, I
never once encountered a youth worker. The estates were
already ghettos. The things said behind closed doors were

now repeated openly on street corners, and mobs of youths roamed around in gangs and cliques, identified by a street or their colour. The BNP was the only service offering free literature and counselling from their minibus, passing in the dead of night, putting out stickers and leaflets and free newspapers.

The Woolwich, Eltham and Thamesmead area used to have a fairly small but violent British Movement and skin following. The Nazi band Squadron lived and practised quite openly and drunkenly from a flat in a tower block on the Ferrier estate with a Union Jack across the window. Most grew up knowing an informal gang called the Nutty Turn-Out that made its name in the 1980s for being drawn from Charlton's tiny B-Mob hooligan firm, and Millwall's infamous Bushwackers. Nutty Turn-Out was just a name for young white guys, including NF members from across the river, who liked a ruck, would smell the trouble brewing and head for it. One night the Nutty Turn-Out was in the area looking for trouble, looking for a victim. They found one: a young black boy by the name of Rolan Adams. And stabbed him to death.

The television cameras arrived in Thamesmead quicker than a council plumber on overtime, pointing at the grey buildings built in the 1960s, when Thamesmead was a model environment for nice white families, with a large recreational boating pond in the middle, where I had gone canoeing while at school. Slowly a new picture began to emerge, of a community under attack from within. A community fuelled by the presence of an openly Nazi organisation on its doorstep, preaching hatred, offering sporadic solutions to random problems. Not all the boarded houses there were empty. Some had tenants inside, living in terror. What an insightful decision the BNP had made to open its office so close by. The BNP protested it was merely a gang fight. The murder resulted in swift condemnation, but what stuck most was the description: racist murder.

Thamesmead became a cause célèbre for the local news bulletins. It produced soundbites, ten seconds of people claiming Thamesmead was being marked by racist activity, and ten seconds in the BNP shop with Richard Edmonds, denying all guilt and all responsibility. Tensions were delicate, to say the least.

A group of local anti-racist activists made contact with The Reverend Al Sharpton, a firebrand black preacher from the United States. He heard what nobody else wanted to. Away from New York, blacks were still being downtrodden, this time in England. Blacks not stolen from Africa, but settled by invitation. He got on a plane and surrounded himself with young black men wearing sunglasses. Edmonds was delighted by Sharpton's arrival. It was going to stir the pot, and get up the noses of more Thamesmead residents. The stuttering old Teddy Boy who stood for the BNP in Greenwich, Ian Dell, not long out of the nick for killing an old couple in a road accident, organised a welcoming party for him.

Sharpton was to address a meeting at Friends House in Euston. I never thought for a minute anyone, even Dell, would dare walk into a meeting packed full of angry blacks and let off a smoke bomb. But that is just what he did. Two seconds later, the meeting was in uproar and Dell was hit by a car as he made his escape. The BNP minibus deserted him, leaving him bleeding and in the hands of the police. During the search of his house, Dell played the officers Nazi marching tunes and showed them his impressive collection of Nazi regalia and newspapers, swastikas and CS gas canisters. While tapping his foot along in time, the search officer is alleged to have said, 'Get rid of these [CS gas canisters]. After us, it's the [Special] Branch that comes calling.' How friendly were the Metropolitan Police in those days, eh?

More publicity followed the meeting, and again the BNP were elevated in the minds of the people unaffected by racism in their homes, who had watched an American black man accuse them of racism. Even I admired Dell's guts, and joined in the warm applause for him and his actions the next time he made it to Brick Lane.

'It's this easy,' said Edmonds. 'Matthew, the people are angry and we will fight back.' What were they fighting back against? I'm not sure anyone was clear about it.

And so I continued, more dedicated than ever before, to be the centre of attention. Blackham had begun to warm to me again, particularly as the NF was shrinking so dramatically. *Searchlight* was encouraged by the amount of information coming out of the far right. It was at this time I met another *Searchlight* mole, Tim Hepple, answering the phones at BNP HQ. Neither of us knew then what the other was up to.

'They say there is a race war going on around here,' said Edmonds, having showered in the kitchen. He mopped his bald head with the same towel he used to dry the special BNP coffee mugs, 'But that's not true. He [Adams] was just another nigger with a penknife. We did not create this, this has always been here.' But BNP activists were sure going to exacerbate the problem. 'They're calling the white people of Thamesmead racists, like it's a crime, like it is the worst thing you could ever be. A black kid lies dead, what about all the white kids, or the pensioners? We're going to march in Thamesmead, tell these coons and cops that we don't accept their prejudices. Join us and march, march with the BNP, Matthew, join a winning side. The spirit of National Socialism will provide for everyone.' Edmonds had that mad twinkle in his eye, like it was the most important thing in his life. Poor trash, he and I, but my life had to start looking rosier soon or I'd be as mad as Edmonds, with nothing to cling to.

Leaving behind those thoughts of race-hate and very slowly approaching light was like leaving a prison. It was only ever a day release though, because I now had to live a lie. I could tell no one about my new choice of direction. The level of excitement in my life had grown, but it was now fraught with danger. Even now I shudder when I think about the close shaves I was having, barely able to do anything a normal person would do in my situation. I felt like a cheating husband while my poor colleagues were like my wife at the kitchen sink. Meanwhile my new lover, *Searchlight*, wanted me to keep fucking my wife, keep bending her over the dishwasher. And that was all fine, all fun and rewarding, but if I met the girl of my dreams, what should I tell her? So I continued having tea with Edmonds, then meetings with the man from *Searchlight*, who I apparently infuriate with my miserable tales of woe.

Leaving London one Saturday, Anderson drove the new NF minibus up to Hemel Hempstead for an election meeting in support of our perennial losing candidate John McAuley. Begged and persuaded to join us, Eddie came along with the same camera he'd been using to capture the proposed future victims of a burgeoning mainland UDA.

Everyone is hoping we'll find some reds to slap, and we don't have a bad little team out for this one. Sheffield, Birmingham, Luton and London have sent their finest remaining young men to campaign for John. Eddie finally gives the order to head to the pub, where we find McAuley holed up in a corner, with Anderson attempting to dissuade him from his planned assault on the local reds. Eddie filmed us drinking, smoking, farting and clowning around, while outside the police gathered to escort us to the meeting hall which is, again, a local school.

As I left the pub there was a cool breeze making me feel unsteady on my feet. The air was filled with chants of 'Nazi scum off our streets,' and a few of the plump

Brummies tried to veer off to confront the couple of dozen protesters outside the school gate. One punch, though, and *Searchlight* would drop me like a bag of shit. 'No reds are to be slapped, in fact nobody. Not by you or anyone if you can help it. Stay out of trouble, keep your eyes and ears open.'

'I don't do that fighting thing. I'm a lover, not a fighter,' I told him, and again he raised his eyebrows, but this time he laughed: 'Don't tell me so many fucking lies, either.'

A hundred metres separated the school building from the school gates. There were no more than two dozen protestors, a mixed bag of old ladies and gobby hippies with black flags and underperforming facial growth. There was an almost carnival atmosphere as NF members milled inside and outside the school hall shouting, 'Let them in, we'll fucking hammer them.'

The protesters were demanding that they be escorted into the meeting. Anderson brushed past us and out to have a chat with the head plod. Eddie and I decided to accompany him to eavesdrop on his conversation with the plod. Inside the school hall the members had been in Ian's ear, demanding that the reds be allowed inside and Ian was sent out to make sure it happened. Behind us we could hear the growing bravado of the lads getting ready, picking and choosing for themselves whomever it was at the school gates that they wanted to fight, while Eddie and I were trying to find someone with half-decent breasts to focus the camera on. Ian was halfway between us and them, chatting away calmly, when through the gates came thirty or so rather large men, pushing their way through the protesters.

'Ooh Eddie,' I say rather grimly. 'We've got a bit of bother at hand here.' The large men are waving at Ian and getting closer, walking in almost slow motion. 'Hello Ian, how the fuck are you?'

The panic went up behind us as the plod were closing the school doors, trapping the NF members inside as Ian took his first blow from the group. 'It's fucking Red Action,' gasped Eddie, dropping the camera to his side and turning to me with horror on his face. Ian had rolled himself into a ball while the rest of the mob made for us. Eddie and I stared blankly at each other.

'Run?' I asked, as Eddie hid the camera inside his over-coat. We ran to the school, banging on the doors to be let in, while a couple of NF members climbed through the windows to get outside at the reds.

'Why are you running, Maff?' asks Eddie as I pass a flustered Blackham trying to get past us and protect the fallen Führer.

There was what could be called carnage in the school grounds, bloody lips and bloody fascists, while inside the school, men who came to fight could only push against police officers. Those who climbed through windows to get out and fight gave a good account of themselves but they were well outnumbered. One red even pulled an NF member out through the window where he was having second thoughts about joining the fray and stamped on his head when he hit the ground.

The reds departed the scene as quickly as they had arrived, seemingly brushing the police aside as they went. We all stood in astonished silence. We had been battered, our leader humbled and humiliated. The police had locked the majority of the NF in the school and watched the fighting from the sidelines.

In the school reception area, national organiser John Hill held an inquest with those assembled. He laid the blame fairly and squarely at Blackham's feet. 'Why wasn't he with Ian when Ian went out to talk to the Old Bill? What fucking use is he politically? He's supposed to mind Ian against red attack, not prance around the fucking area acting tough and then being unavailable when it goes off!'

People sat in corners with their heads in their hands, blood was smeared over the walls. Eddie and I went back outside where the police were examining the broken windows and the school caretaker was measuring up for replacements. Eddie found the whole thing very amusing. Others came outside to show off their battle scars.

'Why do they do it?' asked one young lad. 'Why do they want to kill us all the time, don't they know about the niggers and the Pakis and the IRA? We're supposed to be fighting them, not other whites.' He had a rather impressive boot mark down the side of his face and his eye was all closed up.

Eddie just brushed him off, uninterested. 'If you don't know reds, it's pointless even discussing it with you,' he sniffed. 'Go and clean yourself the fuck up and don't talk to me.' Then he laughed. 'It's the only way these kids are gonna learn Maff. There needs to be a lot more of this before they wake the fuck up.'

John Hill presented me with a squeezy lemon full of ammonia and some dye that he had added for maximum effect. 'When we get out of here squeeze that into some fucker's face,' he said solemnly. It became known as the Goldfish Incident when I poured the contents into the school fish tank instead.

CHAPTER 21

Eddie invited me over on Monday night to watch the video footage that he had shot at Hemel Hempstead. He insisted we go out for tea as he suspected that his flat was now being bugged.

'The phone's been ringing Maff,' he whispered, 'they're going to expel you from the NF.'

That evening I got the expected call from Anderson. He felt it necessary to clear his throat before he spoke. I knew what was coming and I knew my response. 'Matthew, you've been suspended from the party.' I gave a little cough. Immediately I said I wanted to appeal which sent Anderson into a tiz. There was something like a dozen other people wanting an appeal over their own expulsions. 'That means we have to convene a special committee or something, I can't do that,' he said. Then there was a deathly silence.

'I'm afraid you'll have to,' I said, finding my confidence. I knew a fair amount of party protocol. No committee was convened and I undertook a solemn oath not to bring disrepute on to the party ever again.

The staff at *Searchlight* had watched the video fifteen or sixteen times over a few cold beers, continually winding to where Anderson goes to greet the team at the gate, before falling to the floor in fits of laughter. I concentrated my attentions on the forthcoming BNP Thamesmead march, which if I was to attend, would finish me off in the NF once and for all. There was fury in the NF that I had disobeyed an instruction to squirt ammonia in someone's eyes, to atone for Anderson's humiliation. It was all part of the victim mentality; fancy poisoning some

MATTHEW COLLINS 227

school fish when I should have sought justice by blinding some lefty.

The phone rang again. 'This is Keith Thompson, you may have heard of me.' Actually I had, but I said that I had not. I hate people who announce themselves like that. Thompson was one of those secretive Nazis that young boys like me had once dreamed of coming to our rescue with bundles of cash, style and influence.

'I'm from the League,' he announced. Thompson had watched the video of Eddie and I playing up at Hemel Hempstead and had concluded, along with McAuley, that Eddie and I would work well inside his organisation. In its heyday, the League of St George had been a very influential Irish Nationalist group liaising between British and European terrorists. Italian terrorists in particular were keen to use the League when on the run from their own authorities. The League of St George provided safe houses for just about any international Nazi that wanted one.

'Rather than going to the BNP march at Thamesmead, a rather awful affair, I wondered if you and Eddie Whicker would care to join John McAuley as my guests, at a meeting of the League being held at Kensington Library?' I said I'd think about it. Obviously I would have to check with Whicker, and with *Searchlight*.

Eddie was already choosing himself a shirt to wear when I called him. 'This is a step toward sthe big time,' Eddie said excitedly. The man from *Searchlight* described it more a step towards the old time, but the League of St George was full of pure out-and-out National Socialists, all ageing, but still with some behind-the-scenes influence internationally. Underlining this was the fact that Tony Lecomber was also going to address the meeting on behalf of the BNP, and Steve Brady was billed to appear in his individual capacity as a former leading light in the League before he joined the NF. A lot of other fringe dwellers, including old associates and supporters of Oswald Mosley, were also billed to appear. Basically, anyone considering themselves too sinister to poke their head above the parapet would be there, including the Italian terrorists living in London and very close to the old Griffin/Harrington wing of the NF.

That Saturday, The BNP bussed in dozens of thugs from the East End and Essex for their march in Thamesmead, where they were to pass only a few hundred metres from the scene of Adams's murder. Three or four pubs around Eltham and Greenwich were attacked and patrons assaulted as the BNP tried to prevent counter-demonstrators getting at the march. The team was led by hardened BNP activists and joined by the south London British Movement, who had to make a decision about what to do with the BNP, now fully ensconced in their area. Around 300 BNP marched, which was considered a huge success. The news was just breaking of trouble at the march when Eddie and I were at Euston Station waiting for McAuley's train to arrive.

McAuley was more flustered than usual when we met, claiming that Anderson had banned Brady from speaking at the last minute. Kensington was at peace. It was a sunny day and the beautiful people were dining al fresco, or walking their pampered pooches and greeting each other with hugs and kisses on the pavements.

We found the library off the high street with Thompson and an overweight minder in full Nazi regalia, standing to attention outside.

'Heard about the fish incident,' said Thompson as a way of breaking the ice. 'An unfortunate error of judgement probably,' he continued. I was pushed for something to say until it dawned on Whicker there was no security at the venue. 'Who's doing the door here, Keith?' he said, sounding concerned.

Thompson motioned to the overweight man in Nazi

regalia and said, 'You guys are very early, there won't be any trouble. Why don't you go for a drink?' This seemed like a marvellous idea to me and McAuley, but Whicker didn't drink, and wanted to stay. He realised that by standing on the door he would receive adulation from those old Nazis who had heard of his fearsome reputation.

'What about reds though Keith, aren't you worried?' Whicker persisted. Thompson was having none of it. He had every faith in a fat little man dressed all in black, with foreign badges and oversized boots, who really would have been better off at home in an armchair with a bottle of light ale resting on his belly. It was a warm and balmy evening, the only noise was that of the wind rustling the leaves in the trees. We stood on the little square outside the library and there seemed no reason whatsoever to think there would be trouble.

'The reds are in south London and as I hear it they've taken a pounding all day long,' Thompson crowed. He really was a greasy man, square-headed and unshaven, with a mop of stiff, black hair. He had incredible confidence seeing as how we'd only just been turned over ourselves the week before. Like a petulant child, I began tugging on Eddie's sleeves. 'He said it's fine Eddie, let's go for a pint,' I begged.

Now my drinking has got me in a lot of trouble in the past, still does sometimes, but had I not insisted on 'one for the road', then we would have run smack into a no-holds-barred orgy of blood and guts. Just as Eddie's Coca-Cola joined the two pints on the bar, we could hear ambulances and police cars in the near distance. Immediately we looked at each other in horror. 'Finish your drink Eddie,' I pleaded, but both his and John's were left firmly on the bar and off they rushed in the direction of the library, with me lagging behind chuffing on a Woodbine.

The man in the Nazi regalia had done a runner at

the sight of fifty or so anti-fascists crashing towards the meeting hall. They had appeared like a swarm, brandishing tickets to the event, sending Nazi-man on his way. They then split into two groups, one group manning the doors and letting unsuspecting old-timers into the downstairs meeting room where they were to be addressed, not by fellow Nazis, but by Gerry Gable himself, who had taken over the meeting.

As the meeting was settling down to a bit of harsh banter, some skinheads had arrived upstairs and, sensing something was wrong, tried to battle their way in. By the time they made it downstairs, the place was in uproar and everyone was running for cover. When the skinheads made it into the library meeting room, they battered anyone they could see, which included many old-time Nazis. Gable appealed for calm but it must have been useless, and the skinheads were in an awful mess sprawled out on the pavement when the anti-fascists fought back. As the fascists tried to fight their way out they came across more reds fighting their way in and they were done for good.

As Gable left the building, Thompson had apparently thanked him for his restraint, which I thought was a bit strange. I lit another Woodbine as we surveyed the mess of bloodied Nazis telling the lone black paramedic to 'Piss off nigger.'

The fat doorman returned, to derisive howls, while the shaken Thompson tried to explain what happened. 'Gable tried to keep it calm, but it was useless. We didn't have enough security, we never thought this was going to happen.'

Lecomber appeared late, bringing the news that the BNP had fared little better themselves in Thamesmead and, despite a good start, had been turned over there too by the sheer weight of reds. On seeing the bloody mess that was there to greet him, he went all pale, while John McAuley and I drew breaths of relief that we had not been standing on the door with the great Eddie Whicker when the reds had turned up.

Whicker though, seemed genuinely disappointed. 'I knew we should have stayed. Bollocks!' Lecomber quickly made himself busy instructing everyone to blame Gable and to give statements to the police saying as much.

'We'll get Gable for this, we know where he lives,' he went on to tell the meeting. Indeed he did. Not long before, Lecomber had been arrested for going to Gable's house. The cop was the very same officer who had arrested poor Tony some years previously, at the beginning of his criminal career!

The meeting eventually started and droned on and on for a good two hours, which had even Eddie wishing that the reds had done a better job. The room of 100 of Britain's most brilliant and committed Nazis was a sea of bandages and broken glasses. Fire extinguishers remained strewn across the floor, having been pulled off the walls and used as weapons earlier in the evening. Police officers lined the walls, too bored to even be shocked by the bile they were listening to.

Two things came out of this meeting however. Firstly, the end of a long and undistinguished career for Thompson, and a decision by Whicker to play a major part in the formation of a professional security team for the far right, something akin to Le Penn's in France. If they were to keep getting turned over, the UDA would drop them like a sack of the smelly stuff, and permanently dent the plans he and Frank had for forming a tough loyalist street army on the mainland.

The phone rang very early the next morning, before I headed to Brick Lane to hear the heroic tales from the day before. It was *Searchlight*, chatting away but not apologising for letting me nearly walk slap bang into a red rent-a-mob.

Overnight a discussion had already begun between various people that the reds had gone too far, turning over the far right twice in one day. Old Nazis being humiliated and having their protectors being battered was a serious matter.

'These people are our history, a true link to our past. If we can't protect them what use are we? We need to understand the reds, what they want and how they operate. They're smart fuckers. It ain't the SWP or the Communist Party we're running from, it's blokes who look just us, talk like us. Fuck the Labour Party and the Pakis, they're not doing anything. There's a fucking war going on. We've got to clean these fuckers up, have a go back at them. I ain't gonna let fucking reds dictate where and when our people can meet, no way.' The speaker, Charlie Sargent, was getting the twenty-odd blokes in the pub riled up good and proper. This is what Eddie had been on about at Hemel Hempstead. They wanted to know the enemy intimately and up close.

Gerry Gable was likely to be arrested. They were really out to get him. But why, I had to ask, did Thompson shake the hand of the man he and every other Nazi in Britain hated the most? After all, Gerry Gable had made it his life's mission to humiliate and expose Nazis. And Keith was the leader of the notorious Nazi League of St George. Would you believe that the two of them went back a long, long way? I was astonished by Thompson's behaviour, and wondered whether he had given the reds the information to come into the meeting.

Gable was arrested three months later, though his trial stopped after four days of Nazis lying through their teeth. Every piece of evidence against him was concocted and in fact, very few Nazis knew what Gable looked like, even the ones that claimed they'd been there. Thompson, of course, is now in the BNP.

The only independent witness, the library caretaker, identified some BM supporters in full uniform as the men who had turned up for the meeting, armed to the teeth. Most of the witnesses against Gable had some previous for violence. To add insult to injury, Thompson got landed with the bill from the council to have the carpets and hall cleaned of his comrades' blood stains.

The Kensington Library events were significant as they would eventually lead to the formation of the murderous Nazi hit-squad, C18.

Charlie Sargent, who had spoken at the Lane about the street army he envisaged taking the fight to the reds, was an overweight, knife-carrying, drug-peddling lout. Sargent and Whicker became the London UDA commander's lieu-tenants in the far right.

CHAPTER 22

Initially, Derek Beackon, who went on to become the infamous first-ever elected BNP councillor, was put up for the job of head of the new security team. Despite his advancing years, Beackon had never been involved in the NF but had come to the BNP in the late 1980s, after drifting in and out of versions of the old British Movement. I warned *Searchlight* that, now that the BNP was taking its security seriously, maybe I would be better off on the outside. *Searchlight* and I never sat down and properly talked about an agenda for me. I mostly met with them because I was drawn to the new – to me – art of adult conversation and the occasional posh cup of tea, served on a saucer out of a teapot. Of course they were judging me, but they never let me know it. If they wanted me to go somewhere, I knew I had to go. I knew deep down that I was spying on the people that spied on me and that someone, somewhere was telling them the stupid things that I did, but they never told me about it.

We took tea with club sandwiches and talked about music; it's how I got to own my very first Billy Bragg CD. They were proper people who read books. And I know that sometimes when I left wherever it was we were meeting, they followed me all the way home or to whichever pub they thought I was safe in. I must have told them a hundred times that I was walking away, and a hundred more times, a phone call from a fascist colleague would drag me back in, because all I had was angry mates and polite conversations with *Searchlight*.

Over at the BNP office-cum-bookshop in Welling, Tony

Lecomber was pushing very hard for the death of the NF and he gladly saw me as a willing contributor. The BNP was growing fast and Edmonds was always at the front of the shop entertaining the curious and the voyeurs alike. Some people knocked on the door and wanted to chat in the doorway, some even panicked as Richard tried to hurriedly usher them into the shop. He may have been tall, bald and imposing and perhaps a little mad, but he was polite, educated and generous too. He'd give anybody goods straight off the shelves, whether they wanted them or not.

Out the back of the shop, Lecomber immersed himself in his own business. He'd begun writing long and tiresome articles for party publications that were as monotone as his conversation. His grudge against the NF was personal. After his release from prison, he'd tried to ingratiate himself with the NF. He'd been shunned and privately accused of being state. He was a serious weight around the neck of the BNP's precious public image. Tyndall, himself no stranger to wanting to blow things up in his youth, encouraged Tony not to let his conviction weigh him down. In public, the BNP would refer to it as an 'experiment in fireworks' gone wrong, or in Tyndall's own words, 'youthful indiscretion'. But a conviction for something so militant, particularly when he had been so young, was something Lecomber was immensely proud of. There was always an onus to prove yourself and the courage of your convictions, so he was not happy with people claiming he had rolled over for the state for a reduced sentence. It's largely ignored now or, they hope, forgotten, but it was Lecomber who began pushing a slightly modern approach in the BNP in the early 1990s.

Tony recognised that no matter how the party as a whole may have felt politically, it was not going to grow further when, along with some people's receptiveness to their anti-immigration policies, the party also had a completely justifiable image as mad Nazis. He wasn't becoming anti-Nazi in any way, and he most certainly was not against the organisation being militant but he seemed to want to sit halfway between what the BNP had and what the NF wanted.

The NF was bankrupting itself continuing with profess-ional-looking publications and attempts at an image makeover. Lecomber had pushed for the BNP's party paper, *British Nationalist*, to go monthly like *The Flag* and volunteered to help write and edit it, slowly reducing the grip of Tyndall's hands on everything the party produced.

Lecomber had been pushing the BNP to fight more elections, to take on the NF and destroy it. Eddy Butler's 'Rights for Whites' campaign in the East End had seen large numbers of disaffected locals flock to, often violent and always confrontational, BNP demonstrations and marches and this had to be transformed into votes. No one else in the BNP was particularly keen on the idea of elections, but they were doing slightly better than the NF was, as proved by selectively comparing election results.

Where Edmonds and Tyndall scoured the newspapers for evidences of Jewish conspiracies and 'alien crime', Lecomber scoured the same newspapers for opportunities, picking out instances of racial tension or inequalities that might offend whites. Edmonds scoured the court section, looking for Jewish names up on fraud; I stuck to the sports section and poked my nose around for membership lists. Parties like the BNP and NF always lied that their member-ship lists are well hidden, but they never were.

Lecomber even wrote to the very NF branches he had regularly antagonised, offering his services as a speaker at any forthcoming meetings. There was already some resent-ment against Lecomber over his meteoric rise, particularly as it seemed to come at the expense of the untainted Eddy Butler, an equally monotone but skilful organiser. Surprisingly, some of the more militant people in the BNP were the ones who hated Lecomber most. Tyndall was not daft however. He might have had convictions himself for running around with guns and Nazi uniforms in his distant past, but he knew that even Lecomber could not think of himself as leadership material.

A decision had been made to form a strong-arm security group – and news eventually reached Anderson. 'What position are you and Eddie [Whicker] taking on this new security group?' he shouted down the phone. I said that I didn't know if it was up and running properly or whether it was mainly just an East End thing. Immediately he wanted me to spy on it and refuse to be a member at the same time! I told him flatly that he'd lost Eddie and he sighed. 'Is there no hope on that front?' Once more I was summoned to East Ham for 'discussions'.

'I've known Charlie Sargent for years,' Anderson told me, while sitting on his couch. 'I'm telling you he is not to be trusted. He's into drugs in a big way and it wouldn't surprise me if he was state.' Why was everyone state? And why was the state supposedly so interested in us all of the time? We had a lot of tough talkers, lunatics and hard nuts but we hardly ran large-scale terrorist operations. We took, on the whole, a voyeuristic and occasionally helpful interest in our European colleagues' violent terrorism and occasionally the odd idiot got himself caught playing with a gun in his bedroom or back garden, but we were responsible for little more state subversion than perhaps a gang of third division football hooligans. We were criminally inclined pub brawlers and occasional drunken racist attackers, but it was not as if we had organised the Poll Tax riots or London bombing campaigns like some of our opponents on the left had. Politically, we were little more than a poorly organised pressure valve built around obsessive personality cults.

A situation was developing in outer west London and

Ian was wondering whether either Eddie or I could bring muscle over to help. I doubted it. The NF's new branch had been run off its patch by a combination of the lefties, and young black males threatening them with knives. In any other instance ordinary people would just walk away and dump the idea of even attempting to make a breakthrough there but in the face of an enormous and exploitive BNP in both the south and the east of the capital it became necessary to defend the patch.

Despite instructions to 'find out where' by *Searchlight*, Anderson ventured nothing more. 'It's out of my hands,' he said. I'd almost forgotten about it until Terry Blackham arrived on my doorstep early one morning a week or two later.

'Fancy a drive to Hounslow?' he asked, hopping from one foot to the other and rubbing his unshaven chin. I grabbed my favourite dark-green jumper and joined Terry and some of his mates for the drive. On the way over to Hounslow I broke the awful uncomfortable feeling in the car by acting the clown and cracking jokes. 'You're Matthew aren't you?' asks one of the blokes. 'I used to get your bulletins, they were funny.'

The sweet sounds of Skrewdriver blasted out of the speaker as we sped up. Well, I was fucked now. I knew it was to be a 'hit' on some reds. Perhaps the long arm of the law would intervene as we all sipped lager and travelled as fast and dangerously as London's roads would allow.

We parked the car in a back street and walked through town. Hounslow had a pretty poor, pretty un cosmopolitan market on a bland pedestrianised street. We strolled through town, only stopping so that Terry could make a phone call from a phone box. He returned with a smug grin on his face.

'Ginger Rick's with the local lads, they'll be along in a minute.' It was only just after ten and the sun was already burning. In the middle of the high street outside the main entrance to an arcade we found our pitch. The local lads were not to be seen. There were a few other people milling around, a collection of lefties from different parts of the Judean People's Front who were remarkably late in setting up themselves. We went and stood right in the middle of them, Terry dropping his sports bag with a large thud, but they hardly noticed we were there. They were in their little sects, avoiding looking at each other, never mind bothering with us. Within a minute of us starting selling our papers, the number of reds began to grow, a good mix of ages and sexes but all white and all middle class, not the sorts of people that had been turning us over in recent months.

By now the lefties were getting organised, beginning to sort themselves into proper teams to sell their various papers. There were nearly twenty of them and we were right in the middle of them, just the four of us. Terry even managed to sell a paper. The buyer went straight to the lefties and waved it in their faces as he walked past. The penny dropped, albeit very quietly.

A young man from one of the groups walked around us to talk to another of the groups, who in turn followed him back to his group for a mini-conference. Then they walked towards another bunch of lefties who had already decided to pack up and go home. 'Militant,' said one of the NF blokes, nodding at the reds. 'They'll have a go.'

Everybody was a little twitchy. Terry had an enormous grin on his face, a grin that I knew meant he was about to explode into violence. I started getting nervous.

'We're too outnumbered if they're gonna have a go,' I hissed. 'Don't panic yet. There's more to come,' Terry replied, still grinning. From down the road come three members of the local NF, laughing and shouting stupidly, 'Alright Terry, alright lads?'

Shoppers passed by oblivious to either group of political

extremists preparing to do battle. The local lads were
very, very cocky and began pointing out those amongst
the reds those who had run them off their patch in the
previous weeks.

The reds eventually began a chant of 'Nazi scum off our
streets' and then I really started getting nervous. They were
drawing attention to themselves, they were preparing to
attack. From behind us, two cars pulled up and out jumped
half a dozen men for our side. It was on.

Blackham let out a huge 'Yeeees' and off we went. I was
mesmerised for a second because I couldn't work out who
was who but I did see the old pool ball in a sock being
swung, and ducked for cover. The entire high street came
to a standstill, as twenty-odd people rolled on the floor,
screamed and threw punches. *Searchlight*'s instructions
were in my head, 'No bashing reds, no bashing anyone,'
but a cocky little bastard knocked me to the floor then
came back for more, so I dove right into him. We fall on
the floor in a grapple. Seconds later, the sirens started wail-
ing and our cars started pulling away, leaving only six of
us BNP and a lot of bloody, messed-up people. My green
jumper was torn to buggery and my jeans had blood on
them. It was time to depart.

As we ran down Hounslow High Street, some public-
spirited citizens tried to stop us.

'They were IRA supporters,' I protested.

'Fucking IRA supporters, mate, that's why we gave
them a kicking,' said Terry in tandem.

My legs were so heavy I could barely run. A red grabbed
Terry's arm again, so Terry threw a fistfull of loose change
at him and brandished a hammer in his face and we made
our escape. At the time there was no back exit from Marks
and Sparks in Hounslow, so if you're ever shoplifting
there, don't try and make your escape through it. We ran
around the store for a second, before we ventured back

out onto the pavement and walked past four running bobbies. I dumped the bloody jumper in the bin and began to walk calmly down the road, but the noise of the sirens was coming closer and someone was shouting 'Roadblock, there's a fucking roadblock.'

I fixed my eyes firmly ahead, confident that without the jumper no one would be able to pick me out. 'The police might put one of them in a car and come looking,' Terry warned and calmly walked into the first pub he saw, heading for the beer garden. I suggested we jump over the back wall, but it led nowhere so I then suggested a drink to calm matters down. The barmaid told us knowingly, that the police were everywhere, so she'd give us this drink but then we'd have to call a cab and leave.

We took cabs out of town, passing close enough to see the police cars and ambulances at the scene. At another watering hole, we dissected the punch-up. 'We had to give a little back to the reds,' said Terry, standing over the group. The order had obviously come from up top that the dogs had to be let off the leash for the day. It was like sex for a married man.

CHAPTER 23

Whilst the NF were turning over a small group of Trotskyite reds in Hounslow, BNP stalwart and South African-born racist, Steve Tyler, was beaten up while delivering leaflets advertising a BNP demonstration due to take place in Bermondsey. This made Eddie very excited when the news was relayed to him. As we exchanged gossip about another weekend outbreak of violence, Eddie said, 'The word's out Maff, things are getting really fucking heavy. The reds are going to get it, bad.'

Next, Edmonds rang me in similar whispering tones. 'Look, my advice to you is to lie low, that's what we're all doing. The reds and the Jews are putting our members in hospital. Lie low. I'll see you at the shop.'

Edmonds had also been attacked recently. Someone had gone for him in the lane behind the shop where he had been parking the BNP minibus. 'Good reconnaissance on their part,' someone offered by way of praise to the reds. The far left took assaulting what they called 'the fash' very seriously. Red Action even ran seminars where they instructed their members who worked on building sites to smash people cracking racist jokes in the face with the nearest available brick.

The shop was full of people tutting about poor Steve Tyler's beating. Beackon was there, scratching his head with one hand while his other rested on the hammer in his pocket. Everyone was scared of getting off the train at Welling in case there were reds waiting around. 'There's going to be retribution,' Beackon growled. 'This state of affairs is not on. They're fucking cowards.' And with that everyone began hatching plots to attack reds in their beds while they slept.

In their coverage of the Hounslow attack, August's *Searchlight* referred to us as an NF goon-squad and ran a photograph of Terry and me. It also outed previously unnamed NF members and my arse began to quiver. We met in a bar over Kensington way. Gerry Gable bought me another Billy Bragg CD, so that small indiscretion was forgotten. *Searchlight* had named the people involved in the attack so that those who were hurt would know who had attacked them. Blackham would be furious about this, but hey, my name was there too. I relayed the information from the bookshop, but it was only that any red could be hit at any moment, and to look to Beackon if there was any major incident.

The charges against the Curry House Five were dropped when none of the student doctors involved in the incident were prepared to give evidence. Once they'd been reminded that they would be up against NF members, they must have decided against going ahead with it. The name NF could still fill people with fear, particularly when they found one of them on their doorstep with a large hammer.

In response to the growth in far-right violence, AFA made a decision to get the far right off the streets in east London permanently. Both sides were now prepared for a long, drawn out confrontation. The far right was already upping its game for this battle, still not interested in wining council seats or seats in the European Parliament. The race war was still about control of the streets. People from all over the country were converging on an east London market on a Sunday to engage in ideological bloody street fights.

On my return from a week's holiday in Devon, Edmonds greeted me at the shop. There had been much excitement during my week away over plans by a black-led organisation to march in Bermondsey.

'These niggers,' said Edmonds, holding up a black community newspaper, 'are going to march in Bermondsey, *our* Bermondsey, complaining about racism. We've really got the locals on our side, come and join us. Let's send these niggers a clear message like in Thamesmead, that whites will not be intimidated into giving in to black demands.' Edmonds stretched out a little, speaking warmly of Bermondsey. 'They don't want coons and Jews telling them they can't live the way they want to. It doesn't make sense. These blacks, these *blacks*, they're just the tool of the Jews anyway.'

I passed *Searchlight* the crude leaflet that the BNP had been distributing in Bermondsey about the march by the National Black Caucus. I couldn't see why, but the march was also attracting much criticism from the left. Apparently, even though I had been a white racist, I still failed to understand English ethnicity. Wouldn't most people just go shopping for the day, ignore all the fuss and commotion and continue with their ordinary lives?

I agreed I'd go to the demonstration. I agreed to go for *Searchlight*, I agreed to go with the BNP, and when Blackham and then Woods both rang independently of each other, I agreed to go with the NF.

We met at the Blue Market. Ginger Rick was the first to arrive. The usual faces began to crawl their blinkered ways into the area in threes and fours with their hands shoved into their jean pockets. Bermondsey was awash with white faces that day, even more so than usual. There was a torturous expectancy in the air. It wouldn't help the National Black Caucus that Millwall were playing at home that day. Sure enough, the BNP produced a handy-looking thirty or so lads who stood staring at the NF's half a dozen. 'There's going to be a huge fucking riot today,' said Terry confidently. It was as if we were minutes from all his Christmases coming at once.

I actually doubted there would be a riot. I was certain there would be an angry and vociferous demonstration and no doubt someone somewhere would end up with their face being kicked mercilessly by some brave, boozed-up Nazi. But as a rule, we didn't do riots, as we didn't have the numbers or the organisation. What we could do though, was get other people to do those things for us.

We split from the BNP and headed for a nearby pub, which was breakneck full of football casuals. This was nothing to do with us. I did not feel welcome and surprisingly, neither did Terry. We decided to stay away from the football supporters, but then Nick Cooper turned the corner with a group from the Nutty Turn-Out.

'There'll be no football today until we've cleaned all the niggers out of the area,' he said confidently and with real menace. With him were hardened street fighters, the rent-a-mob I had dreamed of back in Enfield the year before. We mixed it up with the Millwall supporters, who generally agreed that they would not join the BNP or NF demonstration, but would use their presence to really have a go at the marchers. Hooligans will fight for any cause.

'It ain't a racist thing mate, it's a Millwall thing.'

There were few police in the area this early, so it must have dawned on them pretty late, that the usual crew of a couple of hundred from the Old Kent Road were strangely absent at the football ground. Eventually they began to scour the Bermondsey pubs close to the march, and found a 300-strong crowd of pissed-up yobbos with Union Jacks and fascist newspapers getting aggressive. Probably because it was a football crowd, the police asked for the pubs to be closed. Hundreds of angry young white men in designer jeans and trainers poured onto the streets, lagered up without the promise of a kebab or a Vindaloo this early.

While the mob milled around without direction, the BNP appeared as if by magic to stand at the head of the throng,

and led the mob towards a pre-arranged static picket which
the police had set up and not manned adequately. Football
was definitely off the menu as everyone crushed against the
barriers and waited for the march to come up the road. At
first Blackham decided not to join the static demonstration
so the few NF supporters hung around, away from where
the BNP were leading choruses of *Rule Britannia* and *God
Save the Queen*.

As the march got closer, police began running along
the pavement to where the mob was starting to rattle the
barricades, and the football mob began a chant of *South
London* as if it were West Ham supporters marching past.
We ended up being swept into the back of the mob. The
more police that turned up, the more aggressive it became.
The police began to look nervous; their training might give
them the warning signs that a riot is imminent, but I only
became certain that it was by the looks on their terrified
young faces.

The NF lads were grinning. From the back of the mob,
we watched the crowd push as the march got closer and
began to turn away into the park around the corner.

'Niggers, fuck off niggers,' began the abuse, and the NF
pushed their way towards the front, causing a crush where
Edmonds and his BNP generals had positioned themselves.
The BNP were chanting: 'Tool of the Jews, tool of the Jews,'
but that did not catch on with the football supporters. The
shoving became more persistent and more aggressive as the
march came into close eyeshot. I did not see how many of
them there were, but my stomach tightened as I realised
the police were not able to control the bloodthirsty mob
behind these barricades.

Up on the balconies behind us, old ladies hung out
their Union Jack tea towels and watched the black marchers from their vantage point. The police began to move
against the barricades, looking us in the eyes shouting,

'Come on fellas, calm down, don't start,' when from the back, another huge push saw the barriers collapse onto them. A huge cheer went up and the mob stormed towards the park. The police were beaten. Some of the football fans stayed to fight with them, and the anger, the alcohol and the sun began to boil up in everyone who headed towards the park and after the marchers.

By the time I got into the park, there was already a trail of destruction. Blacks in the park for nothing more than some nice weather and a read of the paper were nursing bruised faces as hundreds of pissed and racist hooligans ran past them, pretending they were on an international football excursion. The march was stuck and unable to move. The BNP positioned themselves for photographs. It was going to be their day.

It shouldn't have been about the march. Surely they were angry because they wanted to know where were *their* jobs, where were *their* new homes, where was *their* hope? Why did no one listen to us? I was after all, one of them; an angry white face continually pushed into the dirt. None of us were living in the new homes with riverside views and burgeoning youth, music and cultural projects.

The police wanted to negotiate. 'That's enough now lads. We can't move on if you're blocking the way. You've had your fun, please disperse.'

Word spread immediately that the black marchers were not to be allowed to leave the park unharmed. 'These black cunts will never leave the park alive,' one bloke said, sidling up to me spreading the message. Nick the Nazi pressed past me and said, 'Terry wants you right at the front.' There was a lingering standoff. The mob was only catching its breath. Still there were no sirens announcing police reinforcements, as wide-eyed and panicked police officers shouted angrily into their radios in anticipation of a bloodbath.

I pushed my way through rank after rank of football hooligans until I reached the front where Blackham stood with the BNP goon squad. I took in the faces of angry strangers gasping for breath, planning in their hushed tones and secret football code what was to happen next. Steve Tyler proclaimed into a loudhailer that the blacks should 'Go back to the jungle.' The crowd cheered loudly.

'Get on the loudhailer and shout NF,' barked Blackham. Tyler obliged, probably through fear of Blackham, by giving me the loudhailer. 'We are the National Front, you are not...' and with that Eddy Butler grabbed the loud-hailer from me and begun a chant of 'Rights For Whites!' which, once the rest of the BNP goons had begun, got the whole crowd up and chanting. The police didn't know who to negotiate with. I assumed it was their football hooligan spotters who were pointing people out, but there seemed to be more people swelling the ranks of the mob than the ranks of the boys in blue. Millwall's ground was not that far away, where were the rest of the Old Bill?

A mixed-race couple held hands and came and danced close to the fascist demonstration, causing the policemen to start getting anxious.

'Come on guys, get back, give us room. Don't be wound up by them.'

A stupid plod announced to us that the march was going to be marched back out of the area, so we would wait where we were and then be allowed to have a rally ourselves. That seemed to please the BNP, this was a good result. Could we not go back home now, try and catch the highlights of the Millwall game on TV? Before Edmonds could step forward and accept plod's kind offer, someone from the Millwall mob spoke up:

'Let's do the fucking march!'

A huge cheer went up from the crowd and off they ran again to confront the marchers from a side street.

Edmonds and some of the BNP hung around, splitting the police's resources, while into the streets ran the angry white mob, arming themselves with anything they could grab. It was a simple question of circling the park to get back to the front of the retreating march. As the police tried to move the march out of the park, 300 young men stood in their way. Then the rocks started flying and the aggression boiled over as people ran right up to the police to throw their missiles into the march. The police began to move forwards towards the mob but all the mob did was throw their stones and bottles from further back, mainly hitting the police, something which has never really bothered Millwall hooligans too much.

Around me grown men, not just kids, stood with their fists clenched around objects, screaming venomous hate at the marchers and the police. Edmonds walked past me saying, 'Don't throw stones at the police!' As if I would! After a while the police regained their numbers and began pushing back at the mob. The mob began to retreat, but only because they wanted to go into the familiar series of railway tunnels in the area. From behind came police on motorcycles. Voices begun shouting, 'Get the police on the bikes,' and more rocks and bottles flew in their direction, causing them to spin their motorcycles around and retreat from the hail.

Hundreds of angry whites were now in the tunnels grouping together before splitting off, without any police there to control them. Further up the road a good 100 metres away, officers were trying to group up to come into the tunnel and push the mob out of the area. Nick the Nazi ran past me shouting, 'We're moving onto the estate, we're gonna flush out some niggers.'

On their yellow-bricked estate, locals stood at their open doors, nodding at the mob running past their homes swearing and shouting. The estate led into another maze of tunnels. In one tunnel were cars, unable to move as marauding thugs ran through, banging car bonnets. As they ran a large skinhead pointed out that one of the cars had black occupants. Nick and I watched as a mob jumped onto the car and began to try and pull the occupants out. Someone dumped a dustbin onto the bonnet and a huge cheer went up as another car was overturned. I could hear windows breaking and people pointing out shops not owned by whites – 'This one, this one's a Paki shop,' followed by a smash and more cheering. And in amongst it all, among all this mayhem, a photographer walked, taking photographs calmly and discreetly, taking his time to position himself for a good picture of cars being trashed by fascists and football hooligans.

'Shall we do the fucking photographer?' Nick asked, wide-eyed and panting. He was standing within feet of him, with a knife in his hand.

'Don't be so fucking stupid,' I said with horrified panic in my voice.

His eyes closed for a rare moment of deep thought. He leaned forward into me, 'I've got to stick this in some cunt, some cunt's gotta get this.' I'd misread the situation, the fascists weren't supposed to be as angry as the locals, the fascists were just meant to wind up the locals.

'Come on Matt,' he urged me, spitting his anger onto the floor. His large forehead was pushing against mine. 'Some cunt has got to get done today.'

All around us cars were being attacked and shop windows were being smashed as the police were getting closer and closer. Rubbish bins were bouncing off shop windows before they were systematically kicked in.

The Millwall mob was now regrouping at the bottom of the street for a charge against the police. 'People *are* getting fucking done,' I said, raising my arms. The photographer had gone and bricks and bottles were raining over our heads towards the advancing police. Things were now totally out of control. The air was filled with the noise of things breaking, smashing and crashing, people being beaten up, police sirens and encouraging shouts from the flats overlooking us.

First it was the photographer, then another one of our own, and slowly the football mentality turned on itself and rival groups within the mob began to confront each other, throwing bottles, fighting over somewhere to hide as they ran out of objects and individuals to attack. I left, as I became more and more concerned for my own safety. I paused to catch my breath in the car park of Lewisham Tesco. I was shell-shocked. I walked for what felt like miles to find a bus stop. I feared upon my return home that my bags would have finally been packed for me, that the world would have stopped to witness the white riot.

No bags were packed. The house was empty except for my brother's girlfriend sitting miserably at the dinner table.

'Any news on the television while I was out?' I asked as casually as I could.

She looked up sheepishly and sighed. 'Your father's been sent to prison for drink driving.'

CHAPTER 24

The riot only rated a couple of small column inches in the *Independent On Sunday*, with a large photograph by the photographer who I had persuaded Nicky not to stab. Maybe if it had been Brixton and not Bermondsey and the marchers white not black, the pages would have been full of condemnation. What a strange place we lived in though, in the 1990s we still had black and white areas and everybody who lived in them lived in some kind of endless tension that seemed only to be exacerbated by their relationship with the police.

I met *Searchlight* outside the train station near my home. I handed over a typed report of the Bermondsey riot and read a day-old copy of *The Guardian* on the drive into town. Tea and scones lightened the mood a little as we went through the details of the riot. The ability to get away with a march in Thamesmead and cause a riot in Bermondsey were huge successes for the BNP. This was to mark a swing in direction. Some demanded that the BNP jackboot must now tramp much harder south of the river, it must pay attention to the distraction of racism and not to the attraction of racist votes in east London. For the anti-fascist movement, Bermondsey appeared to represent a complete disaster. Poorly planned and executed, it had hammered home the very message it was trying to conquer; Bermondsey was white and must remain so.

The BNP in the East End was now huge, larger than the entire National Front. Once Edmonds and the rest of the BNP's London leading lights decided to move their main activities south of the water, the BNP membership still continued to drink, meet and rampage up and down Brick Lane most weekends. Some in the BNP felt they should encourage violent mobs in south London, rather than bore themselves with trying to govern people in the east. Lecomber couldn't see why they couldn't do both, but BNP members found electioneering a painful distraction. When it worked, it raised their profile and attracted people to the cause, but so few of these new people were ever prepared for the disastrous election results that followed. The electoral evidence still pointed to the fact that the fascists needed a race riot.

There were also sporadic riots breaking out in areas like Cardiff where there were BNP members present. They weren't all racially motivated but significantly, a large number of rioters were young and white.

Over in Welling, Edmonds was talking big about Bermondsey. The NF's presence had been a little annoying to his members from the East End, who had been assured the NF was finished.

'Can't you persuade them to lay off Bermondsey? We're finding NF stickers covering ours,' he told me, stooping forward. 'Some of the young men we have are pretty aggrieved about the way the NF are following our activities. Tea?'

Anderson had also planned to stand NF candidates in the East End at the next general election, including the seats where Tyndall and Edmonds were planning to stand. In retaliation the BNP were going to stand against NF members in the Midlands. With the NF's campaign now wavering and falling well below the intended fifty candidate mark, it looked as if, between the two parties fifty-odd people would stand in thirty-odd constituencies. Lecomber even began advocating, in a ludicrous article in *Spearhead*, that in areas where there was no racist candidate, nationalists should vote against the incumbent to cause instability. A couple of thousand wasted votes nationwide were hardly going to destabilise the country, I thought, but from behind his glasses he looked serious. 'If you hold any sway at all in the NF these days, dissuade them from standing against our members. We're hardly large enough between us to afford this.'

I went and got a job, which pleased and shocked everyone but me. In return for a reference, Anderson insisted I run the NF's bookstall at this year's AGM. He had as good as begged to me to do it. The Curry House Five had booked themselves a celebratory trip to Spain and poor little Ginger Rick was just not up to the job of handling cash transactions. Plus, people had been asking questions as to why I had not been at various meetings that the NF had been trying to throw together over the last few months.

The NF as good as died on its feet at the Ibis Hotel, Euston. Whicker and I manned the redirection point at Euston Station as the sixty attendees shuffled off to the hotel, looking bewildered. Where was everybody? Was this it? I had ruined the NF. Months and months of leaks and cock-ups, ambushes and arrests had destroyed their confidence. I knew everyone in the room, knew their aspirations, their fears, their perversions. Martin Wingfield had declined to attend, as had Tom Acton as a protest at Anderson's decision to stop *The Flag* being printed at Hancock's. The Nashes did not turn up either. Croydon NF sent the only three people who wanted to still be members, while Birmingham sent a dozen of its drunken finest, most of whom were out on bail. Leeds had hired a car to get them to London, but the designated driver had got so pissed the night before he had failed to pick the car up in the morning and left the other members stranded outside Leeds train station.

It was appalling. Anderson sat at the top table with a miserable look on his face, surrounded by the few remaining supporters he could trust, and stared blankly over the heads of the remaining few. Even his bodyguard and lapdog Blackham hadn't bothered to turn up, having headed off with the other Curry House hooligans to Spain. The NF was dead.

Anderson began his Chairman's address by attacking the BNP, 'the imbeciles' who had stolen his moment. The BNP was the enemy of the NF, not the state, not the immigrants who had taken his members' jobs, not the Jews who controlled the media, the real threat to him was the BNP.

As we stopped for light refreshment, in barged Lecomber, Eddy Butler and a few BNP heavies. They wanted to come into the meeting but Anderson instructed Whicker to throw them out.

'Call this democracy? Everyone is welcome to attend the BNP AGM in October,' shouted Butler, as Whicker and I moved them out of the room. No one inside wanted to come out and fight them. Instead, Eddie and I stood at the bar with them and took their leaflets.

'Where's Blackham, then?' asked Wells, pretending he wanted to fight someone who, if he had been present, would have ripped his head off and shit down the hole. The remnants of Croydon NF came out into the bar, embarrassed at having been in the room. They were leaving, they'd seen enough.

CHAPTER 25

1991 ended as frantically as it had begun. I was now working up on Oxford Street. The new job had provided me with personal confidence and slowly I reverted back to the cheeky kid on the fruit market, with a disposable income, silly haircuts, a new orange coat and a belly full of more alcohol than a star substitute should really drink.

Racism and fascism were irrelevant here and my old friends were more than willing to welcome me back into the fold. I realised I had not spent much time in the company of normal, single women, so my jokes about helmet cheese, Roundheads or Cavaliers only ever attracted blokey interest.

A brief love affair popped up for a couple of weeks and all my pent-up poetry came gushing out as I gazed at her arse and listened intently to her go on about unilateral disarmament, the impending Labour victory at the next election, and how jogging and a strict diet would save my waistline. Then my mate from the army came home on leave and shagged her.

In October I agreed with Gerry Gable that I would go for one last bang on the drums with the NF at that year's Remembrance Day Parade. I was looking forward to my lunches with the 'old monster' Gable. He'd been both a Communist and an alleged burglar during his lifetime of fighting fascists. Things were changing, things could be about to become far more dangerous for me now that I'd toyed around with paramilitaries and C18 was flexing its muscles.

Searchlight wanted me to follow Eddie out of the NF entirely, follow him into the UDA, whilst still keeping an eye on Blackham. It was a natural course for me to follow. The BNP annual rally (as opposed to the annual conference) was approaching. Getting in there and reacquainting myself was an important first step. Gable and I spoke for hours. He gave me a long list of everything to look for and who to talk to. There were things I wanted to ask him about *Searchlight* but it was obvious that if I didn't know them, I couldn't trip up. Time after time I asked to be told who else worked for *Searchlight* within the far right. He did not say.

On 19 October Paul Ballard and I met at Euston with a few others for a couple of sneaky snorkels. 300 Nazis hung around the area, mixing with plain-clothed police and football casuals, providing security. A few NF hung around with their faces covered in case they were photographed by NF spies, while in the pub the walls were covered with stickers from home and abroad carrying the legend: 'Niggers Beware' or 'Stamp out homosexuality, stamp out the AIDS menace'. The chief BNP steward 'Daddy' Derek Beackon, took me aside. 'We've got a really useful team waiting up at Bethnal Green. Can you lead the first party up there?'

Forty of us made our way east to Bethnal Green. As ever, with everyone lagered up and jingoistic, trouble was already in the air. They stopped people getting on or off the tube when they wanted to. At one stop a black woman got on. 'Sorry luv, this is a no-nigger train,' they told her, shoving her off onto the platform. The bemused woman pushed her way back on and through them, her eyes widening in confusion. Did she not hear them? 'Are you deaf?' one lad said, leaning into her. Beackon joined us on the journey. The tube was jam-packed with terrified and embarrassed passengers staring at their feet or avoiding looking at us. Out of the corner of my eye I saw a young girl mouth to her friend, 'Who the fuck *are* these people?' As the train pulled

away from the platform we began Nazi saluting people on
the platform and making monkey noises at black youths
still on the platform. The shaken woman took her seat and
Beackon barked that nobody was allowed to touch her.
'Keep it all bottled up for now boys,' he said excitedly. He
turned to me grinning. 'Wait till you see what we've got at
Bethnal Green,' and remained grinning for the rest of the
journey, like a fucking idiot.

On the platform at Bethnal Green, a team of smartly
dressed casuals greeted us and directed us to one of the exits
from the station where, resplendent with BNP armbands
for identification, there was another group of men only
allowing BNP supporters to pass through. The precision
and the absolute front of their behaviour was stunning.
They pointed and barked instructions at civilians walking
towards them to 'use another exit' and the vast majority
of them happily obliged. Beackon and I hung around for a
while as the stewards pointed everyone in the right direction, towards York Hall, the famous boxing venue.

Could the BNP really just turn up in armbands and
commandeer a tube station like this? If they were true
to their fascist beliefs, they should also have checked
our tickets.

York Hall was booked under a false name and the bar
was filling up rapidly. It's an impressive venue, large and
long with a balcony that runs around the top. Edmonds
ran up and grabbed my arm excitedly. 'Welcome to the
Nuremberg rally, Bethnal Green style,' he beamed, proudly.
Already, a hundred or so drunk men were falling around
the place with more piling in, sharing tales of racial violence
dished out since we all last got together. Nazi CDs were for
sale, as were books rewriting the Holocaust. Once more I
could smell the white men's drinking club. In the last twelve
months the BNP had as much as trebled its membership.
They were proud to be here, in their full moronic glory.

Today we would hear from the regions how the party had grown in stature, how violence and intimidation were the key BNP strategies.

Its pride and joy was its new Scottish branches. Scott Maclean was the BNP's leader up there and he droned on and on about his achievements, wearing a shirt straight out of its wrapper. How could I be here, how could I still be doing this? The whole idea was to get away, and yet, these were still the only people I knew. The events were lightened somewhat when a spurned female admirer of Edmonds' tried to storm the stage as he rose to speak. He held up the *Jewish Chronicle*, which he described as a 'piece of shit' and loudly plotted the BNP's intentions to continue aggravating the racial tensions in both east and south east London. Edmonds sat down to warm applause. He looked almost apologetic and embarrassed for his popularity with the supporters. No, I did not want to be friends with Richard any more.

The bar was forcibly emptied for the Leader's speech. Tyndall rose to foot-stomping, Sieg-Heiling and chants of 'Leader', which became 'Führer' in a roar. He allowed himself a small acknowledgment of his pumped-up stature, before crashing down upon us with thunderous words. Men should be real men, women should be women. These blacks this, those Jews that, my men this. His speech was like a huge wave continually crashing down upon us before receding, to come crashing again. He accused the Tories of only flying the national flag because it had 'Israeli blue' in it, which everyone loved. York Hall was alive, nothing was held back as, from the seats facing Tyndall, people raised their right arms to salute their hero.

CHAPTER 26

The morning after the rally, the traditional paper sales pitch just down the road at Brick Lane was occupied by anti-fascists. I did not have much time for them, either. What was it that Orwell said about intellectuals and lefties hating their own countries? The left filled the pavement three deep and would not budge. They had come to fight the ever-growing BNP. No doubt they knew that the day before, hundreds of people had Nazi-saluted and swore obediently to ethnically cleanse areas like Bethnal Green, Whitechapel and Brick Lane. They believed that physical confrontation was the only way to stop the BNP in its tracks.

Another huge confrontation loomed between the powers of good and evil, light and dark. A vicious brawl ensued. Bethnal Green Road came to a standstill as railings were flung and BNP members battered to the ground. The reds had stolen someone's Union Jack and began to burn it, which led to another charge into their ranks. The police had set barricades up on both sides of Bethnal Green Road so that both sides could shout abuse at each other. There were torn up posters and newspapers everywhere. That afternoon, C18 was officially launched. I had not gone to the launch meeting. There were questions *Searchlight* wanted answered, which I didn't have the answers for.

For the rest of October I avoided all contacts. I met *Searchlight* to give them my report on the rally, and was informed that a Jewish schoolteacher, attacked by Lecomber for ripping down BNP stickers on the day of the rally, had identified him from photographs in *Searchlight* and footage from Thames Television. He was sentenced to three years' jail in November.

Both the BNP and the NF were making preparations for a general election in the near future. Tory Prime Minister John Major could seem to do absolutely nothing right. He was so bland, so boring, so straight down the line.

The silence between the NF and me was broken by Terry a week before the Remembrance Day Parade. He called to ask about my plans for the big day. The NF had a nice, big, polished drum just waiting for me. I agreed to drum, even agreed to wear black pants with a white shirt and polish my shoes. I rang Woods, who was surprised to hear from me. I said I would drum in their silly march.

'You're gonna be expelled,' he said excitedly. 'It's over the BNP rally. It was the last straw for Anderson. Once you've drummed they're going to kick you out.' So I rang around and said I wouldn't drum, and that the NF was finished.

Murph agreed to come to the parade with me. Only fifty people were forming up where the NF wanted them to. The Chelsea Headhunters had gone over to east London to join a BNP mob trying to attack an anti-fascist march. I rubbed my hands with glee, but Murph looked shaken by the size of the parade. He quickly turned to me in horror. 'This is your doing, Matthew. All those things you've done and said, you've ruined the NF!' I never spoke to or saw Murph again after that day.

CHAPTER 27

The Beautiful South released *Old Red Eyes Is Back* in the New Year of 1992, trying to get a hit song during a period of traditionally low record sales. The two copies I purchased could not even nudge it into the top twenty.

John Major called the 1992 election for 9 April. Surely Labour would win this one, everybody ventured. Back down to Bermondsey and Bethnal Green I went, to take part in more abuse of the democratic process. In Bermondsey, the NF and the BNP kept a subtle distance from each other. The new Croydon BNP was out in force with the rest of the far right in support of Steve Tyler, while Blackham, standing for the NF, had a motley crew of football hooligans and psychopaths to back him up. Anderson did not make an appearance. For a long time John Tyndall had refused to allow BNP members to stand in elections. Like many old Nazis, Tyndall had little faith in or respect for the electorate. The poor results achieved and the enormous amount of money spent for no return, as well as the obvious humiliation and Tyndall's own beliefs about democracy meant that, although the BNP were good at rabble-rousing and inciting racial hatred, coercing people to put a tick or a cross next to their names, was often impossible.

The BNP was growing at such an enormous rate now though, that Tyndall had to allow this new mood to go to the ballot box, even if only to show those people that elections were a waste of time. He even selected a good seat for himself in the East End that had a dedicated branch to campaign for him. The long hot summer of racial hatred that the BNP had fermented in London and other parts of the country last year had to pay some dividend.

Across the board, Edmonds said that Tyndall was hoping for an average of between 2.5 and 4 per cent. The BNP held a violent and vicious election meeting three days before polling. Using York Hall again, John Tyndall and Richard Edmonds addressed a hundred-strong public meeting, while BNP stewards Nazi-saluted demonstrators and attacked photographers. Inside, Tyndall and Edmonds were ferocious in their speeches against the multiracial society. Their rhetoric even surprised some hardened campaigners.

Blackham lost to the BNP in Bermondsey by about 300 votes, and gained only 0.4 per cent of the poll. Across the country, 29 far-right candidates struggled around, but mainly below, 1 per cent. Edmonds polled 1,310 votes in Bethnal Green (3.6 per cent), and Tyndall got 1,107 (3.0 per cent) in Bow & Poplar. Eddie, keeping his promise to Birmingham NF, polled 370 votes, just under 1 per cent. John Major, standing on a milk crate to make himself heard, was re-elected as PM. Billy Bragg, I'm told, stayed in bed for a week.

Blokes in white vans, blokes off the building sites, plumbers and the odd squaddie began paying attention, thinking that the BNP was some sort of legitimate party with new ideas. The new idea was simply to create as much chaos as humanly possible and simply let the race war take off. Meetings and paper sales became more daring, and the violence more indiscriminate. The very lowest of society had a voice. Years of bitter resentment about the real and perceived injustices of their lives fed the BNP.

Pubs were filled seven nights per week as the thirty or so members of C18 strolled around Bethnal Green like gangsters. Sargent himself had taken to drinking in the Blind Beggar in Whitechapel, a shallow tourist attraction for those who liked to pop in and see where the Kray twins had murdered George Cornell, nearly thirty years before. Sargent had already been to prison four times for possession of guns and drugs. From the pub he used the public call box to muster his troops, arrange meetings and meet people getting off of the tube at the nearby station. With more and more people finding themselves out of work, Charlie paid for their drinks with his drug money. His money and muscle made people sit up and take notice, none more so than John Tyndall, the uptight BNP leader who needed someone like Charlie on his side.

In response to this sudden growth in far-right activity, the SWP re-launched the Anti-Nazi League, something that seemed to do little more than provide more young, wide-eyed victims for Sargent and his gang's appetite for violence against the left. We were certain that Charlie Sargent was running the BNP security team as a UDA front. That would also explain the plentiful supply of drugs.

Gable also asked whether I knew anything about the American book clubs flooding the far right with their literature. The BNP had always sold certain books published by the National Alliance, a well-financed and seedy organisation, including the blueprint for terrorism, *The Turner Diaries*. At the moment, I knew nothing. 'Sargent's pushing this stuff too,' he told me, 'he has his hands on every bit of poison that the right seems to be producing at the minute.'

In May, London UDA and the BNP held a joint demonstration against a march through Camden and Regents Park led by the future Mayor of London, Ken Livingstone, against racism. Edmonds and his small band of BNP supporters waved flags and shouted abuse. A small group of Charlie Sargent's supporters broke away to try and attack the front of the march. Five Jewish students were hospitalised.

Next up, the Reverend Ian Paisley was going to be in Bristol for a march in the summer. London UDA was going down to Bristol to guard the parade of loyalist marching bands and a selection of Orangemen and mainland Apprentice Boys, to the park where Paisley would speak. A council minibus was procured, and at eight in the morning I was at Croydon Station waiting for the minibus with an already drunken Ulsterman and his busty English girlfriend. The drive down to Bristol was a serious affair. Liverpool and Birmingham UDA units were also going to provide security and/or intimidation along the route of the march. As ever, Frank was trying to come across as sinister and secretive, while Eddie kept his eyes on the road. Only a year or so earlier, the NF had gone to Bristol, drunk and aggressive, for a rally. We were kicked from pillar to post, until the day ended with an enormous punch-up with the left at a train station. Two gangs of Bristol football supporters had even taken sides, of which we were the less supported.

The social event that followed the march was a nightmare. We sat at one end of the room, staring at Liverpool UDA who were sitting with the team from Birmingham UDA at the other. An auction was held, including an artefact from the Maze Prison, signed by Michael Stone. As the evening grew drunker, lips grew looser. A major row had been brewing on the mainland about the active or inactive role of certain UDA commanders. Previously, London UDA had been a haven for show-ponies, but the arrival of Frank Portinari and a serious group of far-right thugs, was causing friction. The change in the UDA leadership in Belfast had led to new alliances and favourites. Portinari had been to Belfast to talk his group up and was forming a cell structure akin to that being used by the UDA in Northern Ireland. Portinari had been sticking knives in the back of every other commander and here he was, sitting with the well-known Sargent and Whicker, two trusted, big-hitting, fascist hard-men, plotting the downfall of the other mainland loyalist commanders. They were, according to Portinari and his chubby Italian-looking sidekick, 'Hollywood Prods', while we were lapsed Catholics, drug dealers and Nazis. The standoff lasted until we were safely on the motorway and Portinari was plotting their downfall. But I still had no idea exactly how important London UDA was.

I met with *Searchlight* on the following Monday. Gerry Gable leant across his table and asked me again if I had heard anything about the book clubs that seemed to be springing up around the place, pushing hard-line American Nazi theoretical journals alongside bomb manuals. I confessed to still not knowing anything except for having heard of and read all the material he mentioned.

'It's no longer under the counter stuff, Mattie, some of this stuff is quite serious. Go to see David Irving speak, and see who's pushing this stuff.'

CHAPTER 28

Throughout that year, David Irving, an upper-class Holocaust denier and racist, was on television quite a bit. Some countries would not allow him in and he was currently in Russia planning to address a meeting before flying to England to speak to a ragbag collection of BNP members in London. A mass security turnout was planned. The BNP would be doing redirection from Euston Station, where I was to present myself for further instruction.

During the week, as Irving's intention to hold a controversial meeting in London was discussed on television, my family gave it a cursory glance and tutted before changing channels. Watching anything mildly political or controversial while I was in the house had become unbearable, plus there was the constant underlying fear that I might actually end up on it, in my full, moronic glory again.

'No point guessing what you'll be doing this weekend,' said Brother Nobby, polishing some army boots at the kitchen table.

Edmonds had the tickets and was the man redirecting the general public to the secret meeting place. 'You're on the door, Matthew, you don't need to pay,' he said. 'You'll be with the security team, ensuring no reds or Jews try to gatecrash things. These meetings are awfully boring anyway, enjoy yourself.' This was obviously quite a result for me as it allowed me to use *Searchlight*'s money for a ticket to supplement my dwindling beer tokens.

A couple of days later I was back at Euston Station again, witnessing the biggest turnout of far-right muscle ever assembled. Not just blokes, but real muscle. Phil 'the thug' Edwards with some former British Movement types, joining up with the east London Nazi crew, the south London Nutty Turn-Out, some handy Yorkshire lads and Charlie Sargent and Rob Hilton along with another twenty or so. I turned up wearing a baseball cap, which seemed to make me popular as all the lads had thought of wearing one as well. Charlie shook my hand warmly, like we were old mates. 'Alright, Maff, you're with us,' and with that we headed off to the secret location while the police and small pockets of reds buzzed around us.

Even I found it slightly amusing when I discovered that we were heading to the International Students' House, where hundreds of European, American and African students sit in the library and study English culture from a textbook. They were about to get an explosive and up-front introduction to the real deal.

A small group of German and American guests were already seated downstairs in what looked like a canteen, all set up for a meeting and video show. The BNP and the Nazi printer Alan Hancock already had their bookstalls set up and for a while I mingled around in the meeting. An American and a preposterous Englishman with an awful plum in his throat addressed the one hundred or so of us. 'Mr Irving has been removed from a British Airways plane in Moscow by forces unknown but is endeavouring to be here as soon as possible. I understand he is flying in with somebody else. There will be no photographing or filming any members of the audience.' Standard Nazi fare. I left the canteen and went into the main reception area, where Sargent was marshalling the security team. This was an impressive, psychotic mob. A gang of heavy boozers and brawlers, together at last, with their large knuckles and thick foreheads finally marshalled in one place at the same time.

'We're expecting the reds to show up at any moment, they're moving *en masse* from Paddington to get here.'

Upstairs in the library, Nick the Nazi and his friends were showing their willies to foreign students, grabbing reference books from the shelves and plonking themselves in the middle of small discussion groups burping, farting and trying to be charming. The library was emptying very quickly when someone jumped up onto a chair shouting, 'The reds are here!' The exit from the library was immediately blocked by Sargent's men. They began barking instructions.

'Nobody fucking leaves, so sit down.' The students gasped in horror at each other as the security team lined up against the windows. A small group of Anti-Fascist Action had gone around the back of the building to look for a fire exit to get in by. The ape noises started, then the Nazi salutes, and the students sat in horror as the sideshow became aggressive.

'Come on you Jewish bastards, come and have it with us,' said one of the men, trying to climb out of the first-floor window to get at the reds.

In the reception, terrified students stood behind the security team trying to get out, while Sargent gave the top policeman there his orders.

'You're not coming in. We've got security arrangements in place, there'll be no trouble from us.' The policeman seemed to scratch his head but I could not hear what he said. Sargent came back inside and told the assembled Nazis that there were 300, maybe more, reds outside wanting to get in. 'I've told the copper we can handle it, but I've also promised that the students can come and go as they please. I want this door properly managed by three or four people, the rest of you continue letting the reds know from the windows that we've got a good team in here.' Phil and his small crew manned the doors with Sargent, while the others, seemingly oblivious to their odious personalities, tried to pick up the female students. Some, not caring too much about the inconsistency with their politics, even tried to pick up a couple of African girls. In the student administration office, a guy called Alan Thompson was following a blonde woman declaring he was in love with her. 'I love you darling, come on let's go for a drink.' She politely refused and shut her office door. Thompson then began banging on it. 'Come out you old tart, come out and make love with me. I love you!' He was already so drunk he could barely stand up, let alone throw one up anybody. There was mayhem all around the building, shouting English hooligans terrifying foreign students while at the same time casually wrecking the building like they were having their own prison riot.

Eventually we were summoned; the historical liar Irving had arrived. The police got him past the demonstration and brought him to the door where we were waiting to greet him. Out in the fresh air, the security team started itching for a fight with the reds. They chased a photographer they thought was Gerry Gable and tried to get face to face with the demonstrators.

I squeezed myself into a seat near John Tyndall, and watched Irving. The suspect historian didn't speak much about history, mainly concentrating on his 'persecution'. He got a standing ovation, of course, and a few Nazi salutes. We walked Tyndall to his car at the end of the meeting and posed for photographs, in the first real photo opportunity for Combat 18. The next big outing would be a return to London for a Skrewdriver gig. Having been physically forced out of London by anti-fascists, they felt that the time was right to return and that the movement finally had enough muscle to make it happen.

CHAPTER 29

The June issue of *Searchlight* had the American Nazi leader Harold Covington on the front and inside, a series of letters he had been writing to supporters while staying in the UK. I'd never heard of Covington, nor had I heard of the massacre of anti-Klan activists by supporters of his organisation some years before. Was this the man behind the book clubs Gerry Gable had asked about earlier? I didn't bring Covington's name up at the Irving seminar, nor, despite the notorious loose tongues of the far right, was he mentioned by anyone else.

Despite his excellent Nazi credentials for leading small handfuls of psychopathic thugs and killers into oblivion, Covington had one stumbling block: Irish Republicanism. Whoever Covington was meeting in the UK while he was studying here – which he was able to having married an Irish woman some years before – would have to be very careful not to get caught out. Covington was small fry compared to the rest of the American right. He certainly was not in the same league as Dr William Pierce, the leader of the National Alliance and author of *The Turner Diaries* but, like with most Nazis, size didn't count. Covington was using the names of some of his more prestigious contacts back home to worm his way inside the fringes of the British far right. Among Covington's friends back home in Dixie was Sean Maguire, a leading American Nazi and supporter of the IRA.

Covington was advocating a strategy of 'leaderless resistance'. It seemed pretty daft to me and Eddie because, although the thought of things being blown up and people being murdered because of their colour or political beliefs struck a huge chord with a lot of people we knew, they also all wanted to be leaders.

'Don't worry about Covington, worry about shifting these,' said Eddie as he dropped another half-dozen dirty videos in my lap. So it looked like I was not going to find anything out about Covington from Whicker. I was sure he knew something, but he wasn't too sure what it was himself. An newspaper exposé of UDA activities in the Midlands was giving Frank a headache, as the local Commander had been shooting his mouth off to the local press about being well prepared for when the gloves came off.

The UDA had now been made illegal in Northern Ireland and perhaps were going to move more of their fundraising to the mainland, where they still remained legal. This would mean far more work and kudos for Frank and Eddie. In realisation of this, Frank had been preparing the London UDA group for over two years, encouraging low profiles and keeping his own near-invisible. The mainland UDA were about to play a huge part in the British far right.

The new Croydon BNP, under the leadership of the former Croydon NF, was not working out as well as they had hoped. Despite Edmonds rushing over to Croydon in his battle bus regularly, the Croydon members were being directed to spend more and more time elsewhere in south London. The autonomy they had experienced under the lacklustre NF leadership was gone. Also, much to the disappointment of former NF members in the BNP, Paul Ballard had been in contact with former NF Political Soldier leader Nick Griffin and asked him to address a few BNP meetings.

CHAPTER 30

12 September 1992. Just about every time I leave the house these days it's preceded by a television announcement of major disruption to London caused by a planned demonstration against Nazis.

They were hardly the Beautiful South, but there was something sickeningly exciting about going to see Skrewdriver. Just about every Nazi in Britain who could walk was expected to be at Waterloo Station in London for redirection to the big event. Their mixture of rock-a-billy and poor white trash blues often got hundreds of skinheads and their girlfriends on the dance floor moshing, punching and kicking each other, smashing glasses and bottles into each other's faces while the hard men stood on the sides bemused, drinking lager and eyeing up the skinhead girls. Donaldson's music career had begun in a band playing Rolling Stones' cover versions, but he saw nothing strange or hypocritical applying race hate lyrics to what was after all, originally black music. Driven from his London bedsit a few years before by a sustained campaign by anti-fascists, Donaldson had also spent time in prison for attacking a black man on the London Underground. He spent his time out of London travelling the world, writing new songs, shagging young girls and doing weights in a German prison.

Skinheads were the only group on the right that were guaranteed a regular sex life. Something moronic and twisted among them didn't seem to mind treating the skinhead girls as trampolines, who went from one painful and pointless relationship to another with a mattress tied

to their backs. Some skinheads had fathered children with
two or three different girls, who in turn had three other
kids to three other fathers, who all played together like one
big happy family. Skinheads were mistrustful of the 'casuals' who hung around skinhead events, because they knew
it was not for the music. Most casuals hung around only
because they were more apt at making money from the
events than the skins. The skinheads who sold t-shirts and
CDs only did so because some casual had manufactured
and printed them on their behalf. 'Political parasites' the
skins called them.

I met Nicky outside the Hotspur pub on Tottenham
Court Road and he had another large scab on him, this
time from being hit in the head with a toilet seat at the
punk gig he had recently attacked. He also had a huge
bruise from a kick to his back, which he gladly pulled his
shirt up to show me. 'I'm fighting reds seven nights a week
now,' he told me brightly as he shadow-boxed his way into
the pub. Five large bruisers sat at the table and all rose
and shook my hand in turn. They'd been snorting shit off
the table and I was suddenly overcome by a previously
unfelt puritanical streak. Fucking drugs. I knew it went
on amongst the football hooligans, but dedicated fascists
weren't supposed to do it. I knew Charlie Sargent sold
drugs, but I didn't think for one minute that the anti-drug
campaigners of the BNP would indulge in them personally.

We made a painful trek across London with our paranoia heightened. When we arrived Waterloo Station for
redirection, the streets around it resembled a battleground.
Having dodged reds on the Underground until we came up
into the station concourse, we were greeted by the sight of
bloodied skinheads sat around dazed and confused, nursed
by their girlfriends while panicked passengers ran for cover.
For the past few hours, huge groups of anti-fascists and
skins had done battle in and around the station. The press

were on the station taking photographs of the mayhem, while Nicky and I calmly walked through the mess to the clock that marked the main entrance. Outside, hundreds of police vans and officers aided by dogs and helicopters overhead hovered around. A footbridge crossing the road into the station was full of skins penned in by the police, while below, hundreds of anti-fascists made a mess of any Nazi not hiding behind police lines.

The skinheads looked so helpless, almost childish in their silly boots with swastikas shaven into the backs of their heads, ripped bomber jackets and Nazi badges torn from the arms. The skinhead security had been given a pounding earlier in the day, and there was no one around to redirect the stragglers who had come from as far as France and Sweden.

A huge roar went up as behind us another load of anti-fascists came into the station from the Underground and laid into the skins who were fleeing for the exits. More fighting broke out outside as the skins on the footbridge tried to make a run into the station to join the fracas and the police started to baton-charge the anti-fascists. 'We've got to meet the Aldershot train,' said Nicky, hurriedly pushing through the police and Nazis struggling on the station concourse. A young girl was shouting from the arrival gate, 'The Yorkshire Grey in Eltham, the gig's moved to the Yorkshire Grey, Eltham,' before turning around and getting back on the train. Was she for real?

Daphne Liddle, a small Communist woman I had for years abused on Lewisham High Street where she sold her papers, came and stood next to me. 'Did you hear that?' I asked. 'The gig's at Yorkshire Grey, in Eltham.' She pointed her camera in my face and muttered 'Nazi bastard.'

I headed for the exit to Waterloo East, just as the police were closing down one of Britain's busiest train stations. On the other side of Waterloo East Station Nicky stood in front of a bus heading for the Elephant and Castle, and would not let the driver go until we had all made it on. Even at the Elephant, we would not be safe as we could see a huge mob of Millwall supporters milling about with black youths heading towards the station. The rest of the bus sat in stony silence as police cars drove past us in the other direction and a helicopter flew overhead. I remembered reading in a local paper about a cab firm at the Elephant and Castle that had recently been prosecuted for only hiring black drivers who 'looked and behaved' like Trevor Macdonald, the newsreader. I told Nicky that we would all have to get cabs from there, and to make sure the skins had got some money. After some threats, the cab firm gave us its four best white drivers, while Nicky and I sat in a cab with a black driver, who looked nothing like Trevor Macdonald.

The Yorkshire Grey used to be an enormous but mainly empty pub near the A20 and the Well Hall roundabout, on a main road facing some of Eltham's more notorious council estates. Nicky stuck more powder on his fist and snorted, until I exploded. 'What the fuck is with the coke, man? What the fuck is with the drugs?' He looked a little bit embarrassed. 'There's just so much of it around, I couldn't help but give it a go, could I?'

In the main bar the C18 team sat trying to catch a glimpse of the aggro still going on at Waterloo on the television. A couple of angry blacks came into the main bar to complain to the landlord that they had been racially abused on their way in. The bar staff were shitting themselves.

The C18 crew consisted of all the well-known Nazi football hooligans from London, dressed to the nines in expensive gear, snorting drugs off the tables and drinking bottled beers. This was madness. I followed Nicky into the toilet where he was using his Switch card to cut up some more coke. He was getting more and more jumpy, but I kept following him until he agreed to talk.

'We're splitting up into teams. Charlie's giving us the orders and we're carrying them out for him. It goes all the way to the top. The UDA, the BNP, the Headhunters. We're gonna be unstoppable.'

We missed the first band and piled into the hall free of charge. A couple of hundred skins sat around the floor while the C18 mob drank at the bar. It seemed incredible but it dawned on me, that C18 deliberately let the skinheads get done over at Waterloo so that they could run Blood and Honour themselves.

Charlie wanted to run everything, he'd named his price for fronting a mass street army and it was the book clubs, the UDA under Frank and Eddie, the football hooligans, the BNP casuals, all falling into order. I stood away from Nicky for the rest of the night as he swayed and jabbered his way around the room, bumping into people. The Yorkshire Grey was a fifteen-minute walk from home, I could leave now and be gone, but outside the reds and the police had arrived. The bemused sound engineer was playing rap music during the interim, which the C18 crew seemed to like, but it perplexed the skins somewhat.

When Ian Stuart took to the stage the whole hall ran to the front to salute their hero, returning to London to play for them. Stuart looked uncomfortable. The lights didn't go down, they never did at these gigs. It was a million miles away from Paul Heaton and his cheeky grin. There was a large flag behind the band and a small gang of hard-men at the front of the stage to protect their hero. Donaldson described it as a victory that the gig went ahead despite more than half the expected turnout not making it. 'And even though he's not here, I wanna thank Charlie Sargent and the boys from Redwatch for making this gig possible. He may look like a naughty schoolboy, but he's the toughest bastard I know,' he shouted into the mic. And with that, Skrewdriver launched into their first song, with lyrics about hating blacks, hating gays, and Jews and foreigners.

Nicky sauntered back over to me. 'He got it wrong. *Redwatch* is our *hitlist*.' From his pocket he pulled out a newsletter. 'Look at this.' *Redwatch* was a tatty piece of paper handwritten in places, with dozens of names of trade union members, teachers, community workers and members of the anti-fascist community. 'All you gotta do is look in the phone book or behind a PO Box and you've got 'em. Then we give them a call or even pay them a visit. In the last couple of weeks, I've done loads.' He grinned at me like the silly bastard I knew he was. But this was what it had been bound to lead to.

How long, I wondered, before my name would appear on such a list?

For the rest of the gig I stood in the middle of the hall while skinheads moshed around the room, breaking each other's noses and battering into the skin girls who sat on the sidelines holding their jackets for them. After an hour I could bear it no longer and was just about to run from the building when the landlady intervened. Ian Stuart was no little boy but he was hardly brave either. She pulled the plug. I nearly cried for her. 'Gig's over,' she said into the mic, then left the hall. Rock and Roll! Ian Stuart walked from the stage without protest. Everything fell flat, there were large groans, but nobody kicked off.

The skinheads insisted I get in the minibus with them because 'London's not safe for a white man.' I didn't mind. Everyone in the minibus had a copy of Redwatch and was scouring it for names and addresses near them.

CHAPTER 31

After one social event, a trip to Bristol with the UDA commander listening intently to my synopsis of the Ulster troubles (from an Anglo-Irish perspective) and a few uncomfortable afternoons and evenings with C18, I was beginning to feel the water passing my chin and a real inability on my part to stop myself from drowning. It was around this time that, as he later admitted, Frank Portinari was purchasing low grade and near ineffective handguns from pubs around Bermondsey. Having established a presence in the area during the ferocious two years of campaigning the far right put into the area, contacts with local hoodlums and off-licence robbers would not have been too hard to cultivate. To the criminal mind, a strong army of tooled-up thugs must be an impressive sight, worthy of doing business with. And Portinari, along with Whicker and a few others, had an imposing presence. I did not want to be even the boy in the back seat of a car laden down with guns, so I slowly eased my way out of that particular circle to concentrate my attentions on the rest of the far right.

C18 was becoming part and parcel of BNP culture. Everyone wanted to be part of it, not that Sargent wanted all of them in the organisation. A quick check through *Searchlight* and any other community newspaper throughout late 1991 and the whole of 1992 reveals a huge upsurge in firebombings, death threats, and racist and political attacks. A team of C18 thugs were even responsible for a witness in a court case against one of their number skipping the country, despite police protection. The theory was that they could do almost anything they wanted and get away with it. *Searchlight* said very little of C18 on its pages, much to the disappointment of those inside the organisation. There were arrests, but poor sentences handed down by the courts. The whole early leadership of the organisation remained at liberty, and were joined by Wilf Browning who had not long been released from prison after serving a sentence for an assault on a gay man. I didn't know much about Browning, though I had seen him around a fair bit before. He went straight into the leadership of C18.

Gerry Gable and I met for a fried breakfast in town and he questioned me about how long I could remain inside. I'd been panicking. Whilst I listened to Billy Bragg singing about the sounds of ideologies clashing in the silly old Houses of Parliament, there'd been a series of bones broken and bookshops attacked. How were they getting away with it? How were they so able, almost without fear of being arrested, to continually carry out attacks in the manner they were, without being prosecuted?

I did not know it but Tim Hepple, another mole, had also been feeling uncomfortable. The pressure was really mounting on the people spying inside the far right. Tim had been involved in a vicious assault where they had dropped bricks onto the heads of some anti-racist campaigners and attacked their lifeless bodies with iron bars and boots. After Hepple came out I wondered how he had coped with what he had done, what he had used to cleanse his mind when he was all alone. For me it was alcohol and furious and frequent masturbation. Tim was a classically trained pianist. In his book, *At War With Society*, there was a fair amount of evidence to suggest he too struggled to come to terms with the whole range of things that went on in his new secret life.

I told Gerry, so far so good, which was a bit of a lie but we were close to something, I could feel it. Firebomb attacks on Communist newspapers, petrol through people's doors, fires, windows smashed. These things had always happened, but they were almost a daily occurrence now. Your name on a letter in a newspaper could easily put you on a hit list. Was I going to follow this right through until someone was murdered?

Two days later I stood with C18 a few feet away from Edmonds and the BNP at Brick Lane. There was no NF there any more so we took their space. C18 were getting people who had never been in the far right before out of bed on a Sunday morning to stand on a side street of a London market. Eddie Whicker stood with us selling *Ulster*.

A string of violent assaults on union members, left-wing paper sellers, demonstrations and meetings were owned up to and bragged about. C18 needed more targets and to increase the high level of their activity. They had even managed to turn over a coach-load of what they had originally thought were IRA supporters outside a tube station at boarding time in south London. It turned out to be some ANL supporters, but that was equally pleasurable for them. Charlie Sargent was ringing people up and putting them into teams during the week and ordering them into violent attacks. Their rewards were drugs and endless supplies of pints when they reconvened at the end of the evenings in bars in and around the East End.

Whereas my racist and self-destructive anger had subsided into a mute and confused sadness, the atmosphere of excited and inflammatory bitter hatred from them was like a tinder box. Everyone and everything that passed was an affront to their delicate sensibilities. They were so eager and willing to cause havoc and destruction that for a small moment you would have thought they were running out of black, Jewish and leftist opposition. Whicker had been promoted to London UDA's number two.

In the pub that evening, Sargent was asserting that C18

was separate from the BNP now and that there was too much danger in the BNP for them. The BNP was C18's political affiliation and C18 would serve the party as its protector, but had to remain under Sargent's control and the UDA's influence. There was a little more coke snorting until in walked Wilf Browning, looking larger than I had remembered him. He'd been working out obviously. Browning walked straight over to Sargent and spoke in his ear, while Sargent nodded his approval. Looking around me, there wasn't one person without a criminal conviction for violence. Their faces were bloated by years of boozing and brawling and their political and football allegiances covered their arms in ink. Eddie shook everyone's hands, making new friends all the time. He and I held court in the corner, dipping into the complimentary sea food and roast potatoes that pub landlords used to lay on a Sunday.

Sargent returned to the group ordering curtly, 'It's on. Let's go.'

'Stay close to me,' Whicker said in hushed tones.

We barged our way through the market streets that operate around Brick Lane, invisible to the throng of shoppers, hippies, street performers, beggars and voyeurs. We came out at a crossroads slap bang in the middle of Brick Lane, where a large table had been set up by an assortment of groups against racism and fascism. People were holding newspapers and chatting amongst themselves. They did not seem to see us among all the bustle and noise as we lined up in one straight line, facing them from the pavement, while behind them Browning's group did likewise.

So here it was. For control of the streets, the most brutal and cowardly acts of violence had to be carried out. C18 was born out of a terrified hatred of the left, whom they never understood, never conversed with and never defeated. I looked along our line at the drug dealers, the gangsters, the football hooligans and wife beaters who believed in their tiny minds that they were going to save the white race from drug dealers, wife-beaters, gangsters, Jews, blacks and Asians.

Browning started running at the lefties from behind with his hand clenched around a bottle, and landed it flat on the head of one of the people manning the bookstall. Hell broke out. 'Fucking Jew,' shouted one of the attackers at his victim, and in went more feet and fists and bottles. The screams started off as shock, then anger, and finished begging for help and mercy. Nobody from the large crowd came to their aid. It was similar to Welling Library; it was a message. The next night there was to be an election meeting at York Hall, and this would reduce the number of opponents by hospitalisation or even murder. People lying on the ground were pulled up solely so they could be put down in an even more violent manner. The women in the group were also shown no mercy, and in the thick of it I saw Browning standing over their bodies with his fists clenched and neck strained looking up to the heavens in rapture. Bottles were used as weapons then discarded on the ground as Eddie and I turned into the crowd and pushed our way out.

It was the signal for everyone to leave, as surely some-one, somewhere would soon call the police. Browning had to be dragged off and the crowd parted in amazement as he strolled through them with his ape-like arms swinging as he scowled and barged his way through. Behind him were the bodies of young men and women lying almost lifeless. Who would grab this man, this evil, violent psychopath? Who would get the man they called 'Wilf the Beast'?

I needed to get away, but it was too dangerous out in the open. Surely the police would be looking for us by now. I hailed a cab and got him to drive me past the meet-up point twice while I watched more and more of the firm arrive. The police were sure to arrive, but if I wasn't inside when they did, I'd be fucked either way. The taxi driver became impatient and as good as shoved me out of the cab.

I pushed the pub doors open and a large cheer went up. Sargent put a pint in my hand and his arm around my shoulder. 'That was very fucking cool, the way you handled that. Are you with us or not?' I mumbled something about having to work night shift this week and needed to get a cab home. 'Not a problem,' said Sargent, leaving the pub briefly. When he came back inside he told me he had ordered a minicab from across the road. 'Finish your pint first, Maff, you fucking deserve it.'

Eddie stood outside with me for a chat. 'What d'you think?' He nodded back inside the pub. 'A bit over the top wasn't it, but still... 'ere, are you alright?' He could tell that I wasn't alright, but what could he say?

CHAPTER 32

Six people were arrested for their part in the Brick Lane attack. It was the second serious attack on anti-fascists in the area in recent months. Among the regular and violent clashes, two particularly brutal and organised attacks had been carried out, one witnessed by Hepple and one by me. By the time I got to meet Gable it was the day after the election rally and the injured parties had been prompted to pick out their attackers from the public gallery the night before.

I was obviously tired and distressed. Night shift always made me emotional so I had to avoid bursting into tears. Eddie had been ringing me at home and leaving messages for me to call him over the past few days. I ignored his calls.

'I'm out, Gerry, this is it.'

He looked unsurprised and even a little grateful that I'd made that decision. Sure, I could go on if I wanted to, but the toll was too much and surely now *Searchlight* had enough information to blow up a huge stink about this. I did not want to go back inside for a moment. I'd said that probably a thousand times for a thousand reasons over the period I'd worked for the magazine, including at our first meeting, but this time it seemed to be a more rational decision. Gerry placed his hands on the table.

'Now is the time for you to go travelling. Think about travelling, think about somewhere you really want to go and save like a maniac. Your time is coming.' I didn't know what he was talking about, though he said we'd discuss it in the New Year if I felt like I wanted to. America? I'd really have to start fiddling my expenses to do that.

Eddie finally caught up with me one afternoon while I

was getting ready for work. Perhaps the biggest indication of C18's dangerousness was the fact that they considered me as somebody with brains.

'Brick Lane was sloppy Maff, but let's not talk about it over on the phone.'

I hid from *Searchlight* too, though they were more used to it when I was feeling stressed or under pressure. Things were going great away from the mad men and their politics. There was nothing like just going to work, coming home and watching a bit of television before letting loose on the weekends. But, like Gerry Gable had warned me, things were taking a turn for the worse. I'd consented to be a part of this and the worst thing was, I was involved, only because I hated the mad fuckers. I was also scared of them though. Charlie Sargent with his ugly face and his penchant for knives, Eddie with his large hands and thick angry neck, not forgetting all the other lunatics who were out seven nights a week destroying things for the sake of a line of coke and some free booze. It was violence for violence's sake. And that was what was most scary about it. It didn't even seem to be about reds and the great white revolution anymore.

'If you're not with us, you're against us.' Eddie was passing on a message from Charlie to me. Of course, all the fascists that knew me had disagreed with Charlie's prognosis, but a lot of others didn't care. Charlie had called a meeting where I was on the agenda after a discussion about the shocking news that there was a documentary team on their case. Word was out that a member of the BNP or C18 was going to come out on television. There were a number of documentaries about the BNP towards the end of the year. Generally C18 was not well known or identifiable enough to the untrained eye, but their violence was. No one in the BNP leadership seemed to mind it either. C18 were kicking the BNP into the headlines, and they looked good and strong while doing it. They were now fully controlling the music scene, and also a fair chunk of the drug sceme within it.

Most of the documentaries were quite lame, just another story about the increase in racist violence and the increase in size of the BNP with a quick soundbite from Richard Edmonds, still acting like a Nazi. I kept my distance and Eddie placated Sargent, in the belief that I would come good once whatever little panic attack I was having wore off. But our almost daily phone calls ended. He too was waiting for me to come good.

I heard nothing from the BNP and hadn't heard from the NF in months. I was going political cold turkey and working eighty-four hours per week doing twelve-hour night shifts, putting money in my bank account and waiting for my big trip. But of course, there was no such thing as a free lunch, even with Gerry Gable.

Before Christmas, Gerry asked whether I'd like to meet Andy Bell, the co-writer of Ray Hill's book, former news editor of *Time Out*, television producer and all-round good guy. 'He'll probably buy you a curry,' Gable suggested. Okay then, curry it is.

We met in Bell's office where he produced documentaries for *World In Action* on scummy people. Paedophiles, murderers, corrupt politicians – he'd seen it all. He also obviously knew a lot about fascists and Nazis, having made *Time Out* an authoritative publication on the London Nazi scene, as well as on its restaurants, live music and other liberal lefty stuff that I normally skipped through whenever I found a copy on the train.

'How do you feel about doing some television work?' Where's my curry? 'Let's have a chat.' Bell's a vegetarian, which put me off a bit, until he pointed out that Hitler was one too. The entire time I've known Bell, like Gable, he was always willing to throw in a comment like that, and to this day still continues to gently mock me when he thinks I've gone too far.

Bell wanted to get C18 onto the television to expose it and try to find its weak spot. I hesitantly agreed, though Gerry Gable insisted I would not go face to camera. I mulled it over for a while, and ate more and more curries with Bell and Gable. Sargent continued to push Whicker to find out who was the mole, if there was one, while still exhorting him to get me on the team.

'They want you on the team,' both Gable and Whicker were telling me from either side. C18's violence continued unabated with firebombings, house invasions and professional burglaries. A steady stream of high-profile names were published for attack. Early in the New Year I finally decided to face Sargent and Whicker at Brick Lane. Sargent was bragging that the January Republican march through central London would see C18 at full strength. He and Browning had contacted hundreds of football hooligans and instructed them to attack anything Irish. 'After we've done the march, we'll set fire to fucking Kilburn. We're gonna send those Paddies home like fucking charcoal.'

I politely declined the offer to attend. My new love interest was from New Zealand and, like most people outside the UK, was under the impression that the Irish were a cuddly, humorous race of people in need of much love and protection. Sargent was incredulous and stormed off, leaving me with Whicker.

'Maff, this is bad, this is very bad,' he sighed as we walked down Brick Lane.

'Tell him I'm not into murder, Eddie.'

He shrugged his shoulders. 'But this is where it is heading now, Maff?'

Fascists were always bragging about how big their numbers were or were going to be but there was a lot to believe in what Sargent was saying. The lull in football-related violence was, believe it or not, attributed to the rise in E culture; supposedly football thugs were too busy gurning and kissing each other to have proper punch-ups anymore but reputations spread on the casual hooligan scene and the name C18 was attracting some interest from hooligan gangs with far-right sympathies. None more so than with the Headunters of Chelsea Football Club, a hooligan gang that Charlie and the rest of the far right had more than a bit of history with.

Over the years Anderson and the NF had demonstrated against every Irish Republican march they could. On the last few, they had only mustered ten or so supporters. Having heard of Sargent's plan, the NF leader immediately made it the gathering point for the NF's small but perfectly formed counter demonstration and then alerted the police. Anderson wanted it to look as if it was a massive NF demo behind police lines, making his organisation look huge. The C18-sponsored mob just wanted to attack Irish marchers.

As promised, C18 organised close on 400 football hooligans and Nazis to attack the march. No banners, no flags, just fists and bottles. They arrived at Hyde Park in London, to find themselves behind an NF demonstration of bright flags and banners. The police lined up coaches and just threw the hooligans into them and drove them off, though not before some Muslim-owned shops on the Edgware Road had their windows put in. Over 300 were arrested and released without charge, but only after they had all been photographed, videoed and had their details taken. The NF was finished and C18 now turned their attentions against the NF.

The morning after, I went to Brick Lane with my girl-friend to see Whicker. We went into a little side street café, where he told me nervously to leave the area. 'I don't know what's going down, but you'd better leave.' I gave him five pounds for a copy of the magazine and headed off.

Eventually news spread that *World In Action* was doing an exposé on C18. Whicker and I maintained contact over the telephone but he was becoming increasingly despondent with me. Terry Blackham had been on at C18 to expel me because I was a 'wrecker' and Sargent had told Whicker to tell me that if I was not with them, I was against them. Bell continued to grill me about everything I knew, then go over it again and again. Whicker claimed that Sargent and Portinari had Bell under surveillance at his office in Golden Square, and even pinpointed a day I had been inside with Bell and Gable, but didn't say they had seen me. Did they know? Did they see me there?

The former head of London UDA had been approached by *WIA* and, despite making some disparaging remarks about Portinari's religion, had bluntly refused to cooperate with them. During one panicky phonecall, Whicker claimed they were going to set Bell up and hit him when he arranged to meet the former UDA man again. I passed the information on to Bell, who seemed mildly confused by the things they were continually getting wrong. As the programme moved into full gear, the panic on the right grew to new and monstrous proportions. C18 stepped up its campaign by attempting to firebomb every possible supporter that *WIA* and *Searchlight* might have, including another firebomb attack on the *Morning Star* in case they were printing *Searchlight*.

My girlfriend announced she was returning home to New Zealand before my twenty-first birthday. She concluded she did not like my work for *World In Action* much, it was far too dangerous and stupid. She begged me to pack it all in and go home with her, that day if possible. We could just leave, just go. 'Come with me,' she pleaded, but before I had even had a week to think it over my clothes were returned to me and she had gone.

The *World In Action* programme was to go out shortly after my birthday. I didn't feel much like having a party, but my brothers did so it went ahead. Bell and his team were painstaking in their research and often had me dragged into meetings to confirm or deny the amazing amount of material that they had collated. Bell took it very seriously and *WIA* had researchers up and down the country recording attacks being carried out. There was extra security added at both the *WIA* and *Searchlight* offices.

Eddie Whicker and Charlie Sargent were doorstepped by Andy Bell and a camera crew on the same day. Whicker's erratic behaviour when leaving his house early in the morning to start collecting the bins caused the crew many problems. He would drive around the block and down one-way streets half a dozen times to avoid anyone following him. They watched him do it three or four mornings before finally catching him face to face. Whicker later told me he thought they were a gang of IRA hit-men the way they all jumped out of a car that stopped in front of him. He handled himself pretty well considering, although he did not deny UDA membership, merely commenting, 'It's not a crime is it?' (It actually was in Northern Ireland.) When Bell said 'Yes, they kill Catholics,' Eddie just shrugged his huge shoulders making no attempt to hide the new loyalist tattoo on his arm, of a rifle and a red hand. He also rather coolly told Bell to 'piss off'.

Sargent on the other hand gave a magnificent performance to the camera. Looking short, fat, squat and angry he played up by trying to smash the camera and demanding money from Bell. Eventually, after he had been asked about his UDA connections he put his fingers into the pistol position and told Bell it would end with a bullet in his head.

Whicker rang me immediately after Bell had left him. He was in a panic, breathlessly shouting that he did not need this. 'Too much trouble, for fuck's sake, too much trouble now. I don't need this.'

The programme was shown in April 1993 and

Searchlight also ran a special edition. Tim Hepple revealed himself to camera as an informer, but it was Simon the other mystery man who caused most concern to the far right. It was me. I knew that, obviously, but as I sat down to watch it I saw that everyone else would know too. Immediately after the programme ended I went to the pub with a friend and drowned my sorrows. Would they be there upon my return? How long would it take for them to get together and come and murder me?

That weekend the BNP held an anti-IRA march through London, which Whicker attended, mainly to soak up his increased infamy. John Tyndall shook his hand warmly and told him how well he came across in comparison to Sargent, who was absent from the march. The National Front had immediately told anyone who would listen that I was the mole. Whicker however, came out on my side.

'I told them, Maff, innocent until proven guilty. There's no proof.' I acted indignant about the whole affair until a copy of the League of St George magazine turned up a couple of weeks later. They claimed that 'Simon' (my character) was really MC, a disgraced member whom Sargent had to discipline for running from the enemy.

Its notices column had the following message: 'Matthew, why did you do it? Get in touch.'

What? I responded by dashing off a lunatic religious address blaming Anderson for making it look like it was me on the programme and pointing out that he and Bell had gone to Oxford together (until of course Anderson dropped out). I enclosed a letter that Gerry Gable had written me offering me money to come over and work for *Searchlight* in the light of the allegations that had been made against me. It seemed to send them all around the bend. At the end of my circular I referred to Hepple living in a caravan in Bognor Regis shitting himself at the thought of being caught. Eddie rang me immediately. 'Is Hepple in Bognor Regis, Maff?'

CHAPTER 33

The programme clearly exposed the BNP as sponsoring a wave of terror being carried out by C18. Whicker, who I thought would deep down be rather pleased with his own performance, seemed to be in a rather inexplicable panic. 'They want Simon, not Hepple. If they get this Simon character he'll be dead,' he told me. They? 'Yes, Charlie and the others. I've got far too much going on to worry about this business.'

Eventually Her Majesty's Constabulary caught up with me. They marched into where I worked and offered me a choice. Come for a drink or come to the nick and be processed on any number of charges. I refused and was arrested under the Prevention of Terrorism act. Fucking hell. I couldn't even stand up and piss ran down my legs.

Charlie Sargent wanted me dead and was geeing people up to do it. Whicker was telling people to lay off me for the time being, but I could not expect Whicker to be around forever. The one thing they didn't yet know for sure was whether I actually was the mole that had been working for *Searchlight*. They were desperate to find out.

It was up to me whether or not I told them I worked for *Searchlight* but it could leave me open to prosecution if I didn't play ball the way the Branch wanted. They could do me for Welling Library and, as the League publication had pointed out, Brick Lane. Over a period of weeks I had to meet them whenever they wanted, if only for a few minutes at a time. If I didn't, they would come and get me, in the pub, at work or at home. If I was doing night shift, I had to meet them an hour before work started. They filled my head with absolute terror and regularly told me that I was going to be murdered. They wanted to know where the guns were and why I had dropped out. There was still nothing but silence from the far right on the subject of my impending death sentence, until one day I was called at home and told not to go to work that day. 'Call in sick.'

'I'm afraid there is probably about to be a change in your liberty.' Thrust before me were photographs taken that morning from inside Eddie Whicker's flat, where MI5 and the Anti-Terrorist Squad had been ripping up the carpets looking for guns. Then pictures of Whicker standing outside a car in a pub car park looking confused, then more pictures of Portinari on a later day outside another pub car park with a sports bag, which it turned out was full of guns. Bingo!

My world came crashing down on me. They were both in prison. Portinari had been arrested in Birmingham meeting a man from Belfast to exchange the bag. Whicker had been there two days before to do the drop off, but had gone to the wrong pub. 'So you see,' said the sergeant quietly, 'your guardian angel cannot protect you any more. As soon as word gets around that Eddie's inside with Frank Portinari, Charlie Sargent will run everything. That can only spell the end for you.'

Funnily enough, I took it quite well. The tea was fresh, the biscuits were chocolate, even the fruit was good – for England. What's the sentence for this? 'Too long for you to hang around hoping you'll be safe.' They laid out on the table hundreds of photographs. 'We need to know everyone's names immediately.' Unfortunately for Special Branch, their photographs are not always as good as *Searchlight*'s. They were, however, taken from quite unusual locations; overhead, from passing cars, from café windows. Taken during weekdays when Nazis are trying to live their everyday lives. Photographs of Bristol, pictures of

Eddie leaving home, pictures of me, Eddie and Frank in a side street at the January Republican march.

While Whicker was being held on remand in Birmingham, he denied knowing what was in the sports bag that his friend Frank had asked him to deliver. Although he'd been arrested at home in south London, he had to face his charges in Birmingham. He was held at Winson Green with the notorious Charlie Bronson, considered the most dangerous man in the British penal system, and now a lifelong friend of Whicker's. His partner Sue was devastated, but not as much as I was, as I was now living on a knife edge. The Branch was filling my head with impending doom and gloom and still no one had shown up to kill me yet.

In the transcript from Whicker's interrogation is a series of questions that go like this:

Q: Do you know Matthew Collins?
A: Yeah.
Q: What's he like?
A: He's a good kid.
Q: So you don't believe he's working for *Searchlight* then?
A: No. He's a good kid. He wouldn't do that.

Neither the Branch nor Whicker ever told me that; it came out a couple of years later when we got to see the transcript. But possibly it was passed on to Sargent, because I never received one threat whilst Eddie was on remand. People inside C18 later told another *WIA* programme, which dealt with Sargent's connection to the Security Services, that he had been adamant that I should be murdered, until Whicker was arrested. Whicker had made it clear that I was not to be touched until he was released and could properly look into the situation. The guns were supplied to Eddie and Frank Portinari by C18 members, along with the ones that Frank had purchased himself in Bermondsey. It's probable that a fair amount of suspicion was falling on the inner circle of C18 and Sargent, although he ran the operation ruthlessly, was himself not beyond suspicion.

Instead he turned his attentions to Quentin McDermott, a reporter for *World In Action*. Sargent instructed his members to put him under surveillance before finally pinpointing the exact location of McDermott's home on an electoral roll later found at Browning's house during a police raid. A C18 member was instructed to shoot McDermott in his own home. The hit was aborted after police raids discovered the plan.

Eddie was released without charge in September, causing much panic in the *Searchlight* team who rang me around ten minutes before the Branch did. Special Branch had slipped up; they lost any respect I had for them by not telling me as soon as they knew. They immediately picked me up and took me to a hotel, where they decided I should ring Whicker's partner to see how Eddie was doing, and then feign surprise at his release. When I rang, Whicker had been at large for three days and said we had to meet urgently. He had not seen me for months and months and there was a lot to talk about. Would I go? The Branch said they'd sit outside, but I'm not bloody stupid. It was a no-no. They got frustrated, but they'd already lost my faith by then.

The wheels were set in motion for me to leave. I was exhausted. The one protector I'd had on the far right was possibly the one who would finally give the go-ahead for C18 to do me in. C18 were beginning to explore new and more advanced terror tactics. In their ranks now were people who were regularly handling guns and others who had spent time in the former Yugoslavia fighting with Croatian, then Serbian militias after Croatia signed a pact with Muslim Bosnia.

I'd accumulated enough fly by points with *Searchlight* for an economy ticket out of the country to a safe haven, and the Branch readily agreed to get me a passport and visa quickly.

I had two more meetings with the Branch before I left. One was a serious meeting with their Inspector, who actually worked on the far left desk and predicted that the BNP were about to win a seat on Tower Hamlets Council in east London. From there you might say, the BNP's life is more of a matter of public history.

My own life since then is pretty much public knowledge, but don't believe all you read on Google.

CHAPTER 34

Aftermath

The changes and modernisation of the BNP was a thoroughly Griffin piece of work. Labour and the left described him as all kinds of things, opportunist among them. That he may have been and be, but he built a fascist party right under their noses on the very council estates that the left were abandoning faster than their ideology. Labour's ongoing dislocation from the working class, in particular in England, was happening during a quite benign economic climate. The far left want us to believe that the national growth of the extreme right was solely due to a difficult economic climate, but how did that explain gains in Burnley, Bradford and Barking and Dagenham for the BNP? Probably the dirty word, class.

The BNP had a clean-up. It swept its outright Nazism under the carpet and gave itself a good old-fashioned over-haul. The Wingfields returned from their mysterious time in France to take up arms with Griffin again, presenting themselves as decent, thoroughly British parents, and not as the degenerate wife-swappers Griffin had previously portrayed them as.

Labour became more and more unpopular and further and further dislocated from its roots. And those in charge didn't seem to really care. Some who did, walked away whilst those who remained seemed to be burdened and consumed with polling figures about the party's polling performance in the middle grounds. It was like catching water with a tea strainer. For some, the warning signs were clearer.

I'd never heard of the Lehman brothers when on warm Thursday night in 2006 I stood not four feet away from the BNP's Richard Barnbrook as he swaggered unsteadily to his feet to attempt to berate the controversial journalist Andrew Gilligan, who had exposed a rather 'arty' film Barnbrook had made in his youth. Barnbrook had just won a seat on Barking and Dagenham Council and throughout the course of the evening I had watched horrified as he was joined by another ten (soon to be eleven) of his moronic brethren on the council. Barnbrook had no idea who I was. I was just a plump, scowling anti-fascist. We'd never met before. Barnbrook was part of the new breed of the BNP. Light on rhetoric and ideology but high on personal embarrassments with an arthouse-film skeleton in the closet.

I was driven to the count by Dagenham Labour MP Jon Cruddas in silent misery as Labour pollsters reported the flood at the polling booths as the evening wore on. What *The Guardian* called the 'White Van Brigade' – angry, white, working-class voters – were rushing home and casting anti-Labour votes with venom. The former architect of New Labour had been one of the first to work with *Searchlight* and its *Hope Not Hate* campaign the previous year when, with only a handful of activists, the *Searchlight* office had emptied into Barking and Dagenham to deliver our *Daily Mirror*-sponsored tabloid to counter the BNP's racist onslaught on the doorsteps.

This night, we were braced for only eight of them (elected BNP councillors): moronic, ugly and idiotic, swaggering and slurring into Nazi folklore and putting B&D in the headlines for all the wrong reasons. If they had stood more candidates, they would have taken far more seats and possibly caused irreparable damage. Barnbrook was trying to berate Gilligan, but he couldn't get the words out properly. Not for the first time when I'd seen Barnbrook in public, I concluded he was pissed; I'd been watching

him the previous year when he took 17 per cent of the
vote against Barking MP Margaret Hodge in the general
election. Some 'Hollywood' anti-fascists had felt it better
to go to an anti-BNP pop concert in Trafalgar Square that
year and not do the hard work on the ground. Failure to
confront the rise of fascism by hard work had long been a
cause of the BNP's rise.

I wondered if Cruddas felt responsible: were he and
the New Labour he'd helped create actually the problem here and everywhere that the BNP was rising? Over
time, his words and actions would go on to prove that he
probably did. Perhaps it wasn't the idea, just the application of the New Labour ideology. Perhaps Cruddas and
co. had a bad midwife of their own? He fought the BNP
tooth and nail, even when it got quite ugly, even when it
made him unpopular with his colleagues. He never backed
down once.

I had returned home to fight the BNP after all. Some
eighteen months before, the BBC had finally given me
my documentary. They'd rescued me from ten years of
barbecues and casual sex in the sunshine of Australia and
followed me home to document me facing my demons and
the rise of the supposedly 'respectable' far right. *Searchlight*
had offered me a small desk in the corner of their cramped
offices from where I could front up their preventative work
in the community, but even on my first day at work I had
trouble getting into their offices because the security guard
thought I looked 'like a fascist'.

The BBC called the documentary *Dead Man Walking*,
probably on account of my mate Noel drunkenly grabbing the TV camera in one of Melbourne's better bars and
declaring that ('A Dead Man Walking') was what I was for
going home. They then filmed Noel and his wife and all of
my closest friends watching another documentary I had
done for the BBC a couple of years before called *Life Etc*

with Rosie Boycott, where I owned up to my previous life in the dark and drudgery of England where I had some thirteen years before had my secret conversion. 'More Austin Powers than James Bond,' Noel's wife had suggested, while 'Big Gay Ray' and Ron, the 'sweet and tender' Samoan, sat quaffing ales in stone cold silence.

My ex-wife declined to be interviewed. My mother and father refused also. My father described the whole idea as 'far too painful'.

I left behind in Australia a lifetime of sunburn, emotional and financial traumas. I crammed into ten years more drama than most people could do in a lifetime. I'd left England with a one-year work visa with near-crippling work restrictions, met a woman, applied to stay and got married and then divorced. Wanked a lot too. I had lived as an immigrant, hardly the sort that faced the innumerable challenges of people of colour or different languages, but I had no qualifications and no repeatable history to offer either a wife or new country.

Initially I settled in St Kilda on Melbourne's Port Phillip Bay. Of course, it would later be immortalised by Billy Bragg in song, but in 1993, it was a rustic, bohemian paradise of heroin cafés, half-dressed prostitutes, Kiwi drug dealers, gangland killers, transvestites and stoned and horny middle-class English backpackers who got mugged and/or hooked on heroin with aplomb.

The ex-pat Irish community assimilated me while I gave rare and aggravating thought to pernicious Albion, so far away and unconquerable. *Searchlight* arrived monthly with horrible reminders of the fate that awaited me should I return home.

In 1997 I infuriated my former friends and colleagues by agreeing to give evidence to the Stephen Lawrence Inquiry. Those Nazis who had previously defended me were driven from the movement as if they had collaborated with me.

And when all the drinking and all the fucking had run its course, I allowed the BBC to thrust me back into a dim spotlight in wet and damp England. Television cameras add forty pounds, you know.

In my absence, C18 had imploded murderously and the NF shuffled off of its mortal coil and then back again. Eddie Whicker had been driven from the movement and forced into early retirement, only partly as a result of his defence of and close friendship with me. Terry Blackham went to prison for gun-running for the UDA and for a while, ran the National Front from his prison cell as Ian Anderson finally exited the tiny stage.

The *Searchlight* I arrived back to had grown enormously. It now had five staff. Gerry Gable had moved himself 'upstairs' to become the magazine's publisher, allowing a younger team to take over the day-to-day running of the magazine and the introduction of campaigning. During my ten years away, Gable had been among a number of people whose house had been attacked by C18, even being the intended victim of firebomb. He'd never moved. He starred alongside me on *Dead Man Walking* though he did insist I kept my trousers on at all times.

Nick Griffin had ousted John Tyndall in 1999 as Griffin saw the growing opportunities available to the far right not just in this country, but all over Europe as the fascist disease raised its ugly head again. If they could just dump their previous ideological baggage and, as he had almost begged in writing a couple of years before, their jackboots too, Griffin saw an opportunity to reinvigorate racism. He sounded exactly like his own nemesis Ian Anderson had done, and in doing so slowly but surely recruited most of Anderson's former leading colleagues to the BNP along with his own and changed the BNP almost overnight.

The BNP's shift to electioneering nearly brought an end to Richard Edmonds too. First he was in then he was out of the party as he struggled to cope without Tyndall's tutelage. Tyndall then died in 2005, facing charges along with Griffin and one other of inciting racial hatred. He had also been involved in costly legal actions with Griffin over his expulsion from the party he had founded himself. He'd missed by a whisker seeing the BNP transformed to almost centre-stage of the immigration debate in this country. C18, who had eventually turned against Tyndall, Griffin and itself was gone. The BNP almost believed itself to be a proper political party.

The violence, terrorism, rapes and lies of the far right continue to this day. Now though, the arena is different. Nick Griffin is now an MEP along with Andrew Brons, formerly of the Flag faction.

Searchlight's new editor was Nick Lowles. An investigative journalist and excellent strategist, but sadly a Leeds fan. To counter the BNP's rise, as well as hammering them monthly along with the rest of the team with excellent exposés of the true nature of the BNP in the magazine, he started the Hope Not Hate campaign, the largest and most effective anti-fascist campaign in the country. He extended the challenge to fighting the far right right across the political spectrum, basing the heart of it in the trade union movement. For me, it was the most excellent introduction into community politics, empowering local people and local groups to defend themselves.

And though these are difficult times, Lowles and Gerry Gable afforded me the opportunities to learn about politics, to learn about real people and to also tour with people like Billy Bragg, work in prisons, travel to Spain with people like the great Jack Jones and have my voice heard, no matter how often they would disagree with what it said.

In January 2010, Nick Lowles promised me that we would remove the BNP from Barking & Dagenham

Council. That seemed impossible. We were more likely to be looking at BNP MPs than a BNP defeat. But he kept his word. Hope Not Hate galvanised people right across the country not just to defeat BNP candidates, but to more than halve their number of councillors across the country. We removed every single BNP councillor from Barking and Dagenham and along the way, Billy Bragg came and confronted the ludicrous Richard Barnbrook on his doorstep. Lowles even confronted Griffin as he attempted to sneak out of the election count with his defeated councillors in tow. Some of the old-time BNP members tried to turn on me, shouting abuse at me. Eddy Butler even said I'd seen better days.

But there's not a great deal of hope in my heart. The BNP isn't beaten yet, they're still churning out people with guns and bombs though we rarely read about it like we do when it is Muslims. These days they talk about a 'civil war' not a race war, and those arguments I had with myself all those years ago about who I am and where do I belong, are now almost like a national obsession. Identity and religion has almost totally replaced class in the minds of everyone. It seems these days that only the middle class want to actually be working class, anyway. Bastards!

Occasionally I get wheeled out to speak about life behind those flags and the grim reality of the BNP and their fellow travellers. More and more we find how little not just BNP voters but also BNP members know about the party; its roots, its history, its goals and what words like 'civil war' really mean. This is where the next David Copeland will come from; it's where David Copeland started. Ignorant, unloved and feeling ignored. There is not and never will be a parliamentary road to what fascists want to achieve and their demands. No matter whether they're wearing suits or jackboots, they are an anathema to me now more than ever. But the national obsession of the English working class of its own dislocation in the UK among the Irish, the Welsh and the Scots is growing.

How identity politics replaced class politics in those ten absent years I spent in Australia is breathtaking. Why BBC3 moved the story of my stupid life – *Dead Man Walking* – to later in the evening to fit in a Newcastle match in the Inter-Toto Cup is still annoying. But the explosion of identity politics from groups like the English Defence League, and the seeming inability of many to understand it as well as counter it effectively, is the most worrying thing we face right now. Because they are working class, because they are overwhelmingly white and from the football terraces, it's almost as if no one wants to tackle their message head-on. And it is the Muslim community that faces their threat, daily.

In 2011 our successful Hope Not Hate campaign separated from Searchlight. It was desperately and personally sad for everyone involved, but ultimately necessary if we were to keep doing the work that mattered and continue to hurt the far right.

My mission had begun back in that library in Welling, where I had finally seen with eyes wide open what fascism really meant. I can remember that split second when everything a young boy ever needed to know about the dangers of the life I had chosen played out in front of me. And yet to be honest, some teenage boys – and even teenage girls – get up to a lot worse these days. Wasn't it just a punch-up between two groups of extremists that got a little out of hand? Didn't my friends and comrades from that time go on to do a lot worse – a lot, lot worse?

But Welling library was the moment everything changed for me. There followed a loss of faith and a further, deeper confusion about where I would go to now, where I would fit in comfortably: if not fascism, what did I want out of life? And here I am, over twenty years on, desperately trying to ensure that somehow there will be no more young kids like me, walking blindly into the dark and soul-destroying path of racism.

But how do I do that? I'm forty now and trying desperately to grow up after years of striving to relive or recapture some of that lost youth. Years of running with and then running from the fascists set me on a road where everything I say or do is coloured by that period. Here I am in England working long hours with people who probably wonder 'Is he cured? Is he genuine?'

I'd once been a nasty schoolboy at the same school, of all places, as Richard Reid, the al-Qaeda 'shoe bomber'. Two sides of the same coin, perhaps? Not really, and of course there would be more to gain from preventing the rise of more Richards than there would be that of other poor Matthews. But our paths had crossed. Often I'd get asked if I remembered him. Yes I did, just about. Unlike me, by all accounts he'd been a spectacularly normal school kid in the year below mine. He'd had a shit old time of it and drifted into petty crime, then got 'radicalised' while in prison – not in the pub like me. Neither of us got an invite to the school reunion.

But standing now in schools, colleges, youth clubs and even universities, I watch those same fears and confusions that I once felt play out in front of me in others. And they don't have to be white to ask themselves those same daunting questions I once did. I ran an 'anti-racist' project in Barking and Dagenham until 2010, where I worked with young people. All the experience and knowledge in the world couldn't do much to improve their lives. We played football, watched films and talked about the dreaded asylum seekers that were taking all of the homes in the borough. Not one asylum seeker had been housed in Barking and Dagenham since 1999, but I was the first person to tell the kids that. They seemed bemused. They were often hungry, often confrontational. The funders had expected them to be swastika-wearing, ideological David Copeland types, but they were not. 'What about us?' was about the most controversial thing they ever said. The kids from Barking were often too scared to go to Dagenham and vice versa. But every summer we'd have hundreds of kids at the town show playing football together wearing 'Hope Not Hate' T-shirts.

On the few occasions that the BNP came canvassing, the kids chased them off with 'devil dogs'. It was not science, it was not a miracle. It was us being on the council estates instead of the BNP. They were bored and frustrated with their lives and the absence of aspiration at home, but they were not bad kids. We offered them hope over hate. The work I did there was singled out for praise and the local and national newspapers said that the project may have helped defeat the BNP. And then they took my funding away.

We're still in trouble. In David Cameron we have a Prime Minister who ascribes what should be 'British values' to 'Christian values'. The left, meanwhile, seems to have abandoned its core beliefs when it comes to religion, yet is almost paralysed when asked to defend secular values. In some cases, they actually do a great disservice to the overwhelming majority of Muslims in this country by not helping communities drive out the extremists. All of this does not make me feel particularly inclusive, and I'm sure it doesn't many others, either – the rise of the EDL is proof of that.

When the EDL really took off in 2010, we found ourselves in the front line against them. Totally devoid of coherent politics (or even thought) thousands of angry white men began taking to the streets like they were on some kind of booze-fuelled religious crusade against Muslims. But rather than waving flags at them or marching in opposition, we found ourselves, somewhat controversially, working against the causes of their rise instead. How did we end up in a position where the most lumpen, racist, sexist and homophobic in society are able to portray themselves as defenders of democracy, women's rights and gay rights? Because some people cannot stomach a real fight. When is someone who isn't a racist dickhead going to stand up and say 'I'm English'?

I'm not in hiding any more. The EDL call me a 'fat Communist' and, bizarrely, the BNP say I'm a liar and an alcoholic as well as a Zionist and a Communist. It's not the sort of fan club I thought I'd have twenty-odd years ago. My dad and I meet once a week for lunch and a pint and he thinks I'm something to do with the Labour Party, and also a Communist, obviously. We don't talk about my child-hood, but we talk about his, sometimes. We're both getting old and I guess I'll end up looking like him in thirty years too. He tells me his neighbours play bongo-bongo music and never go to work, apparently. He says we should send them all back. He's an Irishman and I am an Englishman with two flags.

EPILOGUE

Frank Portinari was sentenced to four years for attempted gun-running in 1993.

Ian Stuart Donaldson died in a car crash the same year.

In 1994 Terry Blackham was arrested with a Czech sub-machine gun on his way to Northern Ireland and sentenced to four years' imprisonment.

Ian Anderson tried to wind down the NF and morph it into a new party called the National Democrats, though upon his release, Blackham reignited the Front. Anderson died of a brain haemorrhage in February 2011. His political career had long been finished, and he remained bitter and angry with me till his dying day.

In 1997, C18 tried a bombing campaign in Britain that was thwarted by the work of a mole, later identified to be Charlie Sargent. Sargent received a life sentence in 1999 for murder committed during the ensuing internal dispute.

In 1999 David Copeland carried out a series of nail-bomb attacks in London aimed at the black, Asian and gay communities, killing three people, including a pregnant woman. *Searchlight* identified Copeland from photographs they had taken as being a former BNP member.

Nick Griffin took control of the BNP with the help of Tony Lecomber and Eddy Butler and expelled both John Tyndall and Richard Edmonds.

Tyndall died in 2005.

In 2009 Richard Edmonds was appointed to the BNP's Advisory Council, but temporarily decided to challenge Griffin to a leadership election in 2011 when the party fell out with itself. Later that year he moved to the National Front, the party he had left some thirty years before.